CLAIMING SOCIETY FOR GOD

CLAIMING SOCIETY FOR GOD

RELIGIOUS MOVEMENTS AND SOCIAL WELFARE

EGYPT, ISRAEL, ITALY, AND THE UNITED STATES

NANCY J. DAVIS
AND ROBERT V. ROBINSON

INDIANA UNIVERSITY PRESS
BLOOMINGTON AND INDIANAPOLIS

This book is a publication of

Indiana University Press
601 North Morton Street
Bloomington, Indiana 47404-3797 USA

iupress.indiana.edu

Telephone orders   800-842-6796
Fax orders   812-855-7931

© 2012 by Nancy J. Davis and Robert V. Robinson

⊖ The paper used in this publication meets the minimum re-
quirements of the American National Standard for Information
Sciences—Permanence of Paper for Printed Library Materials,
ANSI Z39.48-1992.

Manufactured in the United States of America

Library of Congress Cataloging-in-Publication Data

Davis, Nancy Jean, [date]
    Claiming society for God : religious movements and social wel-
fare in Egypt, Israel, Italy, and the United States / Nancy J. Davis
and Robert V. Robinson.
        p. cm.
    Includes bibliographical references (p.   ) and index.
    ISBN 978-0-253-00234-1 (cloth : alk. paper) — ISBN 978-0-253-
00238-9 (pbk. : alk. paper) — ISBN 978-0-253-00714-8 (e-book) 1.
Religion and sociology. I. Robinson, Robert V. II. Title.
    BL60.D298 2012
    305.6—dc23

                                                    2012001044

1 2 3 4 5 17 16 15 14 13 12

FOR OUR PARENTS,
BOB AND EILEEN DAVIS
AL AND ALICIA ROBINSON

CONTENTS

PREFACE

OUR INTEREST IN RELIGIOUSLY ORTHODOX (often called "fundamentalist") movements began nearly twenty-five years ago. In 1982, we moved to the small town of Greencastle, Indiana, where religious orthodoxy has a long reach. Poverty and substandard housing were also not uncommon, and for that reason, in 1989 we became involved in a local chapter of Habitat for Humanity that was just getting off the ground. Habitat builds affordable housing in partnership with people in need. The national organization was begun as a ministry by evangelical Protestant founder Millard Fuller whose "theology of the hammer" was biblically based and called for "no interest, no profit." Our local chapter, however, contained a mix of people, some of whom were drawn by their faith and others, like us, who were not particularly religious.

Generally our Habitat chapter ran smoothly, but occasionally there were disputes. When a member of the board proposed that we hold a raffle to raise funds for our next Habitat home, some objected that the Bible forbids gambling. Debate also arose about whether a lesbian couple—a hypothetical lesbian couple—would be eligible for a Habitat home. The group was divided, with some members quoting Scripture on biblical prohibitions against homosexuality and others arguing that discrimination on the basis of sexual orientation is a violation of human rights. Yet through our conversations with fellow volunteers, many of them on Habitat worksites, we noticed that while we had quite different positions from some of the more religiously orthodox volunteers on matters such as reproductive rights and same-sex partnerships, our views on issues of economic justice were not far apart. Many of the evangelical volunteers felt that the government should be doing much more on behalf of the poor and told us that they voted for Democrats. The religiously orthodox people that we met through Habitat did not fit the common characterization of fundamentalists as not only cultural traditionalists but also defenders of laissez faire capitalism and economic inequality. There is, of course, self-selection in joining a group like Habitat, but we began to wonder whether the common wisdom that religiously orthodox people are consistently "right wing" was correct.

We decided to do a study investigating the cultural (sexuality/family/gender) and economic attitudes of religiously orthodox Americans, relative to their modernist counterparts who subscribe to a more contextual, human-derived morality. Analyzing national survey data from the General Social Survey, we found that the religiously orthodox in the United States, not surprisingly, were more conservative than modernists on cultural issues (such as contraception, abortion, sex education, premarital sex, gay rights, pornography, and gender). But, contrary to conventional wisdom, we found that Americans who were religiously orthodox were more egalitarian than modernists in their economic attitudes—in wanting government to provide jobs for all and spend more on Social Security, in believing that profits should go to workers over shareholders, and in having confidence in organized labor. Our findings, which we published in 1996 in the *American Journal of Sociology* under the title "Are the Rumors of War Exaggerated?," belied the notion that a "culture war" was raging between consistently right-wing religiously orthodox Americans, on the one hand, and their steadfastly left-wing modernist counterparts, on the other.

We began to wonder if what we had found in the United States might also hold in European countries. The United States is predominantly Protestant, and we were curious whether the same pattern would hold in other Protestant-majority countries in Europe, as well as in countries that were predominantly Catholic or Eastern Orthodox. Israel, as a predominantly Jewish country, also drew our attention: Would the pattern we had found in the United States, where the religiously orthodox were more culturally conservative but more economically egalitarian than modernists, also hold in different national settings and in countries of different faith traditions?

By this time we had developed a theory as to why the orthodox tend to be stricter than modernists on cultural matters but more caring than modernists on economic issues. We'll say more about the theory in chapter 1, but briefly, we argued that the orthodox tend to hold a communitarian ethos which involves watching over others, both to make sure that community members adhere to what they see as divinely mandated standards on such issues as abortion, sexuality, and gender and to ensure that those in the community who are in need are looked out for. We argued that modernists, in contrast, tend to be individualistic in seeing it as up to individuals to decide what they believe about abortion, same-sex relations, and the proper roles for women and men and also up to individuals to make their own fates economically—good or bad—without much intervention by the community or state if a person ends up poor, unemployed, homeless, or sick.

On a sabbatical spent in Italy and France, we analyzed data gathered by two multi-country survey consortiums, the International Social Survey Program and the World Values Survey, to test our theoretical arguments in European countries and Israel. As we began our study, we spoke with scholars of religion in Europe and were told by most of them that we would not find the same relationship between religion and political attitudes in Europe as we had found in the United States. In many European countries, secular communist and socialist parties vied with conservative religious parties, such as the Christian Democrats, so we knew that Europe would present a difficult test of our theory. Yet through our analyses, we found the same pattern that we had found in the United States in countries that were predominantly Protestant (Norway), mixed Protestant and Catholic (West Germany), Catholic (Austria, Ireland, Italy, Poland, Portugal), Eastern Orthodox (Bulgaria, Romania), and Jewish (Israel). The religiously orthodox were more culturally authoritarian than modernists in believing that abortion, premarital sex, extramarital sex, and homosexuality are always wrong; in wanting school prayer mandated; and in believing that husbands should be breadwinners and wives homemakers. The orthodox were at the same time more economically egalitarian than modernists in believing that government should equalize incomes and provide jobs for all and that employers should not take into account efficiency and reliability in deciding on workers' pay. We published our findings on religious orthodoxy and economic justice attitudes in a 1999 article, "Their Brothers' Keepers?," in the *American Journal of Sociology*.

By this point we were curious whether the same pattern might hold in predominantly Muslim countries. We wondered whether our arguments about the communitarian tendencies of the religiously orthodox and the individualistic inclinations of modernists would extend to all of the Abrahamic religions or "religions of the Book" (Christianity, Islam, and Judaism). On our next sabbatical, which was spent in France and Australia, we undertook a study of surveys of Muslim-majority nations. The first comparable surveys of predominantly Muslim countries were gathered under the auspices of the World Values Survey in 1999 through 2003. We had to wait for the surveys to be made publicly available, but this gave us time to confer with scholars of Islamic studies. In analyzing these surveys, we decided to focus specifically on the most controversial aspect of our theory—the argument that the religiously orthodox are more economically egalitarian or caring than modernists. In an article published in 2006 in the *American Sociological Review* titled "The Egalitarian Face of Islamic Orthodoxy," we showed that religiously orthodox Muslims in Algeria, Bangladesh, Egypt, Indonesia, Jordan, Pakistan, and Saudi Arabia were more supportive than modernists of government efforts to help the needy, equalize the gap between rich and poor, and nationalize businesses. Although cultural attitudes were not the focus of the article, we also found that the orthodox were more conservative than modernists on abortion, divorce, and appropriate roles for women and men, thus confirming the pattern that we had found in the United States, ten European countries, and Israel.

To back up a bit, in 1997, while we were living in northern Italy on sabbatical, we encountered a movement called Comunione e Liberazione (CL), a Catholic orthodox movement working to restore the Church and the pope to what the movement sees as their proper places in Italian society. CL, the largest lay Catholic movement in Italy, had built a massive network (*rete*) of religious schools, unemployment centers, homes for displaced people, food banks, discount bookshops, consumer cooperatives, and other establishments—all linked with tens of thousands of businesses that were inspired by or affiliated with the movement. The aim of this institution-building was ambitious: to establish a parallel Christian society in Italy that would lessen the need for an extensive secular welfare state. CL's multipronged agenda was very much in line with what we were finding, through our analyses of survey data, about the religiously orthodox in Italy and elsewhere: CL had spearheaded efforts to make the Church's positions on abortion and divorce the law of the land in Italy, but it had also established an impressive array of organizations and agencies to address the needs of the poor, unemployed, homeless, and sick.

Seven years later, while on sabbatical in Sydney analyzing the first national surveys that were coming out of Muslim-majority nations, we became aware of how the Society of Muslim Brothers, an Islamic orthodox movement, had established in Egypt an equally extensive, nationwide network of institutions—mosques, religious schools, clinics, unemployment agencies, factories, legal aid agencies, pharmacies, and Islamic banks—that both scholars and government officials had called a "state within a state." The Brotherhood's institutional outreach aimed to Islamize the Egyptian population, with the goal of using this religiously inspired popular base in establishing an Islamic political order. The Brotherhood sought to implement what it saw as divinely mandated positions on sexuality, family, and women's and men's roles, while also building thousands of institutions to address the needs of the poor and marginalized.

Intrigued by the similarity of the Muslim Brotherhood's strategy in Egypt to that of Comunione e Liberazione in Italy, we wondered whether prominent religiously orthodox movements in other faith traditions and countries were using a similar institution-building strategy. We read about the Sephardi Torah Guardians, or Shas, an ultra-Orthodox Jewish movement and the largest religious party in Israel, which had built a vast network of institutions to push Israeli society in an ultra-Orthodox direction. Shas, like CL and the Muslim Brotherhood, has a culturally strict but economically caring agenda. Thinking of our own country, we realized that the Salvation Army, an evangelical Protestant movement, had used a similar strategy in establishing the nation's largest religion-based social service network. Most Americans are familiar with the Salvation Army's thrift shops and Red Kettle drives on behalf of those in need, but few know that the Army also has culturally strict positions on abortion, marriage, and homosexuality and a religious agenda centered in its corps (churches). We decided to look further into how these four religiously orthodox movements in the Abrahamic traditions of Catholicism, Islam, Judaism, and Protestantism are working to install religion at the center of their societies.

Readers of our earlier work sometimes wanted to know about our religious backgrounds. Neither of us was raised in a religiously orthodox family nor do we participate in a religious community as adults. One of us grew up in a decidedly modernist Congregationalist church and the other as a Unitarian. Our adult lives have been largely secular. On the other hand, religious communities have never been far removed. One of us had a set of religiously fundamentalist (Dutch Reform Protestant) grandparents and the other a Pentecostal cousin who spoke in tongues at his ordination ceremony. While our academic lives have been largely secular, living in rural Indiana most of our adult lives has meant that the ethos and reach of religious orthodoxy—at least the Christian variety—has never been far away. Our experience with the evangelically based Habitat for Humanity is, of course, a case in point.

We have mixed feelings about the religiously orthodox movements that we chronicle in this book. We generally admire what we call the "caring," egalitarian side of their communitarianism—their herculean efforts to improve the lives of the poor, unemployed, homeless, or sick; to narrow the gap between rich and poor; and to intervene in the economy to meet the needs of all citizens. Yet we disagree with their goal of making a particular brand of religion the cornerstone of society and law, and we do not support the "strict" or authoritarian side of their communitarianism—their efforts to limit a woman's reproductive choices, to prohibit same-sex marriage, to prescribe roles for women and men, and so forth. We have tried to tell the stories of these movements without praising what we see as their positive efforts or criticizing what strikes us as their less desirable face. While some readers might prefer us to take a decidedly positive or negative stance toward these religious movements, our aim is to understand them sociologically, as movements that are having a powerful impact on their societies, rather than to judge them.

GREENCASTLE, INDIANA N. J. D.
FEBRUARY 2012 R. V. R.

ACKNOWLEDGMENTS

IN WRITING OUR BOOK, WE HAVE incurred debts of many sorts. For helping us to overcome some of our preconceived notions about religiously orthodox people and starting us on this journey, we are indebted to the volunteers and board members of Putnam County Habitat for Humanity.

As we developed our theoretical arguments, we were influenced by conversations with many colleagues and friends. On our sabbatical in Italy in 1997, Enzo Pace of the Università degli Studi di Padova helped us in thinking about Comunione e Liberazione and encouraged us to pursue the study of religious orthodoxy in Islam. Michael Humphrey and his colleagues in the Department of Sociology and Social Policy at the University of New South Wales and Robert Van Krieken and his fellow faculty members of the Department of Sociology and Social Policy at the University of Sydney provided an intellectually stimulating environment while we were in the early stages of developing our ideas for this book.

Steve Warner, professor emeritus of the University of Illinois, Chicago, read the manuscript and gave us detailed and extremely helpful comments on how to revise it. We thank our DePauw colleagues Jeff Kenney of the Department of Religion for reading drafts of our earlier work and providing important guidance on the Muslim Brotherhood and Egypt, Nahyan Fancy of the History Department for his comments on and support of the project, and Bruce Stinebrickner of the Department of Political Science for his advice on conceptualizing the public sphere and reactions to our various proposed titles. We also appreciate the support for the project provided by DePauw anthropologists Srimati Basu (now at the University of Kentucky), Mona Bhan, and Angela Castaneda, political scientist Brett O'Bannon, and sociologists Tamara Beauboeuf and Rebecca Bordt. Our IU sociology colleagues Elizabeth Armstrong (now at the University of Michigan), Tim Bartley, Clem Brooks, Brian Powell, Fabio Rojas, Brian Steensland, and Melissa Wilde (now at the University of Pennsylvania), and former graduate students Jeff Dixon (now at the College of the Holy Cross), Brian Starks (now at the University of Notre Dame), and Jocelyn Viterna (now at Harvard University) were critically important in reading drafts of our earlier work and serving as a sounding board for our ideas. Sociologist Sadia Saeed, while she was a post-doc at the

Center for Law, Society, and Culture of Indiana University, generously read the manuscript and gave us insightful comments.

We are especially indebted to sociologist and Islamic studies specialist Mansoor Moaddel of the University of Eastern Michigan for his infectious enthusiasm and helpful advice over the years on this and other projects, for arranging the translation of some of our work into Arabic, and for organizing the Workshop on Theoretical and Methodological Issues in the Study of Values in Islamic Countries in Cairo in 2010 that provided much useful feedback from Middle Eastern and American scholars on our work on the Muslim Brotherhood, as well as on political activism more generally in Muslim-majority countries.

We thank Dee Mortensen, senior sponsoring editor at the press, for believing in our book and making many important suggestions. June Silay was the project manager for the book and guided us through the various stages of publishing it. Alexander Trotter prepared the index. We thank also Nada Ibrahim, Ann Levy, and Silvia Repila for their help with translations of Arabic, Hebrew, and Italian, respectively. Israeli journalists Shira Leibowitz Schmidt and Barbara Sofer provided important information on the grassroots work of the Shas movement. Lia Sanicola, a professor of social work at the Università degli Studi di Parma and a longtime activist in Comunione e Liberazione, generously took the time to explain the theology and outreach of the movement. We thank Brandon Vaidyanathan of the University of Notre Dame for allowing us to use a quotation from his study of volunteers at Comunione e Liberazione's 2008 Meeting of Friendship among Peoples in Rimini, Italy, as the epigraph for chapter 4.

We are grateful to the University of Chicago Press for allowing us to integrate into the book portions of our article, "Overcoming Movement Obstacles by the Religiously Orthodox: The Muslim Brotherhood in Egypt, Shas in Israel, Comunione e Liberazione in Italy, and the Salvation Army in the United States," *American Journal of Sociology* 114 (March 2009): 1302–1349. © 2009 by The University of Chicago. All rights reserved.

We owe a special debt to Alcira and Alberto Vasquez for their friendship and generosity in providing a home away from home and much-needed breaks from our writing of this book while we were on sabbatical in Buenos Aires in 2008–2009.

Finally, our greatest debt is to our parents, Bob and Eileen Davis and Al and Alicia Robinson, to whom we dedicate this book, for instilling in us, by their example, a lifelong commitment to learning and exploration.

CLAIMING SOCIETY FOR GOD

INTRODUCTION

ACROSS THE WORLD TODAY, RELIGIOUSLY ORTHODOX, "fundamentalist" movements[1] of Christians, Jews, and Muslims have converged on a common strategy to install their faith traditions in societies and states that they see as alarmingly secularized. While many scholars, political observers, and world leaders, especially since September 11, 2001, see this shared line of attack as centered on armed struggle or terrorism, we show in this book that the strategy-in-common of the most prominent and successful religiously orthodox movements is not terrorism but a patient, beneath-the-radar takeover of civil society that we call "bypassing the state." One institution at a time, these movements have built massive, grassroots networks of autonomous, religion-based social service agencies, hospitals and clinics, clubs, schools, charitable organizations, worship centers, and businesses. Sidestepping the state, rather than directly confronting it, allows these movements to accomplish their multipronged agendas across the nation, address local needs not being met by the state, empower followers as they work toward the movements' goals, and for some movements, establish a base of popular support from which to push their agendas in the arena of party politics.

In *Claiming Society for God*, we tell the stories of four religiously orthodox movements—Jamaat al-Ikhwan al-Muslimin (the Society of Muslim Brothers) in Egypt, Shomrei Torah Sephardim (the Sephardi Torah Guardians) or Shas in Israel, Comunione e Liberazione (Communion and Liberation) in Italy, and the Salvation Army in the United States. Each of these movements seeks to "sacralize" society—to bring members of the public to a new or renewed understanding of faith, to impact public discourse, and to permeate public space—clubs, professional associations, schools, medical facilities, the media, social service agencies, universities, and businesses—with its own brand of faith. All four of these movements work to influence law in their society; two of them—the Muslim Brotherhood in Egypt and Shas in Israel—seek to establish what they see as divinely mandated religious law as the sole legal foundation of the state. The primary goal of these movements—claiming society for God—directly challenges modernity's differentiation of spheres of life into those where religion belongs and those where it does not.

The portrait of religiously orthodox movements that has emerged in recent scholarship, media coverage, political commentary, and public understandings is oftentimes inaccurate. First, the focus of most attention, especially since 9/11, has been on religiously orthodox movements that embrace terrorism.[2] While it is important to understand why some orthodox movements or individuals turn to violence,[3] we argue that many of the most prominent orthodox movements around the world are pursuing a nonviolent strategy that is far more successful in achieving their goal of installing religion at the center of society and throughout the world than are suicide bombings or embassy takeovers. Second, religiously orthodox movements are often characterized as irrational.[4] We argue that, in fact, a consistent communitarian logic underlies their theology and goals. Third, most scholarship and media coverage of orthodox movements has highlighted their theologically and culturally authoritarian side—their efforts, for example, to establish religious law as the sole law of the land, outlaw abortion or same-sex relationships, "protect" marriage by making divorce difficult, or enforce separate roles for men and women, husbands and wives.[5] Often missing in these accounts, we argue, is the caring side of orthodox movements—their efforts, for example, to help the impoverished, find jobs for the unemployed, and care for the sick. It is from this compassionate side of religiously orthodox movements—what we have called their "egalitarian face"[6]—that much of their institution-building outreach stems and to which they owe most of their success in attracting followers and transforming societies. For those who see these movements as a threat to civil liberties, gender equality, the rights of sexual minorities, and/or religious freedom, the failure to recognize their compassionate side reduces the likelihood of successfully countering their efforts.

The movements whose stories we chronicle in *Claiming Society for God* are among the most prominent and successful movements—religious or secular—in the world today. The Muslim Brotherhood is the most powerful Islamist[7] movement in the Muslim world, constituted the largest opposition bloc in the Egyptian parliament before the fall of Hosni Mubarak in 2011 and the largest party in the first post-Mubarak parliament, and has branches in 70 countries. Shas, "the most remarkable electoral success in Israel's history,"[8] has grown since 1983 to become the country's largest religious party and a kingmaker in coalition governments of Labor, Likud, and Kadima alike. Comunione e Liberazione is the "largest [Catholic] renewal movement in contemporary Italy"[9] and has an organizational presence in 60 countries. And in the United States, the evangelical Protestant Salvation Army is the largest charitable organization—religion-based or secular—in the nation[10] and is active in more than 110 countries. In our book we show that that each of these movements, despite considerable differences in their faith traditions, social and cultural environs, and political contexts, has used a similar gradual, long-term, unobtrusive plan of institution-building that the Muslim Brotherhood and Shas view as prefiguring new states governed by religious law, that Comunione e Liberazione sees as building a Christian society that obviates the need for an extensive secular state, and that the Salvation Army views as hastening the Second Coming of Christ.

Why is bypassing the state so effective? Starting small at the local level and side-stepping the state allows religiously orthodox movements to accomplish many of their agendas in ways that immediately and directly confronting the state likely would not. Yet this bottom-up, entrepreneurial strategy is for many orthodox movements not mere reformism or accommodation to the state; it is aimed at nothing less than a fundamental transformation of communities and the larger society. Two of the movements whose stories we tell—the Muslim Brotherhood and Shas—see state takeover through electoral politics as critical to remaking society in the name of God. Comunione e Liberazione and the Salvation Army do not directly seek to capture the state, but the hope is that, as hearts and minds are changed, the state will also. The institution-building of three of these movements—the Muslim Brotherhood, Comunione e Liberazione, and the Salvation Army—is a transnational effort aimed at transforming scores of societies throughout the world.

The success of these movements is all the more remarkable because religiously orthodox movements should have three strikes against them. According to social movement theory and research, movements—religious or secular—with rigid ideologies, extraordinarily broad and multipronged agendas, and a strong reluctance to compromise with other groups to achieve their ends are more likely to fail than movements that are ideologically flexible, that focus on a single issue, and that are willing to engage in give-and-take with other groups.[11] In this book, we show that bypassing the state and setting up networks of largely autonomous alternative institutions helps orthodox movements overcome each of these liabilities. The networks established by these movements allow skeptics to "try on" what life might be like if the movement's ideology and agendas were put into practice, encourage comparison with often ineffective, corrupt, or indifferent current governments, and empower followers as they work to bring the movement's ideology into practice. Building dispersed networks of religious, cultural, and economic institutions from the bottom up that bypass the state allows orthodox movements to bring their ideology to people where they live, demonstrating that it works "on the ground." By having local members identify and effectively address needs at the grassroots level, these movements have been able to bring into the movement, with little compromise or negotiation, diverse groups with different local sensibilities, interests, and concerns. Working on the grassroots level allows the many missions of these movements to be implemented, even if they are accomplished by addressing one issue here, another there.

Although it is widely practiced, circumventing the state as a strategy of religiously orthodox—or secular—movements has received little attention in theory or research on social movements and politics. Political scientists and sociologists of politics and social movements have generally focused on strategies that directly engage or confront the state through petitions, boycotts, lobbying, mass rallies, general strikes, electoral campaigns, violence, and transnational terrorism. Little attention has been given to the more patient, less visible, and less directly confrontational strategy of gradually building alternative institutions or burrowing into existing ones to rebuild civil society and permeate it with a new mission and understanding of faith. The scholars most likely to have recognized this strategy are area specialists working in one country or region of the world or studying one religious tradition or one orthodox movement. Although the work of these scholars informs the accounts that we give of particular orthodox movements, because their research is confined to a specific region, faith tradition, or movement, they have not recognized the commonality and power of this strategy as a pattern that prevails across nations, religious traditions, and movements. We see our contribution in this book as uncovering this strategy-in-common of successful religiously orthodox movements through a comparative and historical analysis of four movements in four different faith traditions in four separate societies.

The failure to understand the significance of bypassing the state is not limited to academics. The leaders of many Western governments were blindsided by the decisive victory of Hamas in the January 2006 parliamentary elections in Palestine. Hamas, an Islamist party and offshoot of the Egyptian Muslim Brotherhood, had established an extensive, decentralized network of mosques, schools, and social welfare organizations in Palestine.[12] Explanations for Hamas's victory focused on the corruption and ineffectiveness of President Mahmoud Abbas's ruling party Fatah and sometimes mentioned the charitable activities of Hamas.[13] But these explanations fell short in failing to recognize the full importance of Hamas's "state within a state" in meeting religious, cultural, educational, and economic needs that the Abbas government was not addressing and in allowing Palestinians, through these institutions, to feel that they already had a sense of what life might be like if Hamas were brought to power.

Claiming Society for God serves as a corrective to the view of many scholars, media pundits, and political leaders, especially in the post-9/11 period, that terrorism is the key strategy of religiously orthodox movements throughout the world. We accomplish this by telling the stories of four movements that are using religion-based institutions as building blocks in constructing new societies and states permeated with faith. While they are not the religious extremist groups whose terrorism has recently attracted much scholarly and media attention, the Muslim Brotherhood, Shas, Comunione e Liberation, and the Salvation Army—with their patient, nonviolent strategy of rebuilding society, one institution at a time—may prove to be more successful in sacralizing their societies than movements that use violence.

Through our analyses of four distinctive cases of religiously orthodox movements around the world that have adopted this institution-building strategy, we show the range of global and local circumstances in which it is being applied and the conditions under which it is most successful. In deciding which movements to feature in this book, we were committed to ensuring a diversity of Abrahamic faith traditions in national settings characterized by different histories, levels of economic development, and political structures. Egypt, the most populous Arab nation, is a predominantly Muslim country and home to the world's leading center of Sunni Islamic learning, Al-Azhar University, founded in 970–972 CE.[14] Egypt was also an early center of Islamist theory, organization, and political activism that became a model for much of the Muslim world. Israel is the only Jewish state and a country where Jewish religious parties play a key role in government. Italy is the home of the Vatican, the organizational and symbolic center of Roman Catholicism, with a long history of Catholic influence in culture and politics. Finally, the United States has strong Protestant roots and was the site of the fundamentalist/modernist split within Protestantism in the early twentieth century that subsequently spread to other predominantly Protestant countries.

In each of these countries we examine a movement of the religiously orthodox that is working to sacralize the public sphere and is widely regarded as successful. As Swiss sociologist Marco Giugni points out, there are many definitions of "success" as this applies to social movements.[15] In describing these movements as successful, we do not mean that they have achieved all of their agendas or objectives. Because their goals are so extensive and "world transforming,"[16] few, if any, orthodox or nonorthodox movements with such comprehensive goals have been successful in all their endeavors. Yet each of these movements has achieved at least some of its broad goals—not necessarily the takeover of the state that some of them ultimately seek, but nonetheless extraordinary success on at least one dimension (theological, cultural, or economic) of their agendas and in most cases, a degree of success on multiple fronts. Only one of these movements (Shas) has, at the time of our writing, directly affected the course of national policy, although the Muslim Brotherhood, with the fall of President Hosni Mubarak in Egypt, is poised to do so. Yet each of the four movements has made inroads in reshaping national consciousness and in providing an extensive array of services to their constituencies at the local level. As sociologists Daniel Cress and David Snow note, "focusing on broad policy outcomes may capture only a fragment of what some, and perhaps most, SMOs [social movement organizations] actually do. It glosses over the more proximate impact that social movements can have for their beneficiaries by missing much of what is pursued in SMO collective action campaigns at the local level."[17] By still another measure of success—survival[18]—each of the movements we analyze has achieved remarkable longevity, ranging from 29 years for Shas to 132 years for the Salvation Army USA. While estimates of membership are imprecise and three of the four movements do not even have formal membership, it is undeniable that each of them has mobilized large numbers of people in its country. And three of the movements—the Salvation Army, the Muslim Brotherhood, and Comunione e Liberazione—are active in scores of countries.

We study these movements through their documents, leaflets, mail-order solicitations, financial reports, position papers, insider histories, official websites, press releases, and the speeches, writings, and press interviews of their founders, current leaders, and members.[19] We also base our accounts on narratives and interpretations of these movements by social scientists, historians, ethnographers, and journalists specializing in specific faith traditions or countries.

The book is organized as follows: Chapter 1 introduces our theoretical argument. Although this chapter is more conceptual than the chapters on the movements which follow, it lays the groundwork for a fuller understanding of the nature of orthodox movements, the obstacles they face in transforming society, and the common strategy that the most prominent and successful movements are adopting in bringing religion to the fore. This chapter shows that the religiously orthodox are motivated by a communitarian logic which entails "watching over" community members, giving their movements both a strict side and a caring one. This inclines orthodox movements to pursue strict, authoritarian agendas on cultural concerns of sexuality, marriage, family, and gender, and to carry out caring, redistributive outreach on economic matters of providing shelter for the homeless, jobs for the unemployed, medical care for the sick, and other such activities. Orthodox movements are impeded in pursuing conventional political strategies by their ambitious, multipronged agendas, their ideological rigidity, and their strong reluctance to compromise, and instead have turned to an institution-building strategy that bypasses the state. The political opportunity structure within which these movements operate, including variable features such as shifting political alignments, competition from other social movement organizations, availability of powerful allies, and more stable aspects of states, such as their repressiveness, political party systems, and spending on social services, can affect whether and how religiously orthodox movements adopt the strategy of bypassing the state to make their interpretation of faith the cornerstone of society.

Chapters 2 through 5, in which we offer case studies of the four religiously orthodox movements, make up the core of the book. In chapter 2, we chronicle the Society of Muslim Brothers in Egypt. Founded by Hasan al-Banna in 1928, the Brotherhood contested the highly repressive Egyptian monarchy installed by the British and worked to establish an Islamic order governed according to the *shari'a* (Islamic law). Faced with a puppet-state of the British and then with often equally repressive Egyptian successors, a multiparty system that only theoretically allowed opposition parties, and a weak welfare state, the Brotherhood is the one movement among those we consider where a segment of it used violence, mainly during the movement's first three decades. Yet from the start, the Brotherhood primarily pursued a patient, gradualist, nonviolent program of building an alternative to the state from the ground up, one institution at a time. The Muslim Brotherhood bypassed the Egyptian state to set up a massive, decentralized network of mosques, religious schools, clinics and hospitals, Islamic banks, textile factories, day care centers, youth clubs, social welfare agencies, services for the unemployed, and legal aid agencies—a model that many of the Brotherhood's branches in more than seventy countries have also adopted. The Brotherhood established its extensive "state within a state"[20] in Egypt through grassroots efforts that allowed members to use elements of the movement's ideology and broad agendas in order to address local concerns and sensibilities. Because its efforts in the political arena were severely limited by government repression, during the 1990s the Brotherhood worked instead to gain electoral control of professional associations and student unions, which gave the movement considerable legitimacy and political influence. In 2005, the Brotherhood used support generated through its grassroots network, and the implicit indictment that its services offered of the state's ability to meet citizens' needs, to become the largest opposition bloc in the Egyptian People's Assembly. After Egyptians overthrew the autocratic regime of President Hosni Mubarak in the "Arab Spring" of 2011, the Brotherhood, as the nation's longest-lived and best-organized political force, won the largest share of votes in the first post-Mubarak elections.

The Sephardi Torah Guardians, or Shas, in Israel, the focus of chapter 3, is distinctive in that it has effectively bypassed the state by directly participating in it. Shas was founded in 1983 by Rabbi Ovadya Yosef as an ultra-Orthodox (Haredi) movement of Mizrahi Jews of North African and Middle Eastern origin. Shas seeks to make Jewish religious (*halachic*) law the basis of the Israeli legal system. In contrast to the Muslim Brotherhood, Shas entered party politics from the start, and through its electoral success in Israel's multiparty system, quickly became the nation's largest religious party and a critical partner in coalition governments of Labor, Likud, and Kadima alike. Originally a primarily theological and cultural movement, Shas has increasingly emphasized its economic mission to its Mizrahi followers, who are disadvantaged relative to Ashkenazi Jews of European and Russian origin. Like the Muslim Brotherhood, Shas has succeeded, in part, by filling a vacuum in the Israeli welfare state. Early on, the movement used its political leverage to win funding and autonomy for a vast welfare and educational network, El Hamaayan (To the Wellspring), through which it runs hundreds of programs—religious schools at all levels, day care centers, hot lunch programs, after-school clubhouses, charitable organizations (*amutot*), welfare programs for large families, rotating-credit societies, jobs programs, discount stores, senior citizen centers, housing projects, and so forth. Shas's "surrogate state"[21] of religious, cultural, and economic institutions gives the ultra-Orthodox the autonomy to separate themselves from the rest of Israeli society. Shas's success in winning educational and economic benefits for its followers has gained it the support of large numbers of "traditional" (partially observant) or secular Mizrahim, leading to further electoral gains and greater leverage in the Knesset.

In chapter 4 we offer the case of Comunione e Liberazione (CL), a Catholic, integrist (traditionalist) movement that seeks greater roles for the Church and the pope in Italian society. CL developed its alternative, religiously infused cultural, educational, and economic institutions in Italy, which has a well-funded welfare state, showing that a weak welfare state is not a necessary precondition for adopting the strategy of bypassing the state. Quite the contrary; CL built its institutions precisely to obviate the need for a strong welfare state, an agenda that has been much shaped by its struggles against secular communist and socialist parties. CL was founded by Father Luigi Giussani in 1954 as a purely theological movement, but since 1986 has built an extensive, nationwide network of 1,100 nonprofit charitable, cultural, and educational institutions linked with 35,000 CL-inspired businesses. The network encompasses unemployment centers, a national food bank, homes for recovering drug addicts and the disabled, hospices for AIDS patients and others who are terminally ill, social welfare organizations, bookshops, consumer cooperatives, and primary and secondary religious schools. The network, elements of which have also been established in branches in some sixty countries, has been built from the ground up; local branches of CL identify community needs and initiate entrepreneurial projects to address these. After CL's political arm, Movimento Popolare, failed in its efforts to overturn Italy's liberalized abortion and divorce laws in the 1970s and early 1980s and was hurt by its association with scandal-tainted Christian Democratic politicians, the movement pulled back some from electoral politics. CL today directs its efforts to the spiritual development of its members and to building a "parallel society"[22] of Catholic institutions that it hopes will demonstrate the ability of largely nonstate ventures of individuals, businesses, and social service organizations to meet human needs.

In chapter 5, we narrate the story of the Salvation Army USA, a branch of an international evangelical Protestant movement founded in England in 1865 by the Reverend William Booth. Although the American branch was heavily influenced by the communitarian theology of its British founder, it developed its own agendas and framing to succeed in the American setting. The founder's decision to eschew party politics and two features of the U.S. political landscape—a winner-takes-all, two-party system that makes it unlikely that a small party will affect public policy, and tax codes restricting the political activities of religious and charitable organizations—made the Salvation Army USA distinctive among the movements whose stories we tell in that it never entered the formal political arena. Yet the Army's purpose has still been broadly political. It challenges Americans' life priorities, materialism, and moral condemnation of the poor and it pushes the state in what it sees as a Christian direction through behind-the-scenes lobbying on Capitol Hill. The first institutions established by the Army—local churches or "corps"—grew out of what was initially a purely evangelical mission. In 1890, when its founder, William Booth, came to recognize the structural causes of poverty and joblessness, a second mission of social service to the downtrodden was added. Gradually, the Army's economic mission moved to the fore in the United States while its evangelical ministry and its strict cultural platform on abortion, homosexuality, pornography, and similar issues were pursued more quietly. The Salvation Army USA bypassed the state in its early years by providing a safety net for Americans that was not offered by the government and in its later years by complementing the modest welfare efforts of the U.S. state. Today in the United States, the Army has an elaborate network of institutions, including worship centers, hostels for the homeless, group homes, hospices for HIV patients, day care facilities, addiction dependency programs, domestic violence shelters, disaster assistance programs, thrift shops, outreach programs for released prisoners, career counseling centers, and medical facilities. This vast network of religion-infused institutions serves what the movement sees as the critically important purpose of preparing the way for the Second Coming of Christ.

We conclude in chapter 6 with an assessment of our theoretical argument from chapter 1 in light of the four case studies. We consider whether the strategy of bypassing the state by setting up networks of alternative institutions is unique to movements of the religiously orthodox or is equally suited to modernist and secular movements. We conclude this chapter by arguing that, regardless of whether one supports or opposes their agendas, the four religiously orthodox movements whose stories we tell are remarkably successful in using a gradual, one-institution-at-a-time strategy, coupled with considerable organizational acumen, entrepreneurial skill, and strategic flexibility, to bring religion to the center of society.

CONTESTING THE STATE
BY BYPASSING IT

Contemporary "fundamentalist" movements[1]—or as we prefer to call them, religiously orthodox movements—have been the subject of much scholarship, media coverage, and political punditry. Missing in nearly all accounts of the nature, strategies, and impact of such movements is an understanding of their underlying communitarian logic, including a compassionate side that leads to much of their institution-building, their outreach to those in need, their success in recruitment, and their popular support. Even when this caring side of religiously orthodox movements is recognized, it is often misunderstood as mere charity.[2] Unrecognized is the fact that, for many of the most prominent orthodox movements, this institutional outreach—such as building clinics and hospitals, establishing factories that provide jobs and pay higher-than-prevailing wages, initiating literacy campaigns, offering hospices for the dying, providing aid to the needy, and building affordable housing—is spread throughout the country and linked with schools, worship centers, and businesses into a dense network with the aim of permeating civil society with the movement's own brand of faith. Yet to overlook or misunderstand this strategy is to seriously underestimate the reach of religiously orthodox movements and their success in infusing societies and states with religion.

While religiously orthodox movements are often portrayed as irrational or reactionary, we show in this chapter that they are motivated by a logic of communitarianism that is neither consistently right wing nor left wing. This communitarian logic leads them to establish places of worship, schools, social welfare agencies, and businesses that ultimately grow into extensive networks of alternative institutions and, in some cases, a parallel society or state within a state. This nonconfrontational, institution-building strategy can be an end in itself, since it can result in the permeation of society with religious sensibilities, religiously based standards on family and sexuality, and faith-based outreach to those in need. Or if state takeover is the goal, it can help the movement build a strong base of popular support that can be translated into electoral victories in the formal political arena.

RELIGIOUS ORTHODOXY AS COMMUNITARIAN

To understand the logic underlying religiously orthodox movements, their political agendas, and their strategies, we begin with a distinction between two "fundamentally different conceptions of moral authority," first made by sociologist James Davison Hunter in his 1991 book, *Culture Wars*. The *religiously orthodox* vision views a deity (that is, Allah, Yahweh, God) as the ultimate judge of good and evil; regards sacred texts (and clerical teachings derived from these) as divinely revealed, without error, and timeless; and sees this supreme being as watching over, affecting, and judging people's daily lives. In contrast, the *modernist*[3] vision views individuals as having the freedom to make moral decisions in the context of their times; sees religious texts and teachings as human creations that should be considered in cultural and historical context along with other moral precepts; and regards individuals as responsible for themselves and as largely independent in making their lives and fates.[4] Modernists need not be atheists or agnostics; in the United States, for example, most modernists believe in God.[5]

In a series of conceptual and empirical articles,[6] we have drawn out the theological and political implications of Hunter's ideal–typical visions of moral authority and have recognized that actual individuals, religious groups, and movements exist along an orthodox to modernist continuum, not necessarily at the polar extremes or encompassing fully every aspect of one or the other ideal type of moral cosmology. Our theoretical model, moral cosmology theory,[7] shows how the orthodox and modernist moral cosmologies differ theologically and how these differences affect the political attitudes and behavior of those who hold these moral cosmologies. Our model applies only to the Abrahamic faith traditions, which include Christianity, Islam, and Judaism—all of which regard Abraham as a prophetic figure. Another common expression for these traditions is "religions of the Book," and we use this interchangeably with Abrahamic religions throughout this book. The key characteristic of the Abrahamic faiths, which is lacking in the Hindu and Buddhist traditions, is having a sacred book that is seen as revealing divine, eternal truths and laws. The existence of the sacred book gives rise to the orthodox, who take the text to be literally true for all times, places, and peoples, and to (at the opposite pole) modernists, who regard the text as requiring human interpretation, adjustment to contemporary circumstances, and integration with other moral and juridical principles in formulating law for societies today. Few Hindus or Buddhists take any of the many sacred books of their faith literally, word for word, and hence the orthodoxy/modernism distinction does not apply well to Hinduism and Buddhism.[8]

Our argument is that the religiously orthodox cosmology is *theologically communitarian* in that it regards individuals as subsumed by a larger community, all members of which are subject to the laws and greater plan of a deity. In the orthodox cosmology, timeless religious truths, standards, and laws are seen as having been laid down once and for all in a sacred book or in teachings derived from this by a supreme being—laws that the community must uphold and that everyone is obliged to obey. Thus there is a strict or authoritarian side to the theology underlying orthodoxy.

At the same time, theological communitarianism entails the belief that the individual's faith can find its full realization and expression only in the context of a larger community of believers. Individuals in the faith have an obligation both to seek out others who have arrived at the same understanding and to share this with those who have not yet come to the faith or who have lost it. This often entails the sense among the orthodox that they are part of a "sacred community." Gabriel Almond, R. Scott Appleby, and Emmanuel Sivan note that among North American fundamentalists, referring to themselves as "'yoked together' [is] the ultimate praise for insiders, for the saved."[9] There is often the notion of individuals as being spiritually equal or potentially equal before Allah, as being "children of Yahweh," or as part of a larger "family of God." The theological communitarianism of the orthodox thus entails elements of sharing, caring, mutuality, and responsibility for others.

Communitarianism, like the notion of "community" on which it is based, has elements of both inclusivity and exclusivity. It involves drawing the line between those who have come to the correct understanding of the faith and those who have not—between those who are "real" or "authentic" Christians, Jews, or Muslims and those who are not. Yet it also includes the potential for everyone to take up or return to the "true" faith, and hence the obligation to proselytize outside the community of true believers.

We argue that the two sides of the theological communitarianism of the orthodox cosmology—the strict and caring sides—have important implications for the politics of those who hold this moral understanding. The strict side inclines the orthodox to an authoritarian strand of *cultural communitarianism,* in which the community must enforce what it sees as divinely mandated standards on sexuality, gender, reproduction, and family life, which in practice has often meant forbidding abortion, homosexuality, or sex outside marriage; making divorce difficult or impossible to obtain; and mandating specific and different roles for men and women, husbands and wives.[10] At the same time, the compassionate side of theological communitarianism inclines the orthodox to *economic communitarianism,* whereby it is the community's or state's responsibility to share with or provide for those in need, reduce the gap between rich and poor, and intervene in the economy so that the needs of all community members are met. The communitarianism of orthodoxy thus entails "watching over" community members, giving it politically both a strict side and a caring[11] one, and inclining its adherents toward cultural authoritarianism and economic egalitarianism.[12]

Orthodoxy, as we (and Hunter) conceive it, refers not to "doctrinal" orthodoxy or belief in the specific tenets of a faith tradition (e.g., the divinity of Christ, the obligation to pay *zakat* or mandatory alms) but to a broad theological orientation toward the locus of moral authority with which the orthodox of all the Abrahamic faith traditions would agree. In other words, orthodox Christians, Jews (with a small "o" to distinguish their cosmology from formal membership in the Orthodox branch of Judaism), and Muslims adhere to some religious tenets that are different, but they share the broad worldview that the locus of moral authority is a supreme deity and that legal codes should reflect absolute and timeless divine law.

Neither orthodoxy nor modernism should be equated with any specific faith tradition or denomination. Among individuals who are Catholic, Jewish, Muslim, or Protestant, we have found in our prior quantitative research that there are those who are orthodox in their cosmologies, those who are modernist, and those who combine elements of orthodoxy and modernism. This is even true in the United States among categories of Protestants such as evangelical, mainline, or black Protestants. Within each of these types of Protestants, we have found a range of moral cosmologies, although of course the range in some cases may tend to lean toward either the orthodox or the modernist pole. Moreover, in analyses explaining Americans' positions on cultural and economic issues, we have found that moral cosmology (ranging from orthodoxy to modernism) usually has independent effects from denomination (Catholic, Jewish, evangelical Protestant, mainline Protestant, black Protestant, other, none).[13]

In contrast to the orthodox, theological modernists are *theologically individualistic* in that they see individuals, and not a deity, as largely responsible for their own moral decisions and fates. Reflecting Enlightenment ideals, the modernist cosmology combines support for individual choice and freedom with the expectation of individual responsibility,[14] inclining its adherents to *cultural individualism* or libertarianism, whereby, for example, the resolution of an unwanted pregnancy is seen as a woman's private decision, individual choice in sexual expression is allowed, and husbands and wives should decide for themselves how to divide their labor or structure their partnership. The theological individualism of modernists also inclines them to laissez faire *economic individualism* and hence less willingness to use community or state resources to help those in need. Since modernists are inclined to hold individuals responsible for what happens to them, the poor and jobless are considered to be largely responsible for their own economic misfortune. Thus, for modernists, the tendency is to see greater effort and initiative by the poor themselves as the solution to poverty and inequality rather than collective efforts by the community or state to, for example, improve their lot, equalize incomes, or redistribute economic resources by nationalizing businesses.

RIGHT OR LEFT?

Our argument in moral cosmology theory about the political leanings of the orthodox and modernists goes against the common wisdom that the orthodox are to the political right, while modernists are to the left. The traditional way of representing political space as a single dimension, running from right to left, is shown in figure 1.1, where we have also located the religiously orthodox and modernists according to conventional thought—a view we reject.

Figure 1.1. One-dimensional political continuum, showing conventional view of the locations of the religiously orthodox and modernists.

In our earlier quantitative research analyzing the positions of the orthodox and modernists around the world,[15] we found that political space is better represented as two-dimensional, with one dimension representing cultural issues and running from culturally communitarian to culturally individualistic and another dimension representing economic issues and running from economically communitarian to economically individualistic (see figure 1.2).

That individuals and groups may position themselves differently on cultural and economic issues has been recognized for some time. U.S. sociologist and political scientist Seymour Martin Lipset, writing in 1981, distinguished between cultural conservatism and economic conservatism, the former referring to efforts to restrict freedoms with respect to sexuality, reproduction, marriage, and family and the latter to efforts to support laissez faire economic principles.[16] Reconceptualizing political space to have a cultural dimension and an economic dimension allows us to locate the religiously orthodox and modernists as shown in figure 1.2. Situating these moral cosmologies in two-dimensional political space shows that the religiously orthodox, relative to modernists, tend to be more communitarian on both the cultural and economic dimensions. Because the religiously orthodox are, in conventional left–right terms, more to the right of modernists on cultural issues but more to the left of modernists on economic ones, the complexity and consistency (in terms of communitarianism) of their position cannot be captured by the conventional, one-dimensional, left–right continuum (figure 1.1) and may lead to their being viewed as irrational or, if the economic dimension—their caring side—is ignored, as consistently right wing.

In the United States, as we show in figure 1.3, neither the religiously orthodox nor modernists are in the same political quadrants as the two major political parties, the Republicans and the Democrats. To win the votes of many of the religiously orthodox, each of these parties must emphasize the issue positions that it shares in common with them and deemphasize the positions on which it differs from them. Thus, in attracting votes of the orthodox, Republicans must emphasize their positions on cultural issues,

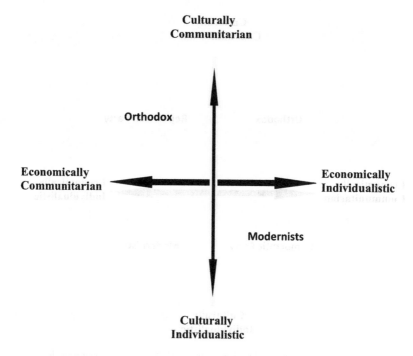

Figure 1.2. Two-dimensional political space, showing the locations of the religiously orthodox and modernists according to moral cosmology theory.

such as legislating against abortion and same-sex marriage, while deemphasizing their positions on economic issues, such as cutting welfare spending, repealing health care legislation that covers all Americans, and maintaining tax cuts for the wealthy. Democrats must take the opposite strategy in winning over the orthodox: emphasize their positions on economic issues but deemphasize their positions on cultural issues.

While these are the dominant tendencies of the orthodox relative to modernists, there are exceptions to these inclinations. Some modernists, such as secular democratic socialists, hold communitarian economic beliefs. And some religiously orthodox people, such as televangelist Pat Robertson in the United States, hold laissez faire individualistic beliefs on economic matters. Nonetheless, quantitative analyses of nationally representative surveys by ourselves and other scholars on the effect of moral cosmologies (orthodoxy to modernism) on cultural attitudes (abortion, homosexuality, birth control, divorce, appropriate roles for women and men) and economic attitudes (poverty, inequality, joblessness) have found in twenty countries that the religiously orthodox are more communitarian than modernists on both economic and cultural issues. This pattern has been found in countries that are predominantly Protestant

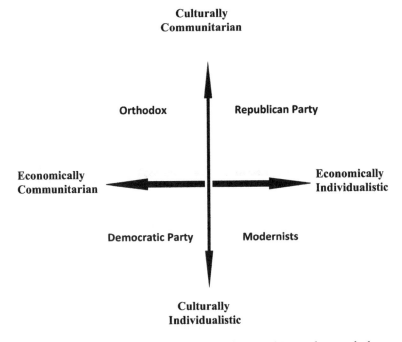

Figure 1.3. Two-dimensional political space in the United States, showing the locations of the religiously orthodox, modernists, and the major political parties.

(Norway, the United States), mixed Protestant and Catholic (West Germany), Catholic (Austria, Ireland, Italy, Poland, Portugal), Eastern Orthodox (Bulgaria, Romania), Jewish (Israel), and Muslim (Algeria, Bangladesh, Egypt, Indonesia, Jordan, Kazakhstan, Kyrgyzstan, Pakistan, and Saudi Arabia).[17] The tendency for orthodox *individuals* to be both strict and caring in all the Abrahamic faith traditions led us to this study of orthodox *movements* that have galvanized around a similar pairing of concerns.

ARE THE ORTHODOX IRRATIONAL?

Understanding the communitarianism of the religiously orthodox and the nuances of its political consequences helps to clear up the misunderstanding—identified in the introduction as coloring scholarship, media coverage, political analysis, and popular understandings of the orthodox—that they are irrational. This characterization, we argue, owes much to rational choice theory. Rational choice theory, popular in economics, political science, and sociology, among other disciplines, assumes that humans are motivated by what is usually framed as economic self-interest. From this perspective, the attitudes and actions of the orthodox appear irrational on several levels. First, the orthodox are motivated by concerns other than purely economic ones: Their theological and cultural agendas cannot be reduced to economic self-interest.

Second, the economic goals of the orthodox are communitarian, not strictly self-interested. Only if one argues that the orthodox tend to be less advantaged economically and that their egalitarian attitudes reflect a desire to help themselves can their economic attitudes be regarded as self-interested. Yet among the four movements whose stories we tell, Comunione e Liberazione draws especially from students and middle-class professionals and the Muslim Brotherhood attracts a wide swath of followers, including students, professionals, poor and working-class people, and the unemployed. Two of the movements we chronicle, Shas and the Salvation Army, do seem to draw disproportionately from the poor and working class, and in this sense it could be argued that their economic positions reflect an element of economic self-interest. Yet our earlier quantitative research on individuals in a wide array of countries, including Egypt, Israel, Italy, and the United States, where our four movements are situated, found that the effect of orthodoxy in promoting economically egalitarian attitudes in favor of government efforts to help the poor, reduce the gap between rich and poor, and intervene in the economy remains significant in these countries even with controls for education, occupation, and income. In other words, the relative egalitarianism of the orthodox cannot be explained away by economic self-interest.

Third and most importantly, our argument above—that there is a consistent communitarian logic to orthodoxy—belies the notion of irrationality. The orthodox are acting in ways congruent with an underlying logic; this logic simply is not the economically self-interested, individualistic logic that rational choice theory assumes.

MOVEMENTS OF THE RELIGIOUSLY ORTHODOX

The four movements of the religiously orthodox whose stories we tell here embody the communitarianism on cultural and economic matters that we have found among religiously orthodox individuals in countries where religions of the Book predominate and specifically in the four countries in which we chronicle these movements: Egypt, Israel, Italy, and the United States. The Society of Muslim Brothers, Shas, Comunione e Liberazione, and the Salvation Army USA share a common communitarian agenda of sacralizing their community, society, and state; legally mandating culturally communitarian or strict beliefs about gender, sexuality, and family issues; and building economically communitarian institutions that look out for the material well-being of those in need. Their theological, cultural, and economic communitarianism is reflected in extraordinarily broad agendas—agendas that could appeal to a wide spectrum of citizens but, as we will see, require special strategy to manage.

In referring to these movements as religiously orthodox, we are not saying that everyone involved with them is religiously orthodox. In our narrative of each of the four movements, we discuss how these movements provide graduated levels of involvement and commitment, from the lowest level, where individuals may agree with only a small part of the movement's theology and make only minimal commitments of time to the movement, to the highest levels, where individuals wholly accept the theology and goals, commit their lives to the movement, give up family and friends for it, and marry others in the movement or remain celibate. We also discuss how at the grassroots level, individuals who do not share the movement's theology and goals may become involved as they work to solve local problems. People's motivations and theological dispositions for becoming involved in, for example, helping the poor may vary widely from person to person, as studies of individuals and congregations in the United States have found.[18] Each of these movements is always in the process of involving and absorbing people who may have originally had little agreement with or commitment to the movement. Moving individuals to greater levels of faith and involvement is one of the ways in which these movements sacralize society.

Of course, not all religiously orthodox movements share the multipronged agenda set that characterizes the four movements whose stories we tell here. Again, we note the probabilistic and not deterministic nature of the pattern we theorize between moral cosmology and cultural and economic agendas. Put differently, we are dealing with tendencies and not certainties. Some religiously orthodox movements seek to sacralize the broader society and promote either a culturally strict *or* an economically redistributive agenda but not both. In the United States, for example, Focus on the Family (http://www.family.org/) is a religiously orthodox group that is pursuing a primarily cultural agenda of imposing a single standard of sexual, family, and gender behavior on Americans, while Habitat for Humanity (http://www.habitat.org/), Bread for the World (http://www.bread.org/), and We Care America (http://www.wecareamerica.org/) are orthodox groups pursuing primarily economic communitarianism or outreach to those in need.

There are also movements of the orthodox which have pursued public agendas of cultural authoritarianism and economic individualism that do not fit with the dominant tendency we have found among the religiously orthodox in our prior quantitative research. These movements, along with the subset of the religiously orthodox who share their political positions, constitute the "Religious Right." In the United States, the Moral Majority of the 1980s and the Christian Coalition (http://www.cc.org/) and the New Apostolic Reformation (http://www.newapostolicchurch.org) today are examples of such movements. While we do not deny the existence and potential or actual political impact of the Religious Right in some societies, our focus here is on movements representing the predominant inclination toward cultural *and* economic communitarianism among the religiously orthodox that we found in our earlier research in a wide range of countries and in all the Abrahamic faith traditions.[19]

THE OVERLOOKED COMPASSIONATE SIDE OF ORTHODOX MOVEMENTS

Most social scientists, journalists, and political pundits focus on two of the agendas of the religiously orthodox—their theological mission to bring people in their society to a new understanding and acceptance of their faith tradition (that is, proselytizing) and their culturally strict mission which may include outlawing abortion and/or contraception, forbidding sex outside of heterosexual marriage, requiring school prayer, restricting the appropriate and legal roles of women and men, making divorce difficult or impossible to obtain, and so on. These theologically and culturally communitarian agendas of bringing the entire community under one theological and cultural standard lead orthodox movements to build centers of worship, publishing houses, television and radio stations, to establish religious schools to socialize children into the faith, and to push for laws regulating sexuality, family life, and gender relations.

What is missing in most accounts of religiously orthodox movements, however, is their caring and compassionate side—what we have called their "egalitarian face."[20] This side often recognizes a need for economic justice in the community and is behind the efforts of these movements to provide jobs that pay living wages to workers, low-cost health care and medicines for the sick, food for the hungry, affordable housing for those without it, and so forth. It is from this caring, egalitarian-leaning side that much of the institution-building undertaken by religiously orthodox movements stems and, undoubtedly, from which much of its public support derives. The failure to see this economic mission leads scholars and journalists alike to miss—or misperceive as mere localized charity—the immense efforts of orthodox movements to establish "state-like" society-wide networks that are motivated by a concern with social justice or entitlement and may far exceed what the state is doing.

Is the compassionate side that religiously orthodox movements display merely strategic—an effort to win people over to the movement by offering services that citizens need? This may be part of the motivation, but because in our quantitative work we have found that this caring, justice-seeking side exists among orthodox *individuals,* most of whom are not part of movements and who would seem to have no strategic motivation for supporting such outreach to the marginalized, we argue that the economic outreach of orthodox movements draws upon a genuine sense of mutual obligation, shared humanity, and compassion, and is not solely strategic.

PUBLIC RELIGION

Religiously orthodox movements develop as a reaction against the secularism, individualism, and materialism that they see as increasingly characterizing modern societies.[21] The rise of orthodoxy itself in the late nineteenth to early twentieth centuries was a response to growing acceptance within the Abrahamic religious traditions of Enlightenment ideals: of scientific explanations and reason over faith and other ways of knowing, of individual autonomy and freedom of thought over religious doctrinal authority, and of separation of religion and state over official state religions. Having recognized and decided to combat these trends, religiously orthodox movements can either disengage themselves from the larger society, as did Protestant fundamentalists in the United States for several decades following their defeat in the Scopes evolution trial of 1925, or become what sociologist José Casanova calls "public religions" that work to remake or sacralize the public sphere.[22] Sociologist Rhys Williams explains why the latter course is more likely:

> Fundamentalist ideological and organizational frames . . . tend to be totalizing. They are predicated on a rejection of differentiation and decompartmentalization of life in the modern world, and as such push toward some form of de-differentiation. The challenge to liberal capitalism's public–private distinction is part of that push. Thus the basic ideological impulse of fundamentalism is toward engagement with the public sphere, including some type of involvement in public politics.[23]

Orthodox movements may also become involved in the public sphere because their communitarianism, which is by nature concerned with the control and welfare of the larger community—spiritually, culturally, and economically—propels them to active engagement with society. The decision to become public movements in pursuit of broad agendas, while maintaining ideological purity and generally eschewing compromise with others, gives such movements several liabilities that scholars of social movements suggest should be serious obstacles to their success.

THREE LIABILITIES OF RELIGIOUSLY ORTHODOX MOVEMENTS

Social movements—religiously orthodox or not—with broad, multi-issue agendas, rigid ideologies, and reluctance to compromise should have three strikes against them. The literature on social movements is replete with theory and case studies illustrating why these are liabilities that often lead to movement failure.[24] Yet today, religiously orthodox movements, many of which suffer from all three of these liabilities, are thriving in all the Abrahamic faith traditions in countries across the world. These movements have agendas on three fronts: theology, culture, and economics. They adhere to a strict, moral absolutism that views the sacred texts, clerical rulings, and teachings on which they base their theology as divinely revealed, inerrant, and true for all times, places, and peoples. And their leaders and followers are highly resistant to the give-and-take with other groups that might make it easier for them to attract a broad following or form alliances and thus advance their agendas. Yet, despite these obstacles to success, religiously orthodox movements are among the most effective and successful movements in the world today.

How can their success be explained? Before answering this question, we explore the problems each of the three liabilities presents for social movements, according to social movement theory and research.

Broad, Multi-Issue Agendas

Writing in 1972, sociologist Roberta Ash proposed that "The broader the goals of a social movement . . . the less likely it will be to succeed."[25] In his classic book, *The Strategy of Social Protest,* sociologist William Gamson tested the opposite hypothesis—that multi-issue groups are more likely to succeed because having "more hooks in the water, it seems that one would be more likely to catch a fish or two." Through his analysis of fifty-three challenger groups in the United States, Gamson found that, to the contrary, single-issue movements were far more likely than multi-issue movements to succeed in winning acceptance from their antagonists and achieving their ends.[26] The potential disadvantages of multiple agendas are many: a greater likelihood of coming into conflict with the state on at least some of the movement's missions; the danger of spreading resources and personnel too thin; the possibility that achieving success on one issue will require inattention to others, thus alienating core members; misunderstandings in the public and membership about what the movement is "really" about; the lesser likelihood that potential supporters will agree with the movement's objectives on all fronts; the greater prospect of schisms developing between those committed to one agenda as opposed to another; and the fear that the agenda is too far-reaching and hence unlikely to be achieved, or if achieved, likely to disrupt predictable, routine ways of life.

The movements we consider here have broad, multipronged agendas, including theological aims, such as bringing the general public of their society to specific religious understandings, establishing religious law as the law of the land, reversing trends toward increasing secularization in education and other realms of life; cultural goals, such as forbidding abortion, contraception, and same-sex relationships, reestablishing "traditional" gender relations, and prohibiting pornography and prostitution; and economic goals, such as addressing the needs of the poor, establishing living wages, providing health care, and equalizing income distributions. Even *within* each of the three issue domains—theological, cultural, and economic—these movements are multipronged movements. In this sense, these movements seek nothing less than a fundamental transformation of the community, society, and state in their countries.

Ideological Rigidity

A second obstacle to social movement success, according to prior theory and research, is ideological rigidity, strictness, certainty, and absolutism, as opposed to ideological ambiguity and pragmatism. In the case of welfare rights organizations in the United States, sociologists Ellen Reese and Garnett Newcombe find that "rigid adherence to strict, highly principled ideologies can discourage SMOs [social movement organizations] from framing their demands in ways that resonate with their targeted audiences and thus constrain their growth and influence" and can "undermine organizational success and survival."[27] Sociologist Vernon Bates, who studied the rise and fall of the Oregon Citizens Alliance (OCA), a fundamentalist Protestant movement with an anti-gay-rights agenda, writes that the rigidity of the OCA's ideology was ultimately rejected by local Republicans in favor of a "Big Tent" ideology. In the words of the executive director of the Oregon Republicans:

> There are a lot of good things in our platform, but the group that came together to write the platform, which is a lot of OCA people, wrote a platform that is preaching. We're not attracting young people. We're not attracting women who think for themselves and the reason they say is that we are very judgmental. Our platform doesn't say you may, it says you can't. And young people say, why would we want to get involved in an organization that sounds like our parents, and teachers and society. . . . Why would we want to join a Party that is also going to judge us, to say you can't think for yourself?[28]

Sociologist Marshall Ganz also identifies the disadvantages of ideological rigidity and the advantages of ambiguity and pragmatism in the "strategic capacity" of social movements. Ganz argues that successful social movements have leaders who, in addition to other talents, "are tolerant of ambiguity" and "rely on multiple sources of resources and authority" in making decisions[29]—both of which contrast sharply with the moral absolutism of the orthodox and their exclusive reliance on what they see as divine authority revealed in sacred texts and clerical rulings. Ganz sees a pragmatic approach to ideology as most efficacious, noting: "Encounters with diverse points of view and ways of doing things . . . facilitate innovation."[30] Similarly, sociologist Richard Wood, in his study of four church-based, economic justice movements in the United States, found that the churches that had a high "capacity for ambiguity" were more successful in pursuing their agenda because they were better able to understand and interact with political officials and less likely to label such officials as "one of them," as opposed to "one of us."[31] Finally, sociologist Elizabeth Armstrong, in her study of the gay and lesbian movement in San Francisco during the 1990s, found that the movement was able to hold together three different approaches (interest group, identity politics, and participation in a commercialized sexual subculture) by structuring in "a high tolerance for ambiguity" and "defining diversity as one of the core commonalities of the movement."[32]

Each of the four religiously orthodox movements we chronicle in this book grounds its theology in a literal interpretation of the sacred text, teachings, or clerical rulings of its tradition, and this constitutes its ideology and the foundation of its theological, cultural, and economic agendas. Members of these movements regard their interpretations of these sources of authority as clear and inerrant, and view these sources as holding truths and laws rooted in divine authority that are true for all times, places, and peoples. This strict ideology allows for little "contextual" reading or decision making; accordingly, morality is not something that is ambiguous and can be interpreted in the spirit of the times or differently by different individuals, as modernists might do. In this book we explore the puzzle of orthodox movements that have been able to maintain their strict ideology on multiple fronts while also winning considerable popular support, transforming civil society, and responding to the political environment in which they are situated.

Reluctance to Compromise

While ideological rigidity refers to strict, inflexible adherence to the movement's ideology, reluctance to compromise concerns a disinclination to engage in give-and-take with opponents and groups that could potentially become allies or coalition partners. Sociologist Neil Fligstein's concept of "social skill" refers to actors (or leaders) who are successful in "getting others to cooperate, maneuvering around more powerful actors, and generally knowing how to build political coalitions," "convincing their supporters to cooperate and finding means of accommodation with other groups," and "building compromise identities that bring many groups along."[33] Support for the strategic importance of compromise is evident in Wood's study of four economic-justice churches in the United States, where having "cultural resources for negotiation and compromise," including the capacity to get beyond seeing political conflicts as "good vs. evil," was critical to the church that successfully pursued its agenda.[34] Those in the midst of political frays—such as, in the next case, the battle over gay rights in the state of Oregon—have also noted the liability of uncompromising stances. Bates quotes an Oregon Republican contrasting his own openness to negotiation with the uncompromising behavior of Lon Mabon, leader of the fundamentalist Protestant Oregon Citizens Alliance: "I am a person who says, I am going to reason with you and if I can't convince you, we can agree to disagree. Lon Mabon believes that if you don't do what he wants, he is going to bend your arm, break it and kick you out and banish you from his presence, kind of an imperial view of politics."[35] While the movements whose stories we tell have occasionally compromised to win over other groups, the primary strategy they developed—that of bypassing the state through the construction of massive grassroots networks that meet citizen needs—allowed local followers to highlight and work on those elements of the movement's agenda that corresponded to local sensibilities and concerns and thus to incorporate people with diverse local interests throughout the country without having to negotiate or compromise in bringing them in.

We do not dispute that comprehensive agendas, ideological strictness, and reluctance to negotiate—key features of the four movements we examine—generally present

significant obstacles to social movements. Rather, through an analysis of four religiously orthodox movements that span the globe, we show that social movements can
overcome these liabilities.

Using a comparative and historical lens, we chronicle a key strategy-in-common
that these orthodox movements have used to handle these dilemmas. Because movements of the religiously orthodox have been understudied by social movement scholars,
much of the theory of social movements has been developed through the study of other
types of movements, particularly secular, rights-oriented, progressive movements—
and usually in advanced industrial societies.[36] The four movements whose stories we
tell do not fit the expectation that comprehensive agendas, ideological strictness, and
reluctance to compromise lead to failure. Our question, then, is: How did movements
that should have failed succeed—and in many cases, become major players in their
country and internationally? Through inductive analyses of these "deviant"[37] cases—
movements that social movement theory would expect to fail—we identify a key strategy
that has allowed these movements to overcome these obstacles.

BYPASSING THE STATE

Each of the movements we recount uses a similar strategy: bypassing the state by
setting up a massive network of largely autonomous, alternative religious, cultural, and
economic institutions. The institutional outreach of the Muslim Brotherhood and Shas
is extensive enough that many scholars refer to the networks they have established as
a "state within a state" or a "surrogate state."[38] Comunione e Liberazione's network in
Italy has been characterized as a "parallel society."[39] The economic institutions of the
Salvation Army's network in the United States complement and bolster the modest efforts of the weak U.S. welfare state. While the motivation for bypassing the state and
the circumstances under which this strategy was adopted vary markedly from movement to movement, each movement focuses its efforts on transforming local communities at the grassroots level—sacralizing society from the ground up, one institution
at a time. This bottom-up transformation, coupled with loose coordination from the
top, resulted in each case in a dense web of cultural, economic, and religious organizations extending to nearly all nooks and crannies of the nation. It was a quiet, beneath-
the-radar strategy of building alternative institutions—schools, hospitals, social service
agencies, clubs, for-profit businesses, and places of worship—to gradually remake or
sacralize society, and sometimes also the state, from the ground up.

Building alternative institutions to sacralize the public sphere portends the future
society, state, or world that each of these movements hopes to establish. It allows skeptics to "try on" the movement's theological, cultural, and economic vision and agendas
and see if they work in practice. It helps allay concerns that the movement's aims are
too sweeping or that it is peopled by fanatics who will overturn all the familiar routines

of life. The alternative institutions, by meeting concrete, everyday needs of citizens, encourage comparison with often ineffective, corrupt, or indifferent current governments that are failing to meet these needs. Sidestepping the state empowers both followers, as they work to bring the movement's ideology into lived reality, and recipients of services, as they recognize their partnership and common interest with those who are providing these services. And working at the grassroots level allows local members to address elements of the movement's ideology and missions to local understandings and sensibilities and thus recruit a broader swath of constituents, avoid schisms, and tackle a wider array of movement concerns, even if these are not all addressed in all localities.

BYPASSING THE STATE TO CAPTURE CIVIL SOCIETY

Much has been written in recent years on the critical importance of "civil society."[40] Although there are myriad definitions of civil society, there seems to be agreement that it refers to a layer of voluntary associations that exists between the state and the family, including political parties, trade unions, professional associations, clubs, charitable organizations, places of worship, and other associations.[41] Civil society has been seen by classical liberals such as John Locke as equivalent to a pluralist democratic government,[42] by Omar Kamil as a "buffer between state power and the citizen's life,"[43] and from a Marxist perspective by Antonio Gramsci as separate from the state and the economy and a means of resistance by the oppressed to the state's and capitalists' efforts to impose their ideology on society.[44] Our analysis of the role of religiously orthodox groups in sacralizing the public sphere fits most closely with Gramsci's, if we define the religiously orthodox, not as a class-based "oppressed" group, but as a culturally based group that oftentimes views itself as oppressed or at the least "embattled"— to use Christian Smith's apt description of Evangelicals in the contemporary United States—in its struggle with what it sees as an increasingly secularized society and state.[45] Moreover, as we will show for the case of Shas in Israel, sometimes orthodox groups have ethnic or class grievances as well, which can heighten their sense of marginality. Of course, from the point of view of theological modernists and members of minority faiths, religiously orthodox groups are often experienced as hegemonic and as already having too much influence on the state.

Bypassing the state can be viewed as an effort to take over civil society so that this can be used in a struggle against the state. For religiously orthodox movements, this effort to capture civil society often follows a common pattern. Most of the movements we consider here began in a local community by establishing a church, mosque, or synagogue, thus reflecting long-established traditions of centering civil society on a local place of worship. They then proceeded to build schools, medical clinics, clubs, or social service organizations linked with the worship center, and eventually established businesses inspired by the movement and linked to the other institutions. Often, the movements built their own, entirely new institutions, but in some cases they took over existing institutions by, for example, renovating and revitalizing a synagogue that had been abandoned or burrowing into existing professional associations or student unions by winning elections to leadership positions. The most successful orthodox movements established a dense network of institutions and organizations that, while it certainly could not be said to encompass all elements of civil society, still comprised a large enough share of civil society to make it an effective challenger to the state.

DOES RELIGION MAKE THESE MOVEMENTS SUCCESSFUL?

Could these religiously orthodox movements have succeeded because they were religious or religiously orthodox, rather than because they bypassed the state? As we will show, religious belief undoubtedly contributed to these movements' successes by providing a transformative vision, a message of hope and inevitability, and a conviction of moral correctness. But their orthodoxy also created problems, giving them the comprehensive, ambitious agendas, inflexible ideology, and reluctance to negotiate that may have necessitated the strategy of bypassing the state. This strategy is not explicitly religious—nor have all religiously orthodox movements used it—suggesting that it could have utility in overcoming movement obstacles for secular movements and that religion or orthodoxy alone probably cannot explain the success of these movements.

Is it possible that faith traditions differ in their likelihood of adopting the strategy of bypassing the state or in the specific form that this takes? As we posit in moral cosmology theory, the specific faith tradition or content of religious texts is not what matters most in the political attitudes of orthodox or modernist individuals. The orthodox of all of the Abrahamic faith traditions tend to differ from modernists in their cultural and economic orientations, regardless of the specific doctrinal positions on these matters in their religious texts or clerical teachings. As we noted at the beginning of this chapter, in our earlier quantitative research we found a similar pattern of effects of orthodoxy vs. modernism on cultural and economic beliefs in many countries where Christianity, Islam, and Judaism predominate.[46] We concluded based on this research that it is not adherence or nonadherence to the specific religious tenets of these faith traditions that is responsible for the effects of moral cosmology on cultural and economic attitudes, but rather the theological communitarianism (with its controlling and its caring sides) of the orthodox and the theological individualism (with its emphasis on individual freedom and individual responsibility) of their modernist counterparts. Following this logic, we expect that many religiously orthodox movements, regardless of whether they are based in Christianity, Islam, or Judaism, will adopt similar cultural and economic agendas, face broadly similar obstacles to success, and overcome these obstacles using similar political strategies. Our purpose in this book is to chronicle the shared organizational and strategic features that we have uncovered in successful religiously orthodox movements around the world, as well as to identify the distinctive elements of each movement, the latter often more a function of the political structures within which each movement is situated than of the faith tradition on which it is based.

POLITICAL OPPORTUNITY STRUCTURE AND BYPASSING THE STATE

While the predominant faith tradition may not matter in the broad agendas and strategy adopted by religiously orthodox movements, we argue that the nature of the political environment in which the movement operates does affect the specific form that bypassing the state takes. According to the political process model in social movement theory, the rise of social movements and their subsequent successes and failures are, in part, a response to variable features of their political landscape, such as the extent of access to the political system, shifting political alignments among parties and their supporters, the support of influential allies, and state repression/facilitation, as well as more stable aspects of political systems, such as the strength of the state, the form of government, and the nature of the state's welfare regime.[47] While many of these factors will figure in our accounts of each of the four movements in chapters 2 through 5, we single out for discussion here four of them that are especially important: the repressiveness of the state, the nature of the political system, the effectiveness of the welfare state, and the state's regulation of nongovernmental organizations.

The political process model posits that open and inclusive political systems which allow citizens to voice their opposition and vote for candidates of their choice should present greater opportunities for mobilization than more restrictive systems. Closed political systems and the use of imprisonment, torture, and murder against government opponents should tamp down political mobilization. On the other hand, repression is, in itself, a source of grievance that could mobilize the opposition, and if electoral avenues for political expression are limited, this may push opposition movements to concentrate their efforts on nonelectoral strategies such as boycotts, mass rallies, strikes, civil disobedience, and armed struggle, as well as the primary focus of our book—bypassing the state altogether.

Research on the relationship between state repression and social movement protest has yielded mixed results. Some studies uncovered a positive relationship between repression and protest,[48] while another found a negative relationship.[49] Sociologist MaryJane Osa and political scientist Christina Corduneanu-Huci found that repression under some circumstances decreases and under other circumstances increases collective action.[50] Sociologists Edward Crenshaw and Kristopher Robison found an inverted U-shaped relationship, such that antigovernment protests rise with democratization, "but subsequently reach a tipping point in which they soon begin to decline, likely because citizens are granted satisfying and co-opting levels of political access, participation and civil liberties."[51] In a study of six Muslim-majority countries, we found that the more open political states have high levels of political engagement. Such political activism declines up to a point as states begin to limit political rights. But then as states become highly repressive, activism increases, perhaps in response to state violence.[52] Political scientist Karen Rasler's study of the Iranian revolution found that repression by the shah reduced protest in the short term but escalated it in the long term.[53] And in a study of Latin American peasant mobilization, political scientist Charles Brockett found that repression was successful in reducing protest if it was enacted early or late in the cycle of protest.[54]

To our knowledge there is no research on how state repression affects the likelihood of a movement adopting the strategy of bypassing the state, and our study is not designed to test this; it includes only one nation—Egypt—which had a highly repressive government through much of the history of the Muslim Brotherhood. We can show, however, that state repressiveness was one of several factors that pushed the Brotherhood to decide to build alternative institutions, and that sidestepping the state proved to be a highly effective strategy in the face of government repression. At the same time, because bypassing the state was adopted as a strategy by Shas, Comunione e Liberazione, and the Salvation Army USA in nations where there was little or no effort by the state to repress them, we can say that state repression is certainly not a necessary condition for adopting the strategy of bypassing the state.

The nature of the political party system may also affect the likelihood of a movement's deciding to limit its participation in electoral politics and concentrate instead on institution-building in civil society. Multiparty systems, such as those in Egypt,[55] Israel, and Italy, theoretically allow even small parties to play a role in policy making because, depending on the levels of support for larger parties, small parties can become important elements of coalitions and may be able to bring down a governing coalition if it does not accede to their demands. Winner-takes-all, two-party systems, such as that in the United States, on the other hand, make it difficult for small parties to affect public policy.[56] Thus, had the Salvation Army in the United States wanted to organize as a political party, as Shas did in Israel and as the Muslim Brotherhood (unofficially until 2011) did in Egypt or even as Comunione e Liberazione's political pressure group did in Italy, it would have had little success in gaining legislative representation. This is one of several reasons why the Salvation Army overwhelmingly focused on building institutions and lobbying, rather than playing a direct role in electoral politics.

The extent and effectiveness of a nation's welfare state can also affect the adoption and success of the strategy of bypassing the state. Because the bulk of the alternative institutions developed through this strategy (unemployment services, clinics and hospitals, hospices for the dying, food banks for poor families, treatment centers for addicts, and social work agencies, for example) stem from the caring or compassionate side of these movements' agendas and are designed to meet human needs, they invite comparison with existing government services. If the movement's services are judged to be meeting needs unmet by the government or as superior (less costly, less stigmatizing, more efficient, less corrupt) to existing government services, they can constitute a tacit indictment of the government's delivery of social services to its citizens, thus giving a political function to institutions that are not explicitly political. This is certainly the case in Egypt, where the extensive welfare network of the Muslim Brotherhood put government services to shame, and in Israel, where Shas's institutional outreach, although partly funded by the government, is seen as filling a vacuum in the Israeli welfare state in meeting the needs of Mizrahi citizens of North African and Middle Eastern descent. Yet the government's failure to provide adequate welfare services does not automatically make a movement's provision of these services a stinging political critique of the government. The Salvation Army is providing services in the United States that have come to be seen—by both the government and the citizenry—as complementing rather than competing with government services. Because "big government" is viewed with suspicion by many Americans, assistance to the needy provided by private—often faith-based—institutions may not discredit the government. In Italy, Comunione e Liberazione initiated its social services, not because Italy lacked a highly developed welfare state, but because the movement saw such services as needing to address both spiritual and material needs and because it wanted to reduce substantially the relative power of the secular state. Thus, a failed or weak welfare state is not a necessary condition for the adoption or success of the strategy of building alternative institutions to bypass the state.

"Institutional channeling" through state regulation of nongovernmental organizations (NGOs) can limit a movement's engagement in the formal political arena.[57] NGOs are an important building block—along with businesses, schools, and centers of worship—of the networks established by orthodox movements. Sociologists John McCarthy, David Britt, and Mark Wolfson show how the U.S. tax code that grants tax-exempt status to churches, mosques, synagogues, and NGOs prohibits them from "engaging in any partisan campaign activities and from most other political activities."[58] Nonetheless, as we will see, the Salvation Army USA is, broadly speaking, political and engages in political activities, including extensive behind-the-scenes lobbying of Congress and, at least once in its history, endorsing a candidate for president of the United States. Even when government regulation is very strict, NGOs may still—at least indirectly—serve a political purpose. In Egypt, for example, the Muslim Brotherhood was forced by the government during the 1930s to separate its Section of Welfare and Social Services from its political activities, and throughout its history the Brotherhood's fear of governmental takeover of its NGOs was a factor in its efforts to ensure that these NGOs did not take an explicitly political stance. This did not, however, prevent the Brotherhood's social welfare organizations from serving as a powerful critique of the government's efforts to address basic human needs.

THE MULTI-INSTITUTIONAL POLITICS APPROACH

Sociologists Elizabeth Armstrong and Mary Bernstein point out that the political opportunity structure (POS) approach treats the state as the central source of political domination and as the primary target of movements for social change. Building on a growing challenge among social movement scholars to the POS approach, Armstrong and Bernstein lay out the parameters of an alternative, multi-institutional politics approach. In this new perspective, the sources of power in society are seen as located in multiple institutions. Movements that challenge these nonstate institutions or combinations of them are regarded as just as political as those that target the state. The institutions within which movements operate are seen as having different, often contradictory logics that movements can exploit in accomplishing their goals, using different strategies in targeting different institutions. Movement goals may include cultural and identity change, in addition to the goal of policy change assumed by the political process model. The multi-institutional power perspective adds to our understanding of the orthodox movements whose stories we tell because these movements target not only the state but also many institutions, such as family life, medicine, the mass media, education, and business, with the primary goal of bringing religion to the fore.[59]

SUMMARY

The argument undergirding our case study analysis of four religiously orthodox movements—the Muslim Brotherhood in Egypt, Shas in Israel, Comunione e Liberazione in Italy, and the Salvation Army in the United States—can be summarized as follows:

- Religiously orthodox movements tend to be theologically communitarian. Culturally, this communitarianism takes a strict or authoritarian side, while economically it has a caring or egalitarian face. Many of the most successful orthodox movements, including the four we chronicle, pursue three agendas—religious, cultural, and economic.

- Most scholarship on orthodox movements captures their culturally strict side but ignores their economically caring side. Yet it is from this compassionate side, which often includes a social justice frame, that much of their institution-building, success in recruitment, and popular support stem.

- According to social movement theory and research, religiously orthodox movements' broad agendas on multiple fronts, ideological rigidity (moral absolutism), and reluctance to compromise should present serious obstacles to movement success.

• Bypassing the state by building vast networks of alternative religious, cultural, and economic institutions at the grassroots level allows religiously orthodox movements to overcome these movement obstacles by letting skeptics "try on" the movement's ideology and agendas; allowing members to use specific elements of the ideology and agendas to address local concerns; empowering members as they work to bring the ideology to reality; inviting comparison with the efforts of inadequate or corrupt state institutions; and helping the movement build a society-wide base of support from which it may launch a direct challenge to the state.

THE MUSLIM BROTHERHOOD
Building a State within a State in Egypt

The Brotherhood is the people. We are struggling. We help the poor. We help the jobless. Where do we get our money? Out of our own pockets. We reach in our pockets to help one another.
—ESSAM EL ERYAN, DEPUTY VICE PRESIDENT OF
THE MUSLIM BROTHERHOOD'S FREEDOM AND JUSTICE PARTY

THE MOST PROMINENT ISLAMIST MOVEMENT in the Muslim world today and the "mother organization of all Islamist movements"[1] is the Society of Muslim Brothers.[2] Founded in Egypt in 1928, the Muslim Brotherhood today has branches in some seventy countries. As Middle East area specialist Barry Rubin observes, "while other Islamist groups have made more dramatic appearances, launched huge terrorist attacks, and fought civil wars, the Muslim Brotherhoods have shown more staying power and better organizational skills."[3]

The Muslim Brotherhood in Egypt is unique among the four movements we chronicle in two respects. While all of the movements encountered resistance, the Brotherhood is the only movement to have faced severe government repression. In the more than eighty years since its founding, the Brotherhood has survived two dissolutions by the Egyptian government, the assassination of its founder, the execution of one of its leading theoreticians, the jailing of thousands of leaders and members, and efforts by the government—at least until the fall of President Hosni Mubarak in 2011—to cripple its institutions and impede its goal of creating an Islamic order in Egypt. The Brotherhood is also the only movement of the four in which a segment of it, in the movement's early decades, used violence, including assassinations of two high government officials. Yet from the start, the Brotherhood's primary strategy was a gradual, reformist one of building religious, cultural, and economic institutions as an alternative to the Egyptian state. These institutions allowed the movement to thrive despite government repression and eventually to win the largest number of seats in by far the first post-Mubarak elections for the Egyptian parliament.[4] That this all has happened in Egypt—the largest and most influential Arab nation and a key U.S. ally in the region—makes the Egyptian case a "bellwether of what might lie ahead"[5] for other Muslim-majority nations and of great interest to the world's policy makers.

How has the Muslim Brotherhood survived and succeeded in many of its goals despite heavy government repression throughout much of its history? Like all the movements whose stories we tell here, the Brotherhood was based on a strongly communitarian vision that saw Muslims as mutually responsible for each other and for their community. This communitarianism, together with the founder's conception of Islam as applicable to all realms of life, gave the Brotherhood the ambitious goal of Islamizing Egyptian society from below, beginning with the individual and moving outward in concentric circles to the believer's family, community, society, and state. Branches of the Brotherhood began by building a local mosque and gradually adding to it other services such as a clinic, boys' club, unemployment agency, and so on. Eventually, businesses serving the community were added. One institution at a time, the Brotherhood established a dense network of alternative institutions that extended to all corners of the nation.

That this "state within a state" was spread across the country allowed the Brotherhood to survive two dissolutions by the government. Decentralization also allowed members to address elements of the Brotherhood's absolutist beliefs to the needs and sensibilities of local communities. Across the country, potential recruits to the movement were able to experience, through the mosques, schools, social services, and businesses established by the Brotherhood, what life might be like if the movement's goal of Islamizing society were achieved. The Brotherhood's provision of much-needed services also served as a tacit indictment of the Egyptian government's efforts to meet its citizens' needs. The Brotherhood's near-capture of Egyptian civil society gave the movement a society-wide base of support from which to enter the arena of electoral politics—a base that propelled them, despite the government's rigging of elections, to become the largest opposition bloc in the Egyptian People's Assembly during President Hosni Mubarak's regime, and the largest party in the Assembly after the first post-Mubarak elections of 2011–2012.

ISLAMIC ORTHODOXY, COMMUNITARIANISM, AND COMPREHENSIVENESS

Founded in Egypt in 1928 by Hasan al-Banna, a twenty-two-year-old elementary school teacher, the Muslim Brotherhood's theological underpinnings are in the Hanbali school of Sunni Islamic thought, the most literalist of Islam's four major traditions in its reading of the Qur'an.[6] Al-Banna's harshest criticism was reserved for Muslims who had their own interpretation of Islam. The Brotherhood's moral absolutism was coupled with an end goal of establishing Allah's law—the shari'a—as the sole legal foundation of an Islamic order.[7]

Like the other movements chronicled in this book, the Muslim Brotherhood was from the start strongly communitarian in its ideology and outreach. Al-Banna saw it as every Muslim's responsibility "to concern himself with the affairs of his community. . . .

[He] can express his Islam fully only if he is political, takes into his regard the affairs of his *umma* [community], is preoccupied with it, and guards it jealously."[8] This communitarianism manifested itself in the movement's cultural and economic positions and actions. On the cultural front, al-Banna founded the movement in reaction to what he saw as "the devastation of religion and morality on the pretext of individual and intellectual freedom"—the result, he felt, of British and Western cultural domination of Egypt.[9] The strict side of the "watching over" that communitarianism entails for the Brotherhood is evident in al-Banna's self-described "campaign against ostentation in dress and loose behavior; instruction of women in what is proper; . . . segregation of male and female students; [prohibition of] private meetings between men and women; . . . encouragement of marriage and procreation; . . . closure of morally undesirable ballrooms and dance-halls."[10] Implementation of the shari'a as the only law of the land—the key goal of the movement—would mean that Islamic tenets on education, marriage, popular culture, and the proper places of women and men would be legally mandated. Regarding the latter, for example, a 2007 statement from the Brotherhood on "The Role of Muslim Women in an Islamic Society" contains the following:

> Women make up half of society and they are responsible for the nurturing, guidance and reformation of the subsequent generations of men and women. It is the female who imbues principles and faith into the souls of the nation.
>
> In most cases, the husband is older and it is the husband who is usually the breadwinner of the family and mixes more, with a wider range of people. Every type of group including the family must have a leader to guide it within the limits of what Allah has ordained for there can be no obedience for a human being in a matter involving disobedience to the Creator. It is the husband who is qualified for that leadership. This role is not one of repression, hegemony, or tyranny but one of kindness, love, and gentleness.[11]

On the economic front, al-Banna had a strong sense of social justice, coupled with a stinging critique of the Egyptian and foreign upper class in his country. In his writings, he often referred admiringly to the equality and restraint that characterized the early Muslims, contrasting these with the excesses of the Egyptian aristocracy of his day, whom he referred to as "prisoners of lust and slaves of their cravings and greed."[12] Communitarian "watching over" on the economic front entailed upholding the Islamic requirement to look out for the poor, widowed, and orphaned. Throughout its history, the Brotherhood has pushed Egypt's authoritarian governments to raise standards of living, redistribute land, abolish *riba* (interest on loans), implement progressive application of zakat (mandatory tithing), establish a minimum wage, and provide unemployment insurance.[13] Writing of the Brotherhood today, the United Nations Office for Coordination of Humanitarian Affairs reports that the Brotherhood sees its economic outreach as a "natural extension of Islamic beliefs."[14] Yet a lengthy article published in 2007 in *Foreign Affairs* on "The Moderate Muslim Brotherhood" fails to mention the Brotherhood's compassionate side, the institution-building that has resulted from this, or the extent to which the movement owes much of its success in winning over the Egyptian population to this outreach.[15] From this rarely acknowledged caring side—what we have called in a study of Muslim-majority nations "the egalitarian face of Islamic orthodoxy"[16]—stems the Brotherhood's drive to build the clinics and hospitals, unemployment agencies, food banks, social work agencies, and so forth that comprise much of its network of alternative institutions.

For founder al-Banna, Islam was "an all-embracing concept which regulates every aspect of life, adjudicating on every one of its concerns, and prescribing for it a solid and rigorous order."[17] The totality of Islam thus extends to all realms of life—giving the movement the extraordinarily broad agendas that it has come to encompass and that social movement theory suggests should be an obstacle to success. That the communitarianism of the Brotherhood extended not just to the cultural and economic realms but to all the pursuits of everyday life is emblematic of the orthodox view that the deity takes an active role in every aspect of people's daily lives. As Sana Abed-Kotob describes the social outcome of al-Banna's interpretation of Islam: "It is the vastness of the territory covered by Islam that has led to the dramatic resurgence of calls for Islam as the solution to all societal issues."[18] A statement translated from the movement's Arabic-language Egyptian website (www.ikhwanonline.com), which reflects the Brotherhood's interpretation of Islam as comprehensive, absolute in its requirements for humans, and applicable to all times, places, and peoples, reads:

> Islam regulates all things associated with life, for all peoples and nations in every period, time, and place. Islam is too complete and noble to deal with only certain aspects of this life, especially as regards worldly matters. Rather, it sets down complete principles for everything, guiding people to a pragmatic way to implement them and carrying on within its boundaries.[19]

To all the problems of everyday life—be they emotional, cultural, spiritual, economic, physical, political, or any other—"Islam is the solution" (*Al-Islam-Huwa-Alhal*) according to the Brotherhood's oft-used slogan. Exhibiting the moral righteousness that is not atypical of the religiously orthodox of all faith traditions, al-Banna saw his interpretation of the "comprehensiveness of Islam" as novel and unique, and regarded the Brotherhood, in the words of the Norwegian historian Brynjar Lia, as "the only Muslim group who had fully grasped the true meaning of Islam."[20]

From the start, al-Banna realized that if the Muslim Brothers were to have any hope of moving Egyptian society to a new understanding of Islam, preaching alone would not be enough. Action and deed were also required, and it is the Brotherhood's coupling of belief and action that has been largely responsible for its success. As sociologist Ziad Munson observes,

> The ideology was . . . not just a set of abstract ideas debated by intellectuals and group leaders; the Islamic message was linked to the real, practical activities of the [Brotherhood]. The activities of the organization and its ideology were thus two sides of the same coin. People came to see the two hand in hand, each reinforcing the legitimacy and effectiveness of the other. . . . Ideas were tied directly to action in concrete, identifiable ways (e.g., "Islam is the answer, so we build mosques," or "the poor must be supported, so we provide widow pensions").[21]

Reflecting the movement's communitarianism, al-Banna saw translating word into deed as the responsibility not only of the Brotherhood but also of every Muslim. Early on, al-Banna successfully "reframed" Islam to entail the duty of every Muslim to bring about the re-Islamization or sacralization of the public sphere, the end point of which would be the establishment in Egypt of an "Islamic order" (al-nizam al-islami), which according to historian Richard Mitchell referred to a Muslim society, whatever its form of government, in which the shari'a or Islamic law was implemented.[22]

How was the Islamic order to be brought about? The Brotherhood did not hesitate to engage in direct action through mass rallies and demonstrations against the highly repressive monarchy installed by the British or against its often equally authoritarian Egyptian successors. And a small minority of the Brotherhood's membership, institutionalized as the "Secret Apparatus" (Nizam al-Khass) in 1940, saw violence as the solution.[23] Sociologist Mansoor Moaddel has shown that the repressive Egyptian state, in contrast to the more conciliatory and inclusive Jordanian state, led the Muslim Brotherhood in Egypt to sometimes adopt violence as a tactic in its early decades, while the Brotherhood's branch in Jordan eschewed this.[24] But generally, al-Banna and the Brothers adopted a low-profile, nonconfrontational, long-term strategy of reforming Egyptian society from below. The process would occur though a gradual expansion of a proper understanding of Islam in ever-widening circles from the individual to the family to the community to the society and ultimately to the state.[25]

While converting belief into action could have involved participation in party politics, al-Banna saw the political parties in Egypt during the first half of the twentieth century as merely pursuing narrow self-interests, rather than what would benefit the Egyptian people as a whole. As a result—and no doubt also because he recognized that there was little likelihood of political success without first building a base of popular support—al-Banna developed for the Brotherhood by the early 1930s a three-pronged strategy that involved: (1) preaching the Brotherhood's concept of Islam as a total way of life, (2) training young people to preach this message to others, and (3) building alternative institutions—mosques, schools, social service agencies, hospitals, and businesses—that would meet the needs of Egyptian citizens—needs that were not being met by the Egyptian state.[26] In the context of highly repressive Egyptian regimes propped up by British occupying forces, al-Banna saw this bottom-up, beneath-the-radar strategy of re-Islamizing the nation as the most viable path to sacralizing all aspects of Egyptian life.

ISLAMIZING EGYPTIAN SOCIETY ONE INSTITUTION AT A TIME: 1930–1948

In Ismailia, the city on the west bank of the Suez Canal where Hasan al-Banna had been assigned to teach in a primary school in 1927 after completing his education in Cairo, al-Banna began by preaching in the city's mosques but soon extended his ministry to local coffeehouses (*qahawi*) where students gathered. Much as we will see that the founders of the other movements whose stories we tell took their messages out of places of worship and into nonsacred places, al-Banna reached out to Muslims where they were, earning the scorn of religious authorities of the day. Al-Banna recruited a corps of committed young men and began to train them in spreading his message throughout neighboring communities.[27]

In 1930, two years after the movement's founding, the Brotherhood initiated—at great expense to the fledgling organization—the building of a mosque in Ismailia. Soon afterwards a boys' school and club were built on top of the mosque, and later a girls' school was added. With the initiation of these projects, the Society of Muslim Brothers was formally registered with the Egyptian government as an Islamic welfare society. Centering civic life on the local mosque was a long-standing tradition in Islam, and Islamic welfare societies were a widespread and vital element of Egyptian civil society in the first half of the twentieth century. Most of these welfare societies were involved primarily in religious activities, as opposed to efforts to meet the economic needs of citizens.[28]

It was no accident that, upon completing construction of mosques in local communities, al-Banna's group built schools. Al-Banna admired Catholicism's Jesuit order for creating an independent schooling system that allowed the order to propagate its message; hence schools were an important part of the Brotherhood's early outreach, as they are today.[29] As we will see with Shas in Israel and Comunione e Liberazione in Italy, studying and borrowing strategy from movements in other faith traditions is not uncommon among the leaders of religiously orthodox movements, calling into question the common characterization of them as parochial and insulated from other faith traditions. Much as we will see for all of the movements we chronicle except the Salvation Army, which did not build schools, the Brotherhood's schools addressed all three of the movement's agendas—they inculcated religious beliefs, taught cultural standards, and offered a rigorous education to advance the economic prospects of students.[30]

The pattern of institution-building established at Ismailia was followed by other branches of the Brotherhood as the movement spread rapidly throughout Egypt during the 1930s. In creating each new branch, al-Banna's followers worked to discover what the local community's needs were and then built institutions to meet those needs. The decentralization into branches, which the Brotherhood shares with the other movements in this book, was key to helping local members identify the different concerns and needs of people in different communities and regions across Egypt—a society that had profound regional differences as a result of uneven rates of urbanization and industrialization.[31]

Centering the branches on local mosques that the Brotherhood built or restored ensured that those who came to listen to the Brotherhood's services in the mosque were already somewhat theologically predisposed to the message. This also lent respectability to the movement and made local branch activities less subject to government repression because the state was reluctant to intervene in religious activities. Later, when the government disbanded the Brotherhood in 1948 and 1954, the movement was able to continue much of its religious and social service outreach because its decentralized structure made it difficult to suppress.[32]

By 1934, only six years after its founding, the Brotherhood had branches in some fifty communities, with a social welfare institution in most of them. Businesses and services were also founded one after another by the Brotherhood during the 1930s and 1940s. Reflecting the entrepreneurial spirit that the movement was showing on the religious and educational fronts, small carpet and embroidery factories were established to provide employment to students while they completed their education in the Brotherhood's schools. A publishing company, operated as a joint-stock company with shares sold only to members of the Brotherhood so that the movement would not be dependent on outside wealthy donors, was founded at considerable financial risk to the movement in 1934 to publish the movement's newspaper, *Jaridat al-Ikhwan al-Muslimin.*[33] The Company for Islamic Transactions, *sharikat al-mu'amalat al-islamiyya,* was established in 1938 according to the principles of "Islamic economics" (e.g., loans given without interest). The Arabic Advertising Company, *sharikat al-i-'lanat al-'arabiyya,* was added in 1947, and in the same year, the Muslim Brothers' Company for Spinning and Weaving, *sharikat al-ikhwan al-muslimin li'l-ghazl wa'l-tansikh,* was established. In the latter company, every worker was a shareholder, and the Brotherhood promoted this as an effort to "revive Islamic socialism."[34] While the communist movement was never a serious competitor to the Brotherhood in Egypt,[35] the Muslim Brotherhood did not hesitate to adopt similar framing of aspects of its economic mission. In Alexandria, the Company for Commercial and Engineering Works, *sharikat al-tijara wa'l-ashghal al-handasa,* was founded to construct buildings, manufacture construction materials, and train workers in the building trades.[36] The joint stock companies, worker shareholding, and loans without interest went beyond mere charity to embody the Brotherhood's redistributive, economic justice agenda.

As doctors and medical professionals were won over to the movement, the Brotherhood began to offer medical services. A Muslim Brotherhood pharmacy was established in Cairo as early as 1933. Two years later, the Brothers opened their first health clinic in Minuf, in the northeast of the country. By 1938 the movement's hospital in al-Mansura, in the Nile Delta, was treating 50–100 people a day and, reflecting a view of health care as a basic right, offering free medicines.[37]

In 1945, the Ministry of Social Affairs, which regulated what would today be called nongovernmental organizations (NGOs), determined that the Muslim Brotherhood was "political, social, and religious," and ruled that, as long as it remained political, its welfare activities would not be eligible for government aid. Even though al-Banna intended for the Brotherhood to eschew government funding for its activities, he decided to split a "Section of Welfare and Social Services," responsible for all of the movement's social welfare outreach, from the rest of the organization, mainly to insulate the economic outreach from government political interference.[38] While this "institutional channeling"[39] by the Egyptian state theoretically meant that the Brotherhood's social service activities could serve no political purpose, in fact, as we discuss below, they had profoundly political effects.

In an effort to reach out to Egyptians further from the movement's headquarters in Cairo, the Brotherhood opened branches during the late 1930s and early 1940s in remote towns and villages throughout the country, addressing the needs of the poor and lower classes—groups often ignored by other movements and by the state.[40] By the end of the 1940s, as a direct result of its vast social service network, the Society of Muslim Brothers, although not organized as a political party, had grown to become the most powerful political force in Egypt. The Brotherhood had some 1,700–2,000 branches and the support of at least one million followers in 1948.[41]

PROVIDING GRADUATED MEMBERSHIP LEVELS

The Muslim Brotherhood was successful in these early years in recruiting members through its institution-building in part because, like the Salvation Army in the United States, Shas in Israel, and Comunione e Liberazione in Italy, the Brotherhood had a membership structure that allowed potential recruits to become involved even at very modest levels of ideological adherence and commitment and then progress to successively greater levels of these.[42] As we noted in chapter 1, those who become involved in these movements are not necessarily religiously orthodox but may agree with some of the movements' theology or aims. Sociologist Philip Selznick, writing in 1952 about recruitment into Bolshevik (communist) cadres in various countries, noted that individuals had to be recruited as "simple adherents" and transformed via the organizational structure into "deployable personnel," who made the commitment to dedicate their lives to the movement.[43] In recruiting new members, the Muslim Brotherhood "did not demand an immediate conversion to a strict moral and religious correctness."[44] Historian Richard Mitchell chronicles how in 1935 the Brotherhood began identifying (1) "assistants," who merely signed membership cards and paid dues; (2) "related" members, who were able to demonstrate familiarity with the movement's principles and pledged "obedience"; (3) "active" members, who demonstrated "total involvement with the movement—physical training, achievement in Qur'anic learning, and fulfillment of Islamic obligations such as pilgrimages, fasting, and contributions to the *zakat* treasury"; and (4) "strugglers," a category "open to only a select handful of the most dedicated." The Brotherhood's graduated membership allowed separation of reformers from more militant members and concealment of secretive, sometimes extralegal operations from those who might object to these. Later, in 1945, the levels of commitment were collapsed to two, "tentative" and "active,"[45] but the functions of tiered membership remained similar.

Important also in the Brotherhood's membership structure was that promotion from the Brotherhood's lower ranks to higher ranks was based on merit. "By defining a wide range of duties and responsibilities and making status directly dependent on the fulfillment of duties, the Society had de facto created a ranking system based on merit and not on social standing and patronage."[46] Hard work and sacrifice were rewarded with higher rank in the movement, making the Brotherhood one of the country's few institutions in which advancement by merit was possible. This was an important way in which the Muslim Brotherhood contrasted itself with the corruption and nepotism of the Egyptian state.

SURVIVING GOVERNMENT REPRESSION THROUGH DECENTRALIZATION

From 1936 to 1939, the Arab revolt against British rule in Palestine absorbed much of the Brotherhood's attention. The movement held rallies in solidarity with the Palestinian Arabs, and when concerns about the possible establishment of a Jewish state in Palestine arose in 1937, the Brotherhood called for a boycott of Jewish businesses in Egypt and published in the movement's newspaper vicious attacks against Jews— both Zionists who sought the establishment of a Jewish state and non-Zionists who did not—referring to Jews as a "societal cancer." In 1940, the movement's paramilitary Secret Apparatus was formed. While it is not known whether al-Banna approved its actions, the Secret Apparatus in 1948 assassinated a judge who had earlier sentenced a member of the Apparatus to prison for attacking British soldiers in Alexandria. A cache of weapons linked to the Brotherhood was discovered by the government in Ismailia later the same year, publicly revealing for the first time the existence of the Brotherhood's paramilitary wing.[47]

Fearing the growing strength of the Brotherhood and the possibility of its mount-
ing a revolution, the government disbanded the movement in 1948. All of the Brotherhood's funds were confiscated by the Ministry of the Interior to be redistributed by
the Ministry of Social Affairs.[48] Following the Brotherhood's dissolution, the first mention of the Brotherhood as a "state within a state" was made in the official government
publication, Akhir Sa'a: "[The government] had done [away] with a society that could
be regarded as its strongest opponent. This was not just a party but rather resembled
a state with its armies, hospitals, schools, factories, and companies."[49] In social science
research on the state, "state within a state" refers to an extensive, society-wide set of
institutions performing functions that could be—but not necessarily currently are—
performed by the state, such as educating youth, helping the unemployed find jobs,
assisting poor families, helping the sick and dying, managing rescue and recovery after
disasters, defending the nation, and stimulating business and the economy. As we will
see, the Brotherhood has been described numerous times since 1948 by both government officials and scholars as a "state within a state" in Egypt.

Sociologist Ziad Munson's careful analysis of U.S. State Department records has
shown that the Brotherhood was not destroyed when it was declared illegal by the
Egyptian government in 1948. The government may have closed the movement's headquarters in Cairo, but the Brotherhood's highly decentralized structure allowed many
branches throughout the country to continue operations, including their economic
outreach.[50]

On February 12, 1949, Hasan al-Banna was assassinated by government agents,
apparently in retaliation for the Secret Apparatus's assassination of Egyptian prime minister Mahmud Fahmi al-Nuqrashi, who had dissolved the Brotherhood in 1948.[51] While
many movements fail after losing their charismatic founder, al-Banna's assassination at
the hands of the state made him a martyr to his followers, galvanizing the Brotherhood's
membership and probably drawing in even more supporters. There was, however, dis-
agreement among the movement's leadership on whether to appoint a successor from
al-Banna's family or from the Secret Apparatus, the members of whom felt that, as the
elite of the movement, the next leader should come from their ranks. After much discussion, the Brotherhood chose as al-Banna's successor Hasan Isma'il al-Hudaybi, an
outsider to the movement but a respected and prominent member of the judiciary.[52] As
a condition for agreeing to be the Murshid (General Guide), al-Hudaybi insisted that
the Brotherhood's paramilitary Secret Apparatus be disbanded. While this was agreed
to, many key members of the Apparatus continued in leadership positions in the movement for a long time afterwards. When four months into his term al-Hudaybi found
that the Apparatus had not been dissolved, he announced his intention to resign, only
to be appeased by the creation of a committee to oversee the paramilitary wing's disbandment.[53]

In this period of government reprisals, the Brotherhood's social service network continued to function as a society-building project with its alternative institutions spread throughout the country, as opposed to a more traditional utopian project located in a single locale and separated from the rest of society. Utopian strands were not, however, completely absent from the movement. Much as we will see with William Booth, the founder of the Salvation Army, who had his own utopian vision in the "Darkest England Scheme," members of the Brotherhood initiated plans for building what they called "the Virtuous City":

> Approximately in 1951 a co-operative society was founded by some members of the organization to begin planning a city which was not only to be virtuous, pious, and peaceful, but would also provide economic security in terms of co-operative ownership of the land and planned facilities. Some 400 feddans [415 acres] of land were chosen in an area of old Cairo . . . and £E20,000 was paid to the government as initial costs. Once the regulations governing the co-operative society were accepted by the government, an "administrative council" was elected and work on the area was started. Land surveys and contour and geological studies were made, and then water pipelines were laid and electric-power stations were started. It was expected to serve 2,000 families in the area. It was at this point (1954) that the [Brotherhood] collided with the government and work stopped.[54]

The Brotherhood supported the July 23, 1952, revolution by nine "Free Officers," led by General Muhammad Neguib, which overthrew the pro-British Egyptian monarchy, but the Brotherhood was almost immediately put in a difficult position. The officers, in an effort to lend legitimacy to themselves by linking their coup to the Brotherhood, as the most popular political movement of the day, invited the Brotherhood to join the new cabinet. After some debate, the Brotherhood's Guidance Council declined, fearing that an affiliation with the revolution would cost the Brotherhood its independence as a "popular" movement and would mean supporting decisions by the officers with which it disagreed. When the Free Officers required that all political parties, except the Muslim Brotherhood, register, only to declare these parties illegal, the Brotherhood was left for a period as the only legally recognized "party."[55] This was an ironic position in light of its founder al-Banna's opposition in the movement's early years to the Brotherhood's becoming a political party and in view of the movement's status during the regime of President Hosni Mubarak (1981–2011) as the nation's most powerful political force that was not officially recognized as a party.

It is clear that after the Free Officers' coup, the Muslim Brotherhood overestimated its leverage on the new government. Apparently believing that through their outreach activities of the past twenty-four years they had sufficiently Islamized the Egyptian population, the Brotherhood demanded that the new government be run according to Islamic principles. Perhaps more seriously, the Brotherhood's Murshid al-Hudaybi appears to have entered into separate negotiations with the British on removing their troops.[56] While Egypt had gained nominal independence from Britain in 1922, British troops had remained in the country, and the Egyptian monarchy they had installed was left in control of the government. From the Brotherhood's founding in 1928, al-Banna had opposed British and Western control of Egypt and the moral degradation that he felt had resulted from their presence. The Muslim Brotherhood had taken a prominent role in the anticolonial struggle.[57] Part of the movement's appeal in Egypt was linked to its early, consistent, and vociferous opposition to Western cultural and economic domination.

Al-Hudaybi's alleged negotiations with the British behind the revolution's back played into the Free Officers' fears about the Brotherhood's political ambitions and allowed the junta to dissociate itself from the increasingly demanding and independent Brotherhood. An apparent assassination attempt in January 1954 on Gamal Abdel Nasser, who had emerged as the leader of Egypt, was blamed on members of the paramilitary wing of the Brotherhood, which had supported Nasser's rival, General Neguib. While most historians accept the government's account of the attempted assassination, some scholars suggest that Nasser himself had much to gain from a failed attempt on his life that could be blamed on the Brotherhood and indirectly on his challenger for the presidency, Neguib.[58] After this, most of the Brotherhood's leadership and thousands of members were jailed, tortured, and put on trial.[59] The movement was again disbanded and its assets confiscated. Brotherhood leaders were tried for the attempted assassination and six were hanged. Al-Hudaybi was initially sentenced to death, but the sentence was later commuted to life.[60] He continued as Murshid of the Muslim Brotherhood from his jail cell until his death in 1974. Devastating as these events were for the Brotherhood, Munson has shown from U.S. State Department records that the movement's highly decentralized structure allowed it to survive once again, even in the face of arrests, executions, seizure of its assets, and official disbanding. Moreover, the Brotherhood's social service network had become so vital in Egypt by the 1950s that Nasser was forced to use government funds and staffing of its welfare organizations to avoid popular unrest.[61]

TWO PATHS TO ISLAMIZATION: SCHISM IN THE NASSER YEARS

The mid-1950s through the late 1960s were dark years for the Brotherhood. Nasser arrested thousands of the Brotherhood's members and executed some of its top leaders. Among those executed was the movement's leading theoretician, Sayyid Qutb, who had characterized Nasser's regime as *jahiliyyah,* a term that had previously referred to the spiritual ignorance that preceded the Prophet Muhammad's preaching in Arabia, because Nasser had not instituted shari'a or Islamic law. In his book *Milestones,* published in 1964 during his imprisonment by Nasser, Qutb applied jahiliyyah for the first time to a Muslim head of state, an egregious insult and one that called into question Nasser's right to rule. For Qutb, *jahili* states were abrogating God's absolute sovereignty (*hakimiyyat Allah*) by establishing human—and specifically Western—laws and values. Since for Qutb any departure from God's rule in legislative matters constituted jahiliyyah, he called upon Muslims everywhere to engage in *jihad* (struggle) against the jahiliyyah in order to establish Islamic states.[62]

While jihad has several meanings for Muslims, including a personal struggle to live up to Islamic ideals, Qutb wrote that this would require armed struggle: "the purpose of *jihad bil saif* [striving by the sword] . . . is to clear the way for freedom to strive through preaching in support of the Islamic movement."[63] Qutb's message had very strong appeal to many in the Muslim Brotherhood, especially the movement's younger members, and after his execution in 1966, he was adopted as a martyr by more militant Islamic movements that split off from the Brotherhood or formed independently of it. Middle East specialist Barry Rubin notes that a "consistent characteristic" of the Brotherhood throughout its long history has been "the constant shedding of radical splinter groups for which the Brotherhood is too cautious."[64]

A contrary, moderate vision, opposed to the strategy of armed struggle, was put forth in 1969 by Murshid al-Hudaybi, also writing from prison, in his book, *Missionaries, Not Judges*. Al-Hudaybi's reformist views appear to have held sway with most of the senior leadership of the Muslim Brotherhood, which remained committed to gradual, nonviolent reform from the bottom up by building alternative religious, cultural, and economic institutions, with the ultimate goal of bringing about an Islamic order.[65] In the many accounts of the Muslim Brotherhood since the late 1960s, there is no convincing evidence that the Brotherhood used violence. To the contrary: Mustafa Mashhur, the movement's Murshid from 1996 to 2002, recounted an incident to historian Hesham Al-Awadi where, during the 2000 election, "a young Brother was severely rebuked for carrying a gun with which he was about to shoot a policeman who had assaulted him."[66] A single mistake like this could have cost the Brotherhood legitimacy that had taken decades to build up.

CYCLES OF STATE ACCOMMODATION AND REPRESSION: THE SADAT AND MUBARAK YEARS

When Anwar Sadat, another of the Free Officers, became president of Egypt following Nasser's death in 1970, he adopted a more accommodative stance toward the Brotherhood. In 1971, Sadat insisted that Article 2 of the Egyptian Constitution state that the shari'a was "a principal source of legislation." This was amended with Sadat's approval in 1980 to make the shari'a *"the* principal source of legislation." While this nominally satisfied the key demand of the Brotherhood, it was a largely symbolic victory since almost none of the proposals of the Brotherhood for specific legislation in line with the shari'a were actually passed.[67] Sadat's assassination in 1981 by the militant Islamist movement Jamaat al-Jihad (the Jihad Group),[68] even though it was not at the hands of the Brotherhood, led Sadat's successor, Hosni Mubarak, to enact the Emergency Law of 1981, which officially banned the Muslim Brotherhood from politics. Since 1984 the Brotherhood has been regarded by the government as a legal religious organization, but until the fall of Mubarak in 2011, the Brotherhood was not recognized as an official political party or allowed to run candidates for parliament under its own banner.[69]

In the 1980s and early 1990s, Mubarak adopted a "selective accommodation" policy of clamping down on militant Islamists while allowing more moderate Islamist movements, as the Brotherhood was now viewed, the leeway to continue their social service activities. Throughout Mubarak's first decade of rule in the 1980s, the Brotherhood continued to expand its society-wide network of social service organizations, schools, businesses, and mosques, and it remained the most popular movement among those Egyptians who identified with the Islamist movement more broadly.[70]

BURROWING INTO THE INSTITUTIONS OF EGYPTIAN SOCIETY

The Brotherhood's grassroots efforts during the late 1980s and early 1990s were not limited to geographical locales or to the creation of new institutions; they also extended to other forms of civic organization and to the electoral takeover of existing institutions. Burrowing into civic, nonstate institutions allowed the Brotherhood to reach diverse, multiclass constituencies and draw them to the movement. More explicit political efforts by the Brotherhood were severely limited because it was not recognized as a political party by the government. But during the 1980s and early 1990s, the Brotherhood, under the banner of the Islamic Trend, ran candidates for and won the leadership of key professional syndicates (associations) of lawyers, engineers, doctors, professors, journalists, and other professions, giving the movement a highly visible and influential role in Egyptian society.[71] Political scientist Carrie Wickham quotes a Muslim activist in one of the professional associations as saying, "We are creating islands of democracy in a sea of dictatorship."[72] Political scientist Raymond Baker called the syndicates "the most vibrant institutions of Egyptian civil society."[73]

As part of the Brotherhood's efforts to gain control of the leadership of the powerful professional associations, the Islamic Trend began to offer assistance to syndicate members in the form of training courses, insurance for emergencies, loans at no interest to pay the growing cost of getting married or starting a business, and subsidized health care, in much the same way that the Brotherhood's social welfare network was offering services to the wider Egyptian public. The Brotherhood-controlled professional syndicates were themselves involved in many social welfare activities in the larger society.

After the devastating 1992 Cairo earthquake, it was Islamic Trend doctors, not the Egyptian government, who stepped in to provide assistance, shelter, food, and clothing for victims, and even gave US$1,000 to each family that had been made homeless by the earthquake.[74] Throughout the rescue effort, banners proclaiming the Brotherhood's slogan, "Islam is the solution," were proudly displayed on rescue tents and makeshift hospitals.[75] Echoing words used by the Egyptian government after its 1948 dissolution of the Brotherhood, the stunned Interior Minister Abdel-Halim Moussa said, "If anyone wants to do anything they should do it through the Government. What is this becoming, a state within a state?"[76]

As we will see with Comunione e Liberazione in Italy, the Muslim Brotherhood also succeeded in the electoral capture of student unions in many Egyptian universities during the 1980s and early 1990s. Much as the Brotherhood offered services to the broader public and to the membership of the professional syndicates, the movement extended services to university students. Using a tactic that was rare at the time, the Brotherhood sometimes even surveyed students via assessment questionnaires to see what services they wanted. At Alexandria University, the Family Medical Project arranged for doctors at the university to provide free medical services to students. On the same campus, a student member of the Brotherhood sold household items such as furniture, refrigerators, and washing machines at discount prices.[77] The services were a logical extension of the Brotherhood's communitarianism and served as a recruiting tool as well. What was offered was often directly tied to accepting the organization's message: Minibuses transporting female students eventually required that passengers cover their heads with a hijab. Similarly, students who could not afford clothing were offered Islamic garments at low cost.[78]

Shahira Amin, reporting for CNN, recently told the story of Iman Abdella, who was recruited to the Muslim Sisterhood, the women's branch of the movement, seventeen years earlier while she was a student at Cairo's Al-Azhar University:

> When Iman Abdella steps out of a black-and-white Cairo taxi in Haggana, residents of this impoverished quarter rush to greet her with jubilant cries. . . . "Alf marhaba (welcome a thousand times)," cries Soad Bekheit, a shabbily dressed mother of four, opening her arms to embrace the familiar visitor. "It's as if the Prophet himself has visited us today." For families in this desolate ghetto, one of Cairo's poorest, a visit from this chubby woman in a traditional Islamic head scarf means they will not have to go to sleep on an empty stomach—at least, not tonight. . . . For years, the Islamist Muslim Brotherhood movement has won over Egypt's poor and working classes with charity work—stepping in to provide many of the services that the [Mubarak] government did not provide, like subsidized healthcare.[79]

The Brotherhood's efforts to recruit students met with great success, especially after the students had graduated and were facing unemployment or underemployment. Years earlier, President Nasser had guaranteed a white-collar state job to every university graduate. Many of those who earned degrees during the years of Hosni Mubarak felt that Nasser's "social contract" was still in effect, despite the government's claim that it could no longer afford to provide a good job to every graduate.[80] Today, in Egypt and throughout the Muslim world, "blocked aspirations"—the inability of university graduates to obtain jobs in their professions—is one of the most common sources of grievance promoting dissent.[81] Political scientist Janine Clark finds through her ethnography of Islamist (not Brotherhood) clinics in Cairo that while such clinics often paid their medical staff poorly, they were a source of jobs or extra income for doctors who might otherwise have been unemployed or underemployed.[82]

The Brotherhood's work among professionals, students, and unemployed graduates was crucial in winning over those who became the most active and successful recruiters for the movement and in increasing its legitimacy with the broader public. An internal document written by Mustafa Mashhur, the movement's Murshid from 1996 to 2002, acknowledged the critical importance of these efforts: "Our activities have become known because of the increase in our public activism and because we are becoming open to sectors of society through effective fronts like syndicates, unions, associations, people's assemblies and local councils. Society has become aware of this activism and of our sincere intentions of seeking to please God by benefiting people."[83]

In 1992, the government raided the offices of the Salsabil computing company and uncovered a large number of documents related to the Brotherhood. Most alarming to the state was the discovery of the movement's Empowerment Project (*mashru al-tamkin*), which the government saw as a blueprint for the gradual takeover of civil society with the aim of assuming power. The Brotherhood was revealed to have, in the words of area specialists Ana Belén Soage and J. F. Franganillo, "recreated the state by setting up sections dealing with all the domains in which they deemed it necessary to have influence: students, professionals, the security services, elections, human rights, and so on."[84] Sociologist Asef Bayat goes so far as to say that the Muslim Brotherhood at this time was

> acting as a though it was a shadow government. The MB controlled thousands of mosques, dominated the major national professional syndicates and the student unions in the north, ran various NGOs, influenced numerous schools, and constituted the most powerful opposition in Parliament. Foreign dignitaries from the U.S. ambassador to Yasser Arafat [chairman of the Palestine Liberation Organization] paid visits to the MB's downtown headquarters. The MB, in short, had captured a sizable space in civil society and was beginning to permeate state institutions, including the judiciary, universities and al-Azhar [University].[85]

Recognizing the threat posed by the Brotherhood's takeover of the professional syndicates and student unions, President Mubarak took steps in 1993 to prevent further victories by the Islamic Trend. Syndicate Law 100 was issued requiring that at least 50 percent of the members of a professional syndicate must vote in a syndicate election for its results to be valid. Two years later, further legislation allowed the judiciary to intervene in syndicate elections. Arrests of Muslim Brotherhood leaders of the syndicates followed in ensuing years, forcing the Brotherhood to take a lower profile in many, but not all, of these associations.[86] The social services provided through the syndicates sometimes disappeared as Islamic Trend was forced out.[87]

The government also took steps to curtail the influence of Islamists in student unions, removing thousands of objectionable candidates from the lists of students running for election.[88] In universities, the government promoted an alternative student organization called Horras. The group's name may not have been a coincidence; Horras was an Egyptian deity in pharaonic times who slew evil.[89] The student organization Horras arranged social functions for students but failed to win much support because it did not provide the welfare services that had been offered by the Islamists.[90] The government also closed down more than 5,000 offices of the Brotherhood across the country and took control of some 60,000 mosques, requiring that their imams be appointed and paid by the Ministry of Awqāf (Religious Endowments).[91]

Asef Bayat refers to the Brotherhood in the post-crackdown period as in "abeyance"[92] or what historian Leila J. Rupp and sociologist Verta Taylor, writing about the women's rights movement in the United States from 1945 to the 1960s, call "the doldrums."[93] Yet even during this period, Bayat notes that religious devotion and piety in Egypt increased dramatically, with more women wearing the hijab, larger numbers of students attending prayer halls in universities, and rising popularity of Islamist preachers.[94]

EMPOWERING AND POLITICIZING THE EGYPTIAN POPULACE THROUGH THE NETWORK

At the turn of the current century, the strategy that al-Banna had formulated seven decades earlier of re-Islamizing Egyptian society from the bottom up—of bypassing the state—was clearly working, despite the obstacles that the government had put in its path. The Brotherhood had established a massive, decentralized, society-wide network of clinics and hospitals, Islamic banks giving higher returns on deposits, textile factories paying better wages and benefits than state-run companies, day care centers, food banks, youth clubs, social welfare agencies, unemployment services, discount grocery stores, legal aid agencies, and much more—a network that both the government and academics regarded as "a state within a state."[95] The network was funded by zakat (a religiously mandated tithe of 2.5 percent of net worth annually) given by supporters; by contributions from Brothers who had fled Egypt during the Nasser era, made their fortunes in the Persian Gulf, and returned to Egypt; and by the profits of the Brotherhood's businesses, hospitals, and clinics. By building a diverse array of alternative institutions spread across the country, the movement had pursued al-Banna's policy of *tamkin* (empowerment) and political education of the umma (community) as a lead up to the establishment of an Islamic order. The Brotherhood's institutional outreach had improved the economic conditions of Egyptians and had drawn supporters by demonstrating that Islamist institutions could outperform the secular, corrupt government in providing much-needed social services.[96] The Brotherhood's network constituted a strategy of "Islamization from below" that effectively bypassed the Egyptian state—a model that was adopted by many of its branches in nearly seventy countries and by other Islamist movements in Egypt and throughout the Muslim world.[97]

Scholars writing on the grassroots outreach of the Muslim Brotherhood see this as empowering both those who delivered the services and those who received them—thus building loyalty to the movement that spanned an array of social classes. Carrie Wickham notes that the involvement of university graduates in Islamist networks in Egypt was empowering in that it "challenged the prevailing climate of fear and passivity by exhorting graduates to obey a higher authority, regardless of the sanctions they would incur as a result."[98] In his ethnographic study of a Jordanian Muslim Brotherhood refugee camp for Palestinians in Amman, Egbert Harmsen, a Dutch scholar in Middle Eastern studies, argues that in the context of Islam, receiving the services offered by the Brotherhood was as empowering as providing them:

> In the more conservative Islamist view, rights and empowerment are not primarily based on the assertive autonomy of individuals, groups, or classes. They can be realized only when Muslim society as a whole achieves an environment of social harmony and solidarity, thus implying that one's rights are necessarily embedded in social relationships of dependency. In this view, a Muslim's duty [to serve the poor] necessarily fulfils another Muslim's rights [to subsistence].[99]

Were the Islamist alternative institutions established by the Muslim Brotherhood explicitly political or critical of the government in their message? By most accounts, no. Egyptian political scientist Emad El-Din Shahin writes of these institutions that "Few are involved in advocacy activities."[100] Likewise, American political scientist John Esposito observes that "Many, if not most, Islamic organizations and NGOs are nonpolitical."[101] In a similar vein, John Walsh, senior editor of the *Harvard International Review*, writes that the Brotherhood's NGOs "give a sense of community to neighborhoods across the country by helping citizens obtain food, jobs, and healthcare. The groups have not tried to gain any formal power in the neighborhoods, but merely to step in where the state has failed and to effect a degree of Islamization in the process."[102]

Political scientist Janine Clark finds that many of the patients of Islamist (but not Muslim Brotherhood) clinics in Egypt in her ethnographic study failed even to recognize that they were run by Islamists, much less that the services came with a political message.[103] Wickham notes that the availability of ostensibly nonpolitical venues for involvement in the project of Islamizing public space meant that recruits did not have to make a direct challenge to the government in order to enter the movement.[104] The existence of these relatively safe venues was, of course, far more important for the Brotherhood in its interactions with the repressive Egyptian state than for the other movements that we chronicle, which faced far less authoritarian states.

In the context of the Egyptian state's "institutional channeling" of NGOs to be no direct threat to the state via laws banning their political activity, the nonpolitical stance of NGOs run by the Muslim Brotherhood during the Mubarak years is understandable. The Ministry of Social Affairs regulated NGOs through Law 32, a 1984 edict that allows the ministry to dismiss the administration of any organization even suspected of political activity, replace their leaders for a period of three years, and decide how their funds are to be spent.[105] While Abdel Moneim Abul-Futouh, a former member of the Brotherhood's Guidance Council, said that "All our associations are legally registered with the Ministry of Social Affairs," the United Nations Office for Coordination of Humanitarian Affairs reported that many of the Brotherhood's NGOs were registered "under different names, and seldom under those of well-known members."[106] Other Brotherhood NGOs were able to avoid some of the restrictions of Law 32 by being under the auspices of a mosque or religious foundation.[107] It is clear that the government's efforts to regulate NGOs did not prevent the Brotherhood and other Islamist organizations from carrying out their missions and profoundly affecting civil society in Egypt.[108]

To say that the Brotherhood's NGOs were not explicitly political does not mean that they did not convey a message that is implicitly political. Referring to service provision by the alternative institutions of the broader Islamist movement in Egypt, Sheri Berman observes:

> Along with the help, however, often came a message: "Islam is the way." Sometimes the message was only indirect and implicit, conveyed through the success of Islamist groups in providing services and fulfilling needs that the state could or would not. . . . Sometimes, however, the message was delivered explicitly, as when social services were run according to Islamic norms (e.g., gender-segregated health care and interest-free loans), or when schools, tutoring, and other educational services were used to inculcate particular values. Islamist primary schools, for example, offered students not only a rigorous education in relatively uncrowded conditions, but also religious indoctrination.[109]

At the least, the Brotherhood's efforts to Islamize all realms of everyday life were indirectly political. This outreach called attention to the secular nature of the state, equating secular with callous, indifferent, and corrupt. Political scientist Carrie Wickham's interviews with university graduates in Cairo working in Islamist (but not necessarily Muslim Brotherhood) organizations, moreover, show that this outreach helped to build a "supportive public,"[110] an outcome very much in line with founder al-Banna's notion of tamkin (empowerment) as a lead up to the establishment of an Islamic order. A 2008 report by the International Crisis Group, drawing on interviews with Brotherhood leaders and the movement's publications, notes that the movement's leaders believe that with "the Islamization of society having taken root in the last two decades, the necessary mass support now exists to create a truly Islamic system of governance. This means, in turn, that the Society should focus on the next stage, gaining political power."[111] As we will see, however, the Brothers are far from unanimous in supporting this change.

CAPITALIZING ON THE NETWORK FOR ELECTORAL VICTORIES

Having established a solid popular base by building a network of alternative institutions and burrowing into others, the Brotherhood was, by the early years of the current century, in a position to convert this support into seats in the Egyptian parliament, the People's Assembly. As we noted earlier, the movement's founder, Hasan al-Banna, was opposed to the formation of a Muslim Brotherhood party. Nonetheless, this did not mean that members of the Brotherhood could not enter politics on their own. In 1941, al-Banna himself declared his candidacy for a seat in parliament, only to withdraw in exchange for the government's taking steps against prostitution and the sale of alcohol.[112] Much later, during the 1970s, 1980s, and 1990s, Brotherhood candidates won seats in parliament running under the banner of legally recognized parties, most remarkably in 1987 when the Brotherhood won 36 seats in an alliance with the 'Amal and Ahrar parties, making them the largest opposition group in parliament.[113] In the 2000 parliamentary elections, Muslim Brothers, running as individuals, won 17 seats in the 454-seat People's Assembly.[114]

The decision on whether to pursue a primarily institution-building strategy or a strategy of involvement in the formal political arena to directly challenge President Mubarak and his ruling National Democratic Party (NDP) has been a major source of division in the movement, threatening to cause a schism between different generations. The older generation, many of whom are in their sixties, seventies, and eighties, holds nearly all the seats on the Brotherhood's Guidance Council. This generation has been made more cautious by years spent in prison during the regimes of Nasser, Sadat, and Mubarak and tends to favor continuation of the institution-building that we have called bypassing the state as a means of gradually sacralizing Egyptian society. The "younger" generation includes members in their twenties, thirties, and forties, as well as even older members, such as the Brotherhood's spokesman Essam El Eryan, who are well into their fifties and some of whom, like El Eryan, have served time in Mubarak's prisons. The younger generation of the movement is more inclined to direct engagement in politics, in the hope of eventually winning the support of the majority of the Egyptian people and control of the state. This generation is demanding a greater role for itself in the movement, as well as less exclusionary policies on women and Christian Copts, and seems to regard Turkey, where the moderate Islamist party, Justice and Development, has electorally won a majority of seats in Parliament, as a model for Egypt. This generational divide has been a source of conflict in the Brotherhood's goals and strategy since the mid-1990s.[115]

In the parliamentary elections in 2005, despite the fact that the Mubarak regime shut down polling places in districts where the Brotherhood was strong, beat and arrested movement leaders, and stuffed ballot boxes, Muslim Brotherhood candidates won 88 of the 150 seats they contested, a fivefold increase from their representation in the last parliament, making them the largest opposition bloc in the People's Assembly.[116] The Brotherhood's gains in parliament were all the more remarkable since, apparently not wanting to push the authoritarian government too far and generate further repression, it had contested only 150 of 444 seats (10 seats are appointed by the president), even though the Brotherhood likely would have won in far more districts.[117]

Each of the movements whose stories we tell relies on modern technology, social science insights, mass media, and economic analysis to accomplish its theological, cultural, and economic agendas. As public religious movements seeking to desecularize or sacralize the public sphere, they are especially likely to adopt the latest mass communications technology, fund-raising methods, and strategies for membership expansion. The Muslim Brotherhood, which rejects what it sees as the individualism, secularism, and immorality of modern society, uses up-to-date medical technology in its hospitals and social science insights in its welfare agencies. As political scientist Amin Saikal notes of the Muslim Brotherhood and other Islamist groups, "They are not necessarily against modernity; but want to ensure that modernity and all its manifestations are adopted in conformity with their religious values and practices."[118] The Brotherhood has established independent publishing presses and bookstores to get *da'wa* (call to God) pamphlets to the public, publishes two journals, *Liwa' al-islam* and *al-I'tisam,* and uses cassette tapes and websites to get the message out to a broad, now worldwide, audience.[119] All of these resources have been marshaled in the Brotherhood's electoral campaigns as well.

Technological sophistication aside, the Brotherhood's electoral gains in 2005 were overwhelmingly the direct result of its decades of involvement in Egyptian civil society. Writing before the 2005 elections, John Walsh observed that "The Brotherhood's evolving social network is probably more responsible than anything else for the enormous power that the organization would now wield in an open election."[120] Reporting after the 2005 elections, the UN Office for Coordination of Humanitarian Affairs notes that "According to many observers, the Brotherhood's devotion to social work was the prime driver behind its astounding results in parliamentary elections."[121] In many senses, the mere fact that the Muslim Brotherhood offered an extensive array of services became an indictment of the government's efforts to meet community needs. As journalist Robert Kaplan observed in describing widely held sentiments about the Brotherhood and the Mubarak regime: "When the Muslim Brothers are asked, they open the drawer and give you something. When you ask government officials, they open the drawer and they ask you to give something."[122]

Even in those areas where the Egyptian government actually was offering social services, its efforts were widely perceived as less effective than those offered by the Brotherhood and other Islamist organizations.[123] As Mary Anne Weaver, a foreign correspondent for the *New Yorker,* observed, "From my own experience, having visited a number of [institutions run by Egyptian Islamist groups], I can tell you that they are far better equipped, the staff is far more professional, the equipment is much more modern, than things you'll find in the typically run-down government facilities."[124] The availability and quality of the services offered by the Islamists amounted to "a quiet indictment of the government's inability to provide" for its citizens.[125] For Hesham al-Awadi, a scholar of Middle Eastern politics and history, the Brotherhood's efforts in setting up its extensive array of services constituted a new "Islamist social contract" that reminded many Egyptians of the failure of recent regimes to uphold the "social contract" that President Nasser had established with the Egyptian people decades earlier.[126]

Translating support gained through social service outreach into electoral victories is not without precedent in the Muslim world, as we saw in the introductory chapter in Hamas's victory in the Palestinian elections of 2007. Years earlier in Algeria, the Islamic Salvation Front (Front Islamique du Salut, FIS) had built a network of educational and social services prior to June 1990, when the country's first free local elections since 1962 took place. The FIS handily won a majority of the seats in the local elections and went on to win a majority of seats in the first round of balloting in the parliamentary elections the following year, only to have the government cancel the second round of balloting, arrest their leaders, and outlaw their party in 1992.[127]

THE BROTHERHOOD IN PARLIAMENT

The Brotherhood's success in the 2005 parliamentary elections and its participation in Egyptian politics have not been without detractors, both within and outside the movement. All of the orthodox movements we chronicle have at least some ambivalence to participation in party politics. The Brotherhood was criticized by some of its membership and especially by leaders of more militant Islamist movements for legitimizing a government that was not run according to the shari'a. Ayman al-Zawahiri, current leader of al-Qaeda (following the killing of Osama bin Laden by U.S. forces) has vehemently condemned the Brotherhood's participation in Egyptian politics.[128]

Brotherhood officials responded on their website that "the *Ikhwan* [Brothers] don't get involved in the parliament to 'make' laws that are non-Islamic, but rather to 'prevent' these laws as much as they can."[129]

In parliament after the 2005 election, the Brotherhood MPs, a good number of whom were professionals in the younger generation of the movement who had developed leadership skills through their involvement in student unions and professional syndicates, did not pursue the Brotherhood's religious or culturally strict agendas, opting instead to push for its economic justice agenda and especially for democratic reform.[130] An article posted on the movement's website details the efforts of the Brotherhood's MPs in their first year after the 2005 parliamentary elections to increase the minimum rate of social insurance, control environmental pollution, reduce unemployment, enact health insurance reform, and reduce illiteracy through educational reform, in addition to raising objections to the government's antiterrorism policy. The only ostensibly religious or cultural issue raised was an objection to "insulting caricatures of the Prophet."[131] It appears that the Brotherhood's MPs were using their service in parliament to display the movement's caring side on economic matters and, perhaps more importantly, to demonstrate to the Egyptian people that, if they were given the reins of government, they could be trusted to support the institutions of democracy. The Brotherhood's MPs lived in their own districts, studied the issues the country was facing by bringing in outside experts from a variety of perspectives to speak to them as a group, attended nearly every session of parliament (in contrast to the ruling party's MPs), and proposed the bulk of the legislation considered by parliament. This led area specialists Samer Shehata and Joshua Stacher to describe the Brotherhood as "Egypt's only operating political party."[132]

Although the Brotherhood's new democracy agenda may have been self-serving since the movement had much to gain if free elections were to be held, John Walsh observed, "The Brotherhood's experiences in the past 20 years have suggested that it may be more capable of providing social services to the Egyptian population, more reliable in keeping the promises it has made, and even more democratic than the secular [Mubarak] regime."[133] Adding the democracy plank could be viewed as broadening the Brotherhood's agenda to reach out to other constituents, including those who did not accept the movement's Islamist ideology but who rejected the corruption and authoritarianism of the Mubarak regime. It could also be viewed as a radicalization of the agenda since it presented a direct challenge to Mubarak's authoritarian rule and perhaps an implicit critique of the autocracy of the Brotherhood's old guard. As we will see as well for the other movements whose stories we tell, the Brotherhood has persisted and thrived in part by being flexible in prioritizing and reprioritizing agendas in response to changes in the larger political opportunity structure—in this case, a brief opening up of the political system.

In the spring of 2007, fearing further electoral gains by the Brotherhood, Mubarak's ruling National Democratic Party pushed through a sweeping wave of repressive, constitutional "reforms" that forbad "any political activity . . . within any religious frame of reference" and severely limited the number of candidates for parliament allowed to run independently (as members of the Brotherhood, not being an approved party, had to).[134] Yet, as the *Economist* observed, "You cannot fault the Muslim Brotherhood for its lack of ingenuity." When the movement's longtime slogan, "Islam is the solution," was banned under the new rules, the Brotherhood changed this to "Reform is the solution,"[135] a change that undoubtedly subconsciously linked "Islam" and "reform" for many voters and continued to function as a critique of the Mubarak regime.

While up until the 2005 elections the Mubarak regime largely ignored the NGOs and businesses of the Muslim Brotherhood, after the Brotherhood's stunning electoral success the regime increasingly tried to clamp down on these. James McGann, director of the Think Tanks and Civil Societies Program of the Foreign Policy Research Institute, observed that "The [Egyptian] regime has conducted a relentless and largely successful pushback against NGOs, featuring such legal measures as funding restrictions and intrusive government monitoring, as well as extra-legal measures, including the suppression and harassment of leaders and threats of violence."[136]

Despite the government's efforts, in the years leading up to the spring 2011 protests that resulted in Hosni Mubarak's resignation, the Muslim Brotherhood's social welfare network continued to thrive in Egypt. There are no official figures, but Abdel Moneim Abul-Futouh, a former member of the Brotherhood's Guidance Council, claimed that roughly 20 percent of Egypt's 5,000 NGOs and associations were run by the Brotherhood.[137] In health services alone, the UN Office for Coordination of Humanitarian Affairs reported that the Brotherhood managed twenty-two hospitals, and political scientist Ghada Talhami estimated that the Brotherhood controlled more than 1,000 medical clinics, including 300 in Cairo.[138] While the Brotherhood was not the only Islamist organization providing social services in Egypt, as the largest and most visible Islamist organization, it may have received much of the credit for the efforts of these other Islamist groups.[139]

THE 2011 PRO-DEMOCRACY REVOLUTION AND ITS AFTERMATH

The pro-democracy uprisings against the regimes in Tunisia, Egypt, Yemen, Libya, Syria, and other Muslim-majority nations that shook the world in 2011 took most academics (including ourselves), media pundits, and heads of state by surprise. In Sidi Bouzid, Tunisia, on December 17, 2010, a twenty-six-year-old street vendor named Mohamed Bouazizi set himself on fire in front of the governor's office after a municipal authority slapped him in the face when he tried to resist her confiscating his fruit, had her assistants beat him, and refused to return his electronic scale. This act of defiance, which resulted in Bouazizi's death after eighteen days, became the spark for country-wide demonstrations that led to the departure on January 14, 2011, of Tunisian president Zine El Abidine Ben Ali, ending his twenty-three-year autocratic rule. Soon afterward, demonstrations began spreading to other countries in the Arab world.[140]

On January 25, 2011, Egyptians began what were to become eighteen days of demonstrations and marches, much of it focused on the occupation of Tahrir Square in central Cairo. The organizers of the protests were young, mainly secular Egyptians, who used Facebook and Twitter, as well as face-to-face contact, to mobilize hundreds of thousands of people against Mubarak. The Guidance Council of the Muslim Brotherhood, consisting mainly of the movement's older, more cautious generation, was seemingly caught off guard and waited until the protests had been underway for several days to endorse the demonstrations. The *New York Times* reported that "the Muslim Brotherhood may have grown too protective of its own institutions and position to capitalize on the new youth movement"—a situation where its vast organizational network may have led to some initial inertia.[141] Yet Ann Lesch, a political scientist and associate provost for international programs at the American University in Cairo who was at Tahrir Square during the protests, reports that younger members of the Brotherhood, who would like to see the movement emphasize its democracy agenda more and become more internally democratic, were involved in the demonstrations from the start.[142] As do other observers of the Brotherhood, Lesch reports growing tensions between the younger and older members of the movement.[143]

While most of the media downplayed the role of the Muslim Brotherhood in the revolution (although not in fears about its aftermath), PBS's *Frontline* program reported that the Brotherhood's years of organizing experience came into play as the movement quietly provided much of the infrastructure for the tens of thousands of protesters in Tahrir Square, from taking responsibility for garbage collection, checking those entering the square to ensure that they had no weapons, and arranging microphones and bullhorns for speakers, to offering medical assistance to the wounded. When plainclothes police and pro-government provocateurs—some riding horses or camels and wielding whips, others armed with stones, knives, or clubs, and still others throwing tear gas and Molotov cocktails—stormed the protesters on February 2, it was the Brothers who took the lead in holding off the effort to retake Tahrir Square. A secular participant in the square's occupation, in an interview with political scientist Joshua Stacher, called the actions of the young Brothers "heroic."[144] In a minor but telling incident, *Frontline* filmed young Brotherhood members asking one of their own to put away the Qur'an that he was waving in front of the TV cameras. The Brotherhood wanted to keep a low profile and did not want the foreign press to see their movement as having hijacked the revolution.[145] Egyptian sociologist and longtime democracy advocate

Saad Ibrahim, who had himself been jailed by Mubarak, told the *New York Times* that the young Brothers who were in Tahrir Square used the inclusive slogan "Religion is for God, country is for all," rather than the Brotherhood's usual mantra, "Islam is the solution." Ibrahim said, "One of the great scenes was of young Copts [Christians], boys and girls, bringing water for the Muslim Brothers to do their ablution, and also making a big circle—a temporary worship space—for them. And then come Sunday, the Muslims reciprocated by allowing space for the Copts to have their service. That of course was very moving."[146]

On February 11, 2011, it was announced that Hosni Mubarak had stepped down as president of Egypt, ending his thirty-year autocratic rule. After much celebration and some uncertainty as to who was actually running the country, the Supreme Council of the Armed Forces took control and promised to move the country quickly to democracy. The council appointed an eight-person committee of legal and constitutional experts, one of whom was a Muslim Brother, to draft amendments to the Constitution. A national referendum was held on March 19 on nine amendments to the Constitution, limiting the president to two four-year terms, requiring that the president appoint a vice president, allowing candidates to run independently of parties, and barring anyone from running who has a foreign passport, among other issues. Egyptians were allowed only two choices in the referendum, yes or no. Perhaps because the Muslim Brotherhood was one of the few organized political groups in Egypt and the amendments called for early parliamentary and presidential elections that would allow only a few months for new parties to organize and campaign, the Brotherhood waged an all-out campaign in favor of the referendum, complete with appearances by spokesmen on popular television shows, door-to-door canvassing, and countless fliers and banners. The Brotherhood stood to gain if other groups—including the young secularists who precipitated Mubarak's removal from power—were given little time to organize themselves into political parties. The Brotherhood initially campaigned with the argument that it was a "religious duty" to vote "yes" on the amendments, but after secular activists objected, the Brotherhood told voters that a "yes" vote was a vote for "stability." Despite the opposition of many young secular activists, as well as both of the leading presidential contenders, Mohamed ElBaradei (former head of the International Atomic Energy Agency and Nobel Prize winner) and Amr Moussa (secretary general of the Arab League), the referendum received 77.2 percent of the popular vote.[147] Brotherhood spokesperson and Guidance Council member Essam El Eryan, declared the vote "an historic day and the start of a new era for Egypt . . . the first brick in our building democracy."[148]

The Brotherhood was now poised to reap the benefits of its decades of institution-building to Islamize the Egyptian populace. In one of the few newspaper articles to recognize the importance of the Brotherhood's social welfare network to the movement's electoral fortunes, *Washington Post* reporter Fredrick Kunkle reported on how the Brotherhood's outreach in rural villages like Awseem could affect the outcome of the upcoming elections:

> For needy families in this dusty village outside Cairo, Mohamad el-Seesy is a useful man to know. A devout member of the Muslim Brotherhood, Seesy, 45, leads an Islamic charity that has burrowed deeply into the community by providing an array of religious and social services. The organization has given a widow an oven for baking bread, bought uniforms for a girls school and even arranged marriages. . . . Theirs is the face of the Muslim Brotherhood. . . . "They are active all year round, active and working," said [shopkeeper] Taha Haroum. . . . If given the chance, Haroum said, the Brotherhood could, over time, steer Egypt toward a society infused with religion, not dominated with it. "Their strategy is that they will go step by step," Haroum said.[149]

To try to allay fears of the movement's sectarianism, the Brotherhood announced that it welcomed Coptic Christians and women to its newly established Freedom and Justice Party (FJP). Essam El Eryan, who gave up his seat on the Brotherhood's Guidance Council to become deputy vice president of the FJP, said, "We are keen to spread our ideas and our values. We are not keen for power."[150] Yet the road to the elections was far from easy for the Brotherhood. Radical Salafi groups, some of whom had used terrorism in attempts to overthrow the Mubarak regime during the 1990s, formed political parties. The Salafi party Al Nour, among other Salafi parties, adopted the Brotherhood's strategy of grassroots organizing and charitable activities to vie for the votes of Islamists. Some 200 younger members of the Brotherhood, who felt that the movement's old guard was unwilling to take their views into account, joined with others to form Egyptian Current, a centrist party that does not insist on the establishment of the shari'a. The Brotherhood expelled the leaders of the new party, announcing that members could join only the Freedom and Justice Party. And when Abdel Moneim Abul-Futouh, who had served for twenty-five years on the movement's Guidance Council, launched an independent campaign for president, he was expelled from the Brotherhood.[151] These autocratic moves did little to allay the long-standing fears of some inside Egypt and in the West that the Muslim Brotherhood would ultimately create a nondemocratic Islamic state. As sociologist Saad Ibrahim said of the Brothers in a February 26, 2011, interview with the New York Times, "Far from taking their word, we should keep demanding that they prove that they really are pluralistic, that they are not going to turn against democracy, that they are not going to make it one man, one vote, one time."[152]

While many secularists, liberals, and Copts in Egypt were concerned about how open the Brotherhood would be to religious pluralism, these groups, together with the Brotherhood, were even more fearful of the intentions of the Supreme Council of the Armed Forces (SCAF). The SCAF maintained that in the next Egyptian constitution, the army should be independent of civilian control, with the authority to intervene in politics as it sees fit. In late November 2011, tens of thousands of protesters in Tahrir Square demanded an end to military rule and a delay of parliamentary elections. While the Muslim Brotherhood initially participated in these protests, the movement withdrew from them when the army and police responded with violence. The SCAF granted some concessions to the protesters but insisted that parliamentary elections begin as scheduled on November 28, 2011. The elections, held over the next month and a half, were widely reported as fair and orderly. When the votes were tallied, the Brotherhood's Freedom and Justice Party had won the largest share—47.2 percent— for 235 of the 498 seats in the new parliament (10 seats were named by the SCAF). The second-largest vote—24.3 percent, for 121 seats—went to the Salafi Al Nour Party. Support for the Brotherhood undoubtedly reflected a variety of motivations, not solely religious ones. As Amna Abdel Aziz, a young mother and office worker in Cairo, said: "If the Muslim Brotherhood run the country, they'll fix everything—health, housing, jobs, girls who walk around with their hair uncovered, girls who walk around in the wrong clothing. God willing, they'll fix everything."[153]

CONCLUSIONS

The Muslim Brotherhood, the most powerful Islamist movement in the Muslim world, has for decades been highly successful in bypassing the repressive Egyptian state to achieve its theological, cultural, and economic ends. Writing for *The Nation*, Stephen Glain observes that "Throughout the century-long history of the modern Middle East, no political movement has proved itself so resilient as the Muslim Brotherhood."[154] The Brotherhood is, in the words of Middle East expert Omar Ashour, "a textbook example of how to survive and prosper in highly unfavourable political conditions."[155]

The Brotherhood shares with the other orthodox movements we document—Shas in Israel, Comunione e Liberazione in Italy, and the Salvation Army in the United States—a strongly communitarian theology of "watching over" community members. The strict side of this communitarianism, which has received the most attention from scholars and the media, leads them to push for institutionalization of cultural dictates on sexuality, the family, and the proper roles of women and men. The rarely acknowledged caring side or economic justice orientation of this communitarianism works to ensure that the economic needs of citizens are met.

Along with its cultural and economic communitarianism, Hasan al-Banna's concept of the "comprehensiveness of Islam" gave the Brotherhood a wide scope of agendas and mandated the sacralization of every aspect of private and public life—a goal that the Brotherhood shares with the other movements we chronicle. For al-Banna, it was the religious duty of every Muslim to work toward the transformation of society. Words alone were not enough to re-Islamize Egyptian society; action was needed. The transformation of society would not take place overnight; it required first that individuals be brought to a proper understanding of Islam, then extending this new appreciation of faith in ever-widening circles to their families, communities, and the larger society. The state would become fully Islamized only when it established the shari'a, or Islamic law, as the sole legal foundation.

In the context of highly repressive quasi-colonial and later Egyptian regimes, directly confronting the state was unlikely to be effective, although the Brotherhood did not hesitate to organize mass rallies against British and Western cultural domination of Egypt, and members of the movement's paramilitary Secret Apparatus assassinated some Egyptian government officials in the late 1940s and were blamed for an attempt on Nasser's life in 1954. But generally, al-Banna opted for a patient, long-term, bottom-up strategy of building alternative institutions—reconstituting civil society—that was not overtly political and thus could often fly under the government's radar. Only when Egyptian society had been sufficiently Islamized would the Brotherhood press for the creation of an Islamic order.

As early as 1948—only twenty years after the movement's founding, the Brotherhood was seen by the Egyptian government as a "state within a state," with its own schools, welfare institutions, hospitals and clinics, mosques, and businesses. The Brotherhood's takeover of Egyptian civil society was aided by the inability or unwillingness of the Egyptian state to meet the needs of its citizens, thus leaving the task of addressing these to the Muslim Brotherhood or other groups. Political scientist Carrie Wickham describes the civil society outreach of the Brotherhood and other Islamist groups as having created

> nothing less than a "counter-society" detached from the mainstream social and political order. To reduce the spirit of this community to one of opposition would be to understate its creative, experimental, and comprehensive character. What defined the Islamic movement was less its opposition to a given regime or set of policies than its efforts to construct, from the bottom up and over time, a new kind of society inspired by Islamic ideals.[156]

The state within a state that the Brotherhood patiently built, one institution at a time, over more than eighty years allowed Egyptians to feel that they could experience what life might be like if the movement's theological, cultural, and economic ideology and agendas were put into practice; encouraged comparison with ineffective, corrupt, or indifferent governments; and empowered followers as they worked to bring the movement's ideology into lived reality. While according to social movement theory and research, the Brotherhood's comprehensive agendas, ideological strictness, and reluctance to compromise should have resulted in the movement's failure, bypassing the state and offering much-needed services to citizens lessened the need for pragmatic changes in the movement's strict ideology and helped win over people and groups that might otherwise have required significant compromise to incorporate.

As with the other movements we chronicle in this book, the success of the Brotherhood's network owes much to its decentralized, society-wide structure. Decentralization allowed the Brotherhood to survive not only government efforts to disband the movement in 1948 and 1954, but also efforts by the Mubarak government to shut down or take over its NGOs. When the Brotherhood's central headquarters were closed down, its branches continued. By creating dispersed, decentralized, grassroots-based networks of religious, educational, and social services, the Brotherhood has been able to bring its ideology-in-action to people where they live, demonstrating that the ideology, even though strict, works "on the ground." The grassroots activism of the Brotherhood illustrates one element of Neil Fligstein's concept of "social skill": "find[ing] ways to get disparate groups to cooperate precisely by putting themselves into the positions of others and creating meanings that appeal to a large number of actors."[157] The Brotherhood's frame of "Islam is the solution" is appealing in a conservative, highly religious country and is multivocal—it means different things to different people, thereby allowing the movement to draw in people across classes, genders, and regions. The frame also suggests that secular government is *not* the solution. This framing, together with the movement's efforts to identify and address needs at the grassroots level, allows the Brotherhood to bring in diverse groups, with different interests and concerns, throughout the country. It also allows the Brotherhood's broad, multipronged agenda to be implemented, even if this is accomplished piecemeal in one community after another.

Having established through its civil society work in Egypt a solid base of popular support, the Brotherhood, in the first truly democratic elections in Egypt's history, has succeeded in drawing on this base to secure a leading role for itself in Egypt's future. Only time will tell whether the Brotherhood is finally able to capitalize on its eighty-year effort to sacralize Egyptian society, whether the movement's Freedom and Justice Party allies itself with ultraconservative Salafi parties or with secularist parties, whether the Egyptian military in fact hands over power, and whether the Brotherhood, at the helm of the Egyptian state, is as committed to religious and democratic pluralism as its leaders proclaim.

THE SEPHARDI TORAH GUARDIANS
Penetrating the Israeli State to Circumvent It

Shas is the only party we see in the street. . . . Shas does not disappear after elections. . . . There is more "soul" to their work.
—YEMINI-BORN SHAS SUPPORTER

BREAKING INTO POLITICS WOULD LOGICALLY seem to come after a movement has used institution-building to win popular support for its political program, as we saw in the case of the Muslim Brotherhood in Egypt. The Sephardi Torah Guardians, or Shas, in Israel shows otherwise. A Haredi (ultra-Orthodox) movement working to make Jewish religious law the sole law of the land in Israel,[1] Shas is unique among the movements we chronicle in having entered party politics in the year of its founding, 1983.[2] From its first parliamentary (Knesset) election, Shas became a kingmaker in Israeli coalition governments. The movement then used its lynchpin position to win government funding for a massive network of Haredi welfare and educational institutions that is almost entirely under its own control. Shas penetrated the Israeli state to bypass it.[3]

Shas has built a largely autonomous—many would say completely autonomous—network of institutions that allows its members to worship in Shas synagogues, educate their children in Shas-run schools, shop in the movement's nonprofit shops, take loans from Shas's rotating-credit societies, invest in mutual funds that include only companies that observe Shabbat (the Sabbath), house themselves in Shas-populated neighborhoods, support their typically large families with child allowances that Shas has won for them, and in general, live their lives in a faith-imbued community. This network, in turn, has allowed Shas to win the electoral support of fellow Haredim, as well as "traditional" (partially observant) and even some secular Jews.[4] Today, Shas is the largest religious party in Israel.[5]

Shas is also unique among the movements we chronicle in that it is an ethnicity-based movement. It is not only a Haredi movement; it is also a Sephardi—or, more accurately, Mizrahi[6]—movement that seeks redress for the cultural, economic, and political subordination of Jews of Middle Eastern and North African background by Ashkenazi Jews of European and Russian origin. The network that Shas built grew out of the communitarianism that all Haredim—Mizrahi or Ashkenazi—share. The strict side of this communitarianism entails rigid adherence to what the movement sees as divinely mandated and rabinically interpreted sexual, gender, and family rules—rules that Shas seeks to make national law. The caring side of Shas's communitarianism sees egalitarianism and mutual support as fundamental Jewish values that must be implemented in state policy. While Haredim are expected to give one tenth of their income to those in need,[7] many are themselves poor for reasons we discuss later in this chapter, making it impossible, based on their contributions alone, to provide fully for the economic needs of their community. This is in contrast to the Muslim Brotherhood, which recruits adherents from across the class spectrum, and Comunione e Liberazione, which disproportionately recruits students and professionals, allowing these movements to rely largely on private donations from within the community in providing economic services to the less well-off. Yet Shas and the Salvation Army draw their members primarily from the poor and working class, necessitating at least some funds from the government, and in the Salvation Army's case, better-off, nonmember donors, to support their economic outreach.

At the same time, Shas wants to keep its social welfare programs and schools autonomous from state control so that they can embody and model the movement's theological goal of bringing all Jews in Israel to *teshuva* (repentance and return to the faith). Combining government support with funds raised within the Mizrahi Haredi community and with much volunteer labor on the part of its supporters, Shas has succeeded in building a civil society in which the movement's strict and caring sides can be realized and which serves as a political base to make further demands on the Israeli state.

ETHNICITY AND MIZRAHI JEWS IN ISRAEL

The rise of Shas is integrally tied to the experience of Mizrahi Jews of Middle Eastern or North African origin, who, facing persecution in the predominantly Muslim states of their origin, immigrated to Israel in massive numbers after the nation was established in 1948. From the start, Mizrahim were regarded as inferior by many Ashkenazi Jews from Europe and Russia and were often relegated to nonleadership positions in Ashkenazi religious organizations, to the lower rungs of economic and political hierarchies, and to impoverished "development towns" in remote areas of the country. Poverty, high dropout rates from school, crime, and family problems were common in many Mizrahi communities.[8] Moreover, "Arab Jews," as Mizrahim were sometimes called in reference to the origins of many of them in the Arab Muslim world, received a mixed message from the largely Ashkenazi establishment: They were regarded as "irremediably Arab" but were encouraged "to see their only *real* identity as Jewish."[9]

Israel's first prime minister, David Ben-Gurion, made the following observations about Oriental (Mizrahi) Jews immigrating to Israel from Morocco and Iran in 1965, two years after the end of his term:

> [Jews] from Morocco have no education. Their customs are those of the Arabs. They love their wives, but they beat them. . . . Maybe in the third generation something will appear from the Oriental Jews that is a little different. But I don't see it yet. The Moroccan Jew took a lot from the Moroccan Arabs. The culture of Morocco I would not like to have here. And I don't see what contribution present Persians [Iranians] have to make.[10]

In the early 1970s, the Black Panther Party in Israel, taking its name from the U.S. movement of African Americans, attempted to organize Mizrahim as "blacks," a term derived from an Ashkenazi racial slur (*schwarze khayes,* Yiddish for "black animals") that was used with pride by some Mizrahi Jews. The party failed to gain enough support to win a single seat in the 120-member Knesset.[11] In the 1981 elections, Tami (an acronym for Tnu'at Masoret Yisrael [Movement for the Heritage of Israel]), won three Knesset seats with Mizrahi support but was reduced to only one seat when Shas first ran for parliament in 1984.[12] Reflecting on the underlying ethnic grievances that led to Shas's founding, the movement's spokesman Yitzhak Suderi said in 1999, "Shas was born from a scream. It was a scream against the system in which the Ashkenazim were the rulers and the Sephardim [Mizrahim] were the black slaves."[13] Mizrahi Jews today comprise nearly half of Israel's Jewish population,[14] giving Shas the potential to become one of the largest political parties in the country were it not for another key characteristic of the movement—its Haredism.

HAREDISM, COMMUNITARIANISM, AND POLITICAL ENGAGEMENT

The Haredim (roughly translated "those who tremble in awe before God"), or ultra-Orthodox, in Israel are a controversial group. They set themselves apart from traditional—or partially observant—and secular Jews by their distinctive rituals and clothing and their efforts to impose on the rest of Israeli society their strict interpretation of the Torah and rabbinical rulings. Their exclusivist definition of the faith extends even to the point of lobbying for "Who is a Jew?" legislation that would treat Reform and Conservative Judaism—referred to in Israel as "alternative Judaism"—as inauthentic.[15] The social welfare and educational benefits that Haredim have won from the state, along with the exemption from military service for students engaged in full-time yeshiva studies, where they study the Torah, Talmud, and other religious texts, have earned them much resentment from many in the non-Haredi population.

After Israel's founding in 1948, Prime Minister David Ben-Gurion made the decision to exempt full-time yeshiva students from military service and to give them government support, provided they were not employed. Yeshiva studies can occupy a man (only men can undertake religious studies) most of his adult life. At the time the exemption was granted, there were only 400 yeshiva students in Israel. Since many Torah scholars had been killed in the Holocaust, Ben-Gurion gave the exemption to stimulate the regeneration of this scholarship. Today, it is estimated that there are 60,000 Haredi men engaged in full-time yeshiva studies—more than 60 percent of the Haredi male population of Israel. Because these men are not employed, and because the ultra-Orthodox have also traditionally strongly discouraged women from working outside the home, the poverty rate among Haredim is very high—56 percent by one estimate.[16] This has generated an increasing need for social welfare for Haredi families and has created a backlash against them among non-Haredi. Cartoons depicting Haredim as lecherous and as bloodsuckers, and verbal characterizations of them as "parasites on the Israeli state" are not uncommon in Israel.[17]

The appeal of Shas to Mizrahi identity could give it a broad base of popular support among the nearly half of the Jewish Israeli population that is Mizrahi. Yet because Haredim make up only 9 percent of Jews in Israel,[18] Shas's insistence on Haredism poses the risk of repelling the overwhelming majority of Mizrahim who are traditional or secular. The success of Shas has much to do with how the movement has been able to use its extensive network of alternative faith-based institutions to draw traditional and secular Mizrahim, and even some Ashkenazi Haredim, to its religious and political agendas.[19]

Ashkenazi Haredism or ultra-Orthodoxy in Central and Western Europe was a reaction against the *Haskalah* (Jewish Enlightenment) of the eighteenth century. Ultra-Orthodoxy did not exist before modernism created the need for it. Judaism in the Middle East and North Africa, however, did not experience much secularization. Thus, there was initially no need for a movement of Mizrahi Haredim to defend the faith against secular influences.[20] As Shlomo Ben-Ami, an Israeli historian born in Morocco, observes, "The secular challenge of modernity didn't exist . . . and neither did the reaction of religious extremism."[21] After Mizrahi Jews came to Israel, many became absorbed in the dominant Ashkenazi institutions and movements, often adopting more secular values and lifestyles. Some of those Mizrahim who rejected the predominant secularism of Israeli society became involved in Ashkenazi ultra-Orthodox movements such as Agudat Yisrael (Israel Union). When they realized that in these movements, as in Israeli society more generally, their interests as Mizrahim were subordinated to Ashkenazi concerns, some ultra-Orthodox Mizrahim decided in the early 1980s to organize a separate movement.[22]

The Sephardi Torah Guardians, or Shas, was founded by Sephardic chief rabbi Ovadya Yosef in 1983. Yosef, born in the Iraqi city of Baghdad in 1920, had moved with his parents to Jerusalem at age four.[23] The new movement Yosef founded had the critical patronage of an Ashkenazi rabbi in Agudat Yisrael, Rabbi Eliezer Menachem

Shach, who recognized the need for the Mizrahi Haredim to organize independently of their Ashkenazi counterparts.[24] Denouncing "the failures of secular Zionism, namely drug addiction, emigration, and individualism,"[25] the Shas movement and party set out to sacralize what it saw as an overwhelmingly secular Israeli society. Rabbi Yosef's slogan, "*Lehachzir Atara LeYoshna*" (Restoring the crown to its ancient glory), referred to restoring faith *and* ethnic identity, as well as meeting social and economic needs.[26] The slogan's multivocality allowed Shas to appeal to multiple identities—to the ethnicity, class, and/or religion of potential supporters.

Like the Muslim Brotherhood, Shas seeks to make religious law—in this case, founder Rabbi Yosef's interpretation of Sephardic *halachic* law—the sole basis of the Israeli legal system.[27] Israel was founded as both a Jewish state and a democracy.[28] Because synagogue and state are not clearly separated in Israel, Shas's goal of establishing religious law in Israel is, in a sense, on the table for political discussion and debate. Shas's party leader, Aryeh Deri, noted in 1998, "It's clear that there is no contradiction between us being a Jewish and a democratic state. It is less Jewish than I would prefer but only democracy determines if we will be more or less Jewish. Politics is the means to achieving the option of living a religious life."[29] In a 1999 survey, two thirds of Shas voters mentioned the desire for a religious state in Israel among their reasons for voting for Shas.[30] As the movement's full name, the Sephardi Torah Guardians, suggests, Shas seeks to sacralize the Israeli society and state by disseminating Torah teachings.[31]

Orthodoxy in Protestantism is based on a literal reading of the Bible, in Catholicism on the authority of Church teachings and papal rulings, and in Islam on a literal interpretation of the Qur'an and other sacred texts. Haredism, or ultra-Orthodoxy, in Judaism is based on intensive, often lifelong, study of the Torah, Talmud, and other religious texts, with an unquestioning attitude toward the correctness of their content.[32] Haredi theology also rests on the authority of rabbinical *responsas* or opinions on halachic law.[33] Shas's founder, Rabbi Yosef, is considered one of, it not the, foremost Torah scholars of his generation.[34] His theological mission is to rewrite the body of halachic law,[35] and his responsas are unchallenged by his followers.[36] A U.S. journalist reports that "In the eyes of Shas loyalists, to undermine the authority and sanctity of Yosef is tantamount to doing the same to God."[37] Yosef's halachic opinions have generally been more strict than those of the Middle Eastern rabbinical tradition of his background and he "advocates strict Rabbinic control—and thus uniformity—in spheres relating to personal habits, such as food, sex, and Sabbath observance, and of course in the crucial sphere of marriage."[38]

The teshuva that Rabbi Yosef and his followers in Shas hope to bring about in Israel has two meanings. As anthropologist Aaron Willis observes: "The double meaning of teshuva (repentance and return) was ideally suited to the Shas message. It represented the process of personal movement away from a less observant and committed past to a future of spiritual fulfillment and enhanced individual destiny. At the same time, it was a symbolic 'return' to the once great traditions of the Sephardic past."[39]

Yet while the return of individuals to faith is important, the broader aim of Shas is to bring whole families, communities, and ultimately all of Israeli society to teshuva.[40] Haredism—Mizrahi or Ashkenazi—involves "sacrificing individuality for the community"[41] and is thus inherently communitarian. Israeli sociologist Nissim Leon writes of Rabbi Yosef's concept of spreading the message to the broader community: "According to him, the obligation to engage in *zikui harabim* [proselytizing] is an integral element in the mission of every rabbi, talmudic scholar, yeshiva student, and simple believer within a religious community facing modernization and secularization."[42]

In the economic realm, the caring side of Shas's communitarianism stems from what the movement reports on its website as the "important Jewish values of equality, charity, compassion, and mutual support."[43] Yet, as Israeli political scientist Yaacov Yadgar observes, "Although its political leadership uses social-justice rhetoric, Shas does not see itself as the representative of any 'class,' in a Marxist 'class-consciousness' and 'class struggle' sense."[44] Because the Labor Party in Israel was strongly associated with secularism, its social democratic rhetoric was emphatically rejected by Shas.[45] Shas's commitment to social justice, we argue, comes from another source—its communitarianism.

Shas does not merely talk about social justice. Since 1985 it has used its lynchpin position in government coalitions with all the major parties (Likud, Labor, and Kadima) to win funding with which to establish a nationwide welfare and educational network, El Hamaayan (To the Wellspring).[46] El Hamaayan is almost entirely under the party's own control. It is also partly funded by private donations and aided by much volunteer labor. El Hamaayan encompasses religious schools at all levels from preschool to university, day care centers, summer camps for children, hot lunch programs, after-school clubhouses in poor neighborhoods, charitable organizations (*amutot*), welfare programs, unemployment counseling services, discount stores, rotating-credit societies, housing projects, programs to aid farmers, and centers for senior citizens, among other things.[47]

The strict side of Shas's communitarianism can be seen in the movement's regulation of nearly every aspect of the sexuality, gender relations, and family lives of its members. David Lehmann and Batia Siebzehner note that "This surveillance or interference is in effect the price people pay for the security and benefits of living in a community protected from market forces, and of taking part in closely knit networks of mutual help."[48] In Shas's schools, the strict side of communitarianism is reflected in the obedience the schools require of students, separate schooling of boys and girls, and a schedule for students' daily hours that regulates almost all their time, inside and outside school.[49] In the political arena, Shas members of Knesset have taken conservative positions on abortion, sexuality, pornography, sexually suggestive advertising, and the media. Shas deputy health minister Shlomo Benizri asserted in 1998 that "Homosexuality is an abomination and disgusting. . . . There are no Orthodox homosexuals. If they are homosexual, then by definition they are not Orthodox."[50] Shas MK (member of Knesset) Nissim Zeev argued in 2000 that representatives of the antiabortion organization Efrat should be included on committees in hospitals that authorize abortions.[51] In 2001, Shas deputy labor and social affairs minister Yitzhak Vaknin complained that sexually oriented material on cable TV "corrupt[s] society." Shas generally condemns Israeli popular culture more broadly as immoral and antithetical to Orthodox beliefs.[52]

In Israeli politics, positions on the boundaries of Israel—on how much land should be returned to the Palestinians in exchange for peace—not economic or cultural issues, are the primary basis of determining political left and right.[53] Historically, Shas's position on the occupied territories, which is based on a responsa given by Rabbi Yosef, was sufficiently abstract and flexible as to allow Shas to work with political parties with a wide range of positions on the occupation question. Yosef ruled that Israel should strive for peace with the Palestinians, even to the point of giving up the occupied territories (except for Jerusalem), if it can be proven that this will save lives.[54] Shas's slogan in the 1992 election, "Not Right and Not Left," reflects not only the party's willingness to work with parties of a variety of ideological stripes on the occupation issue,[55] but also that, like all of the other movements we are considering here, Shas is ideologically mixed in conventional left–right terms—conservative (right wing) on cultural matters but egalitarian-leaning (left wing) on economic issues (see figure 1.2 in chapter 1). What may seem to some Israelis to be opportunism in joining quite different governing coalitions probably reflects the fact that Shas is pursuing somewhat different theological, cultural, and economic agendas from those of other Israeli parties. And, as we will see, even as a coalition partner, Shas has not hesitated to push for its own agendas to the point of threatening to withdraw from governing coalitions if the movement's priorities are not addressed.

BREAKING INTO POLITICS

Of the four religiously orthodox movements we chronicle, Shas has been the most deeply involved in party politics. Historically, the Ashkenazi Haredim in Israel, as non-Zionists (they believed that the state of Israel could only be established after the coming of the Jewish Messiah), had rejected participation as ministers in an Israeli state that they regarded as illegitimate, although their party, Agudat Yisrael, put forth candidates for seats in the Knesset. In contrast, from its first parliamentary election in 1984, Shas, as a party of Mizrahi Haredim, strategically took the opposite position—that it should play a role in governing coalitions whenever possible, thus giving it leverage to push its theological, cultural, and economic agendas.[56] Shas has been part of governing coalitions in all but three of the twenty-eight years since its first parliamentary election in 1984, joining coalitions led by Labor, Likud, and Kadima alike.[57] Although Shas participated in the Israeli state from the start, this does not mean that the movement regards the state as supportive of its theological, cultural, and economic aims. As Lehmann and Siebzehner write, the movement's "discourse is laced with bitter hostility towards the impersonal, liberal [laissez faire] and individualist framework of Israel's legal system in particular, and to what it sees as the secular bias of the state in general."[58]

Both the motivation for and the success of Shas's involvement in formal politics has much to do with the nature of Israel's multiparty system, which allows even small parties to potentially play a key role in policy making. In Israel's history, none of the nation's major parties (Labor, Likud, and now Kadima) has ever won enough seats in the 120-seat Knesset to form a government without bringing in coalition partners.[59] This allowed Shas from the start to use its lynchpin position in most government coalitions throughout its quarter-century history to leverage major financial considerations for the Mizrahi community and to gain key ministerial posts.[60]

Shas's remarkable success in winning state resources for its constituency, which we detail later in this chapter, is also due in part to the corporatist nature of Israeli society. Lehmann and Siebzehner describe Israel as a "society of enclaves" that "allows fiefdoms to exist within the state but largely beyond the control of central government."[61] Prior to the rise of Shas, the trade union movement and the ultra-Orthodox were two of the dominant enclaves. One reason that Shas entered politics was to wrest resources from the state for educational and welfare resources that the Mizrahi Haredim felt that the Ashkenazi-controlled ultra-Orthodox enclave was unwilling to share with them.[62]

Shas first ran candidates for municipal office in Jerusalem in 1983, the year of its founding, winning three seats on the city council. Shas's spiritual and political leadership are separated. The movement's most prominent political leader in its early years, Moroccan-born Aryeh Deri, rose virtually overnight from a twenty-four-year-old yeshiva student in 1983 to become the party's leader in 1988 and minister of the interior in 1989, from which he controlled funds allocated to cities and had an effect on many important domestic matters.[63] Shas won four Knesset seats in its first parliamentary election in 1984, and improved its standing to six seats in 1988 and 1992. New elections were called in 1996 after Prime Minister Yitzak Rabin was assassinated in 1995, and Shas nearly doubled its representation in the Knesset—to ten seats.[64]

Although Shas's target constituency—Mizrahi Jews—were economically disadvantaged relative to Ashkenazi Jews, and an appeal could have been made to Mizrahim based on class, the movement's original themes were those of religion and family, probably because there was much family disruption, youth crime, and loss of respect for parents in Mizrahi communities due to their impoverishment. A return to faith was seen as a way of bringing back the family.[65] Thus, Shas initially concentrated on restoring the Torah and halachic law to the center of the state of Israel and creating a religious educational network. A Shas leaflet handed out in the 1992 election campaign depicted these concerns as a battle between good and evil, showing two photographs: one of the Ramle prison near Tel Aviv and the other of a schoolroom with children studying the Torah. Beneath the photographs was the caption "The curse, and the blessing," representing the disproportionate percentage of Mizrahi men who were in jail as the "curse," and Shas's religious schools as the "blessing."[66]

PENETRATING THE ISRAELI STATE TO BYPASS IT

Although Shas did not begin with an economic agenda, it very quickly used its political leverage as a key coalition partner to establish in 1985—only one year after it entered national politics—what was to become a massive welfare and educational network, El Hamaayan.[67] By 1999, Shas was estimated to have 3,500 branches and 956 organizations throughout Israel.[68] Shas's welfare and educational network functioned in Israel then, as it does now, as a "surrogate state," a "state within a state," or a "parallel and hostile society," in the words of many Israeli social scientists and international journalists.[69] Yet unlike the network established by the Muslim Brotherhood, and more so than the networks built by the Salvation Army and Comunione e Liberazione, Shas's network depends on considerable government funding. By demanding resources for its constituency as a condition of joining governing coalitions, gaining control of key ministries (for example, Interior, Labor and Social Affairs, Infrastructure, and Health) that dispense social welfare and educational funds, winning near autonomy in supervising its network of educational and welfare institutions, and building its own "enclave,"[70] Shas has effectively bypassed the Israeli state.[71]

Shas, we argue, penetrated the Israeli state precisely to sidestep it. As Israeli historian Noah Efron observes: "There is something paradoxical about this: The life apart of the ultra-Orthodox was made possible by the Zionist state itself.... The ultra-Orthodox social services—medical care, money for retirement, unemployment benefits, food stamps—were provided by the government. In a sense, it was the state that made it possible for the ultra-Orthodox to ignore the state."[72] Likewise, in the words of Israeli political scientist Yaacov Yadgar, "Shas . . . 'sends' the party to represent it within the political field and amongst Zionist state institutions in order to secure the flow of resources necessary to ensure the independence of Shas . . . from government."[73] As have numerous others in Israel, Israeli political scientist Zeev Sternhell voices alarm over what he calls Shas's "state within a state," arguing that "You can't provide Shas with the instruments of power to organize independently of the society as a whole."[74]

The largest and most highly institutionalized division of Shas's El Hamaayan network is its educational system, Ma'ayan Hahinuch Hatorani (Wellspring of Torah Education), which was established in 1988.[75] The Education Wellspring offers a (Mizrahi) Jewish-religious curriculum to students at every level.[76] Funded by the state but almost entirely under the control of a group of prominent and respected Mizrahi rabbis (the Wellspring appoints its own inspectors), the Shas schools' very low tuition, free transportation, free or low-cost lunches, and full day of instruction (ideal for employed parents) make them "a serious challenger to the state educational system."[77] Although their low cost draws traditional and secular, as well as Haredi, Mizrahim, the education offered is in accord with Shas theology.[78] Pictures of Rabbi Ovadya Yosef and other Shas sages are hung in sex-segregated classrooms where a portrait of the prime minister would normally be. A Shas activist observed of the schools: "We teach our children the things that are relevant to them: Jewish history, Sephardi religious customs, Torah, Mishna [oral tradition], Jewish values, and not the French Revolution."[79]

Education systems are, of course, potential means of upward mobility in addition to reproducers of cultural systems. Shas originally saw its state-financed education system as more useful to its theological agenda of bringing Mizrahim to teshuva than as part of its agenda to improve their economic standing, preferring to offer content that was more suited to further religious study, which was open only to men, than to advanced academic study and practical careers. By the end of the 1990s, the movement's governing body, the Shas Council of Torah Sages, amended the high school programs so that they could lead to further secular studies, gainful employment, and professional careers, and later, in response to a 2003 requirement from the Education Ministry that Haredi schools teach a "core curriculum," added courses on mathematics, English, the sciences, and grammar. Nonetheless, a 2010 investigation by the Israeli newspaper *Yedioth Ahronoth* found that many Shas of schools were over-reporting the number of hours devoted to nonreligious subjects in order to receive state funding.[80]

In 2001, Adina Bar Shaom, the eldest of Rabbi Yosef's eleven children, with the permission of the Shas Council, cofounded the Haredi College of Jerusalem, which offers programs, primarily to women, in social work, computer science, paramedics, interior design, business, finance, and other fields.[81] Classes at Haredi College are segregated by gender, and modesty regulations for women on sleeve length, hairstyle, makeup, and head covering are posted at the entrance. Because large numbers of Haredi men undertake full-time yeshiva studies and are thus not earning a living, the Haredi community has increasingly recognized the importance of education in allowing women to enter professional fields where they can better support their families. Haredi College founder Bar Shalom says, "I don't know if this is a revolution. But it is possible to talk about a significant change in the attitude of ultra-Orthodox society toward education. The leaders of the ultra-Orthodox community realize that it is impossible to sit on the fence if they don't want the community to wallow in poverty all its life. I entered this field in order to open a door to masses of girls."[82] The increased education and earning power of Haredi women may ultimately change some traditional gender relations or create a backlash against this.

BUILDING AT THE GRASSROOTS

The widespread notion among the majority, non-Haredi Israeli public and academics in Israel is that Shas's welfare and educational network exists only because of the funds it has been able to wrest from the government. Yet to our knowledge no definitive figures exist on how much of the funding for all of the activities of Shas comes from the government. Many of the movement's programs are partly or wholly supported by donations raised among its followers and rely heavily on the volunteer labor of Shas supporters.[83] The focus of much of the scholarship on the movement as the recipient of government largess—on its top-down success—misses the extent to which the activities and programs of the movement often arise from the ground up—through the grassroots efforts of Shas supporters. The failure to recognize the time-consuming volunteer work of Shas activists, many of whom are yeshiva students, also contributes to the stereotype of Haredim as deadbeats who are only taking from society. This tendency among scholars to ignore the unpaid labor of Shas activists also misses the fact that many in the Haredi community do not buy into the logic of the market.

Israeli political scientist Lilly Weissbrod describes how Shas activists established local centers "in poor oriental [Mizrahi] communities and neighborhoods, housed in synagogues and abandoned shelters, staffed with volunteers and providing adult religious education and supplementary free or low-cost religious education for children, hot meals for the needy as well as nursery schools."[84] An example of this grassroots approach is the nongovernmental organization Ma'yanot Hityashvut (Sources of the Settlement Process), through which teams of Shas-affiliated yeshiva students work for free in local *moshavim* (agricultural cooperatives), where they often find abandoned synagogues and loss of faith among the residents:

> Aiming to gradually reintroduce a taste for observance, the teams would begin by cleaning up the synagogues, then they would install themselves there to study, invite the inhabitants to join them, conduct services, teach elementary Torah to the children, [and] run activities for the women. . . . [S]ince the *moshavim* suffer from widespread poverty and governmental neglect, the organization . . . distributes food parcels for Passover, school equipment packages and clothes for the needy. The scheme has operated . . . in 180 out of the 540 *moshavim* in Israel.[85]

As the activities of this NGO illustrate, Shas has built its welfare and educational network around Shas-controlled synagogues, reflecting long-standing Mizrahi practices of centering civil society on the local synagogue, much as the Muslim Brotherhood has centered its outreach on local mosques that they have built or control and, as we will see in chapter 5, the Salvation Army has built its economic outreach around its local corps (churches). Political scientist Omar Kamil describes this pattern as follows:

> The civil society of Shas is self-contained in its own community and centered in synagogues based on Jewish fraternities. The recipe for success of these civil societies is very simple: offer help to everyone who needs it. In order to realize this motto, Shas established an independent educational system, religious schools, synagogues, and *mikvaot* (ritual baths). It rehabilitated delinquents and drug addicts, provided support for large families, created jobs, and improved housing.[86]

Like many successful social movements, Shas has used familiar, preexisting institutions as a base upon which to build an alternative social order.

The sacralization of Israeli civil society that Shas is working toward can also be seen in the movement's efforts to extend its control over existing neighborhoods, a process that parallels in some respects the Muslim Brotherhood's and Comunione e Liberazione's success in winning electoral control of existing professional and student associations. Efron captures the fear that these efforts have engendered among some in the non-Haredi population, citing a pamphlet distributed in neighborhoods by the anti-Haredim group Hofesh (Freedom), which describes what the group sees as the stages involved in the Haredi takeover of neighborhoods:

• Purchase of or rental of one or several apartments by Haredim.

• Torah study in these apartments, involving the importation of students from far away, including other cities and towns, and creating a nuisance for the neighbors and residents of the neighborhood. This leads to erosion of housing prices.

• Purchase of additional apartments from the neighbors at significantly lower prices.

• Transformation of apartments into a *kollel* [a yeshiva for married men] or Talmud academy.

• Leaving the apartments to begin missionary activity; encouraging men to put on *tefillin* [small leather boxes containing scrolls of Torah Scriptures], hand out Shabbat candles and other ritual objects on Fridays at shopping centers.

• Setting up stands proselytizing others to become religious or Haredi, especially near secular schools.

• Transformation of an apartment into a synagogue. Usurpation of a class in an existing school to turn it into a synagogue on Shabbat at first, and then later expansion of religious activity, building a kollel near the synagogue, building a ritual bath, a yeshiva, and eventually, closing a street or part of a neighborhood on Shabbat.

> • Infiltration of religious and Haredi residents into the neighborhood association, numerical domination of the association, and exploitation of the democratic process to make decisions to the detriment of the freedom of the neighborhood.[87]

Although this pamphlet is clearly alarmist, it reflects the concern among many non-Haredim with what they see as Shas's "invasion" of public space. Israeli academics have also noted the Shas tactic of seizing unoccupied building sites and converting them into kindergartens or youth clubs,[88] a tactic that is illegal and explicitly bypasses the state.

Building a strong presence in the mass media is another key element we identify in Shas's efforts to bypass the state by capturing civil society. Up until 1995, the Israeli state did not allow commercial radio. Even today, the government makes only a very limited number of frequencies available to commercial stations. As a result, numerous "pirate" radio stations, operating without license from the state, permeate the airwaves in Israel. The Israeli minister of transportation has called these stations "aerial terrorism."[89] Israeli communications professor Yaron Katz writes that the pirate stations "allow the bypassing of the imposed restrictions on official means [of communication], reaching segmented target audiences and creating direct connection with sectorial groups without restrictions on broadcasting or considerations and preferences imposed by public supervision."[90] Because they are illegal, the more than 200 *piratim* in Israel are understandably reluctant to announce their affiliation with a specific movement or party, but an article in the leading Israeli newspaper *Haaretz* reports that "the stations are most closely associated with the Sephardi ultra-Orthodox party Shas."[91] The pirate station with the largest audience, Kol HaEmet (The Voice of Truth), is widely seen as connected to Shas and, according to Katz, is aimed at "the newly religious and traditional just interested in maintaining the values of religion emphasized by Rabbi Ovadiah Yosef."[92] The stations have also played an important role in getting Shas's message out in electoral campaigns and in responding to the leadership scandal detailed later in this chapter.

In June 2007, several pirate radio stations, including Kol HaEmet, were accused of wandering from their usual frequencies and interfering with air traffic control broadcasts at Tel-Aviv's Ben-Gurion International Airport, shutting down the airport for a day and a half. Kol HaEmet's popular radio personality and one-time Shas candidate for office Rabbi Shmuel Ben-Atar was sentenced to nine months in prison for illegal operation of a station, and the station was closed.[93] Kol HaEmet has, however, been shut down by the government numerous times before and always seems to find its way back to the airwaves.[94]

Shas has a legal satellite TV network that broadcasts a weekly program featuring prominent rabbis, including Rabbi Yosef, as guests. The program is broadcast to some

600 public locations throughout the country, in addition to private homes. Communications professor Yaron Katz notes that these broadcasts allow Shas to reach large audiences without having to organize mass rallies or move rabbis from place to place and "assist in the significant political success of the party in elections."[95]

A good part of Shas's outreach, however, occurs informally, unsupported by government aid, undertaken by people doing what they see as needing to be done at the grassroots level, and embodying the strongly held commitment to mutual support in the Haredi community. Yael Ben-Moshe and her husband, Yisrael, run Yael Falafel, one of most popular falafel shops in Netanya, a city of 176,000 on Israel's Mediterranean coast. Her activities on behalf of Shas have been the subject of two newspaper articles. In an interview in *Inside Magazine* of the *Jewish Exponent* with Israeli journalist Barbara Sofer, Ben-Moshe calls her fast-food stand "an outpost of Shas." Writes Sofer, "This week she's helped a couple find a washing machine and stove, even arranging delivery; she's overcome city bureaucracy for an elderly woman and found her a space in a municipal convalescent home; and today she's meeting with a newly religious woman who has separated from her irreligious husband. She'll remind them all to vote Shas." In addition to running what Stofer calls a "fast food stand cum welfare bureau," Ben-Moshe freely gives advice to those who visit her shop, such as asking a woman wearing a "revealing" dress "why she would want to share what she has with anyone other than her husband."[96]

Also writing about Ben-Moshe's work, *Jerusalem Post* reporter Sarah Hershenson observes that "there are no name plates, award dinners or televised fund drives for this goodwill effort—it is strictly a local affair." Ben-Moshe, who likes the nickname "Falafel Yael," is the center of what she calls a "syndicate of kindness"—a network of friends and neighbors, mainly women, who step in to help wherever they can. If Ben-Moshe cannot take on a task by herself, which she often does, she matches people who need furniture with those who have items they no longer use; arranges help for overburdened young mothers from women who are willing to do laundry, iron, and watch the children; and connects lonely shut-ins with women who bring them medicines, arrange for meals to be sent in, and chat for a while. In her home, Ben-Moshe hosts weekly lectures for women on the Torah and family matters, the result of which, she says, is that "many women have changed their lives for the better by becoming knowledgeable." While running the falafel shop and making her daily rounds in the neighborhood takes up much of her time, Ben-Moshe says, "One needs to get out and do acts of kindness, and by doing them God gives one the strength to do more."[97]

While Yael Ben-Moshe's "syndicate of kindness" is a private, nongovernment-supported effort, many of the activities and programs of Shas are partly or fully funded by the state. As such, just as with the Salvation Army's government-funded efforts in the United States, these state-subsidized activities are supposed to be nonpolitical. Yet in a nation where religion and politics are not separated and where the line between them is a matter of much dispute, efforts to bring Mizrahi Jews, and Israeli society more generally, to teshuva are inevitably political, especially when there is a religious political party—Shas—whose explicit aim is to accomplish this.

Moreover, much as the Muslim Brotherhood's network of services is seen as meeting citizen needs that are unmet by the Egyptian government, political scientists Rebecca Kook, Michael Harris, and Gideon Doron observe of Shas's network:

> Shas has gradually become the prime provider of central social services to its targeted and underprivileged population. This population constitutes the largest Jewish consumer of welfare services. Feeding into an obvious vacuum in the distribution of services by the Israeli welfare state, Shas provides compensation: In [largely Mizrahi] development towns . . . the main social services such as child care and community services are provided by Shas, not by the state. This ability to function as a surrogate state is what laid the basis for its electoral and social success.[98]

In a similar vein, a report published by the American Jewish Committee notes that "Shas has filled the welfare vacuum created by years of government neglect" and in another observation similar to those made about the Muslim Brotherhood in Egypt, "[U]nlike other parties, its activists work with their constituents on a daily basis, not just when elections roll around."[99] Both of these laudatory accounts give Shas full credit for these programs, despite the fact that a considerable part of the funding for Shas's social welfare work comes from the government. Even for those programs that are entirely government funded, Shas's visibility in wresting these funds from the state and its autonomy in controlling and distributing the funds directly to those who need them have undoubtedly put Shas's stamp on the programs, rather than that of the Israeli government or taxpayers.

In a comparison that the movement would surely reject, Shas has been likened to Hamas, the Palestinian offshoot of the Muslim Brotherhood, which has also established an extensive, autonomous grassroots network, as a "'total movement' that caters to the social needs of its marginalized constituency."[100] In some secular circles in Israel, people have rhymed the names of the two movements, "Shas, Hamas," as a foreboding image of what may be to come for the nation.[101]

Shas's massive educational and welfare network helps the movement draw political support from its Mizrahi constituency, including from the many in this community who do not share the movement's ultra-Orthodox theology.[102] Israeli political scientist Etta Bick notes with reference to the 1999 elections that

> Many [non-Haredi Shas voters] have had contact with Shas programmes throughout the year and have become involved in their activities. Many traditional Sephardim switched their allegiance to Shas out of appreciation for Shas' welfare

work and assistance programmes within the communities. . . . The only group visibly helping to alleviate poverty, providing day-care, bus transport to school, afternoon programmes for children, and offering any real assistance was Shas. [103]

Regarding the empowering effect of this activism on the recipients of Shas's services, David Tal, a Shas member of Knesset from 1996 to 2002, said, "We help the weak to survive. We build their self-esteem. That helps them to help themselves."[104]

PROVIDING GRADUATED LEVELS OF INVOLVEMENT

Had Shas been unable to win the support of a larger constituency than its relatively small core of Haredi Mizrahim, its impact on Israeli politics would have been minimal and short-lived. Key to the movement's success, both religiously and politically, was winning the support of Mizrahim who are not Haredi but are traditional or secular in their religious beliefs and practices. Like the Salvation Army, Muslim Brotherhood, and Comunione e Liberazione, Shas offers degrees of ideological adherence and commitment to its followers, through which it seeks to draw less religiously committed Mizrahim to support its electoral efforts and to teshuva (repentance and return). This flexibility allows Shas to bring in groups that normally would require significant compromise to be incorporated. As social scientists David Lehmann and Batia Siebzehner observe, "the Shas leadership did not try to mobilize these 'intermediate' [traditional] votes by softening their stance on religious matters."[105]

Despite its unwillingness to compromise theologically in bringing in new followers, Shas has been highly successful in incorporating Mizrahi Jews who do not share the movement's ultra-Orthodoxy, initially at minimal levels of commitment and later at higher levels. Etta Bick describes Shas's constituency as made up of

concentric circles in terms of religious observance [with] . . . a relatively small nucleus of hard-core fundamentalist supporters who are strictly observant, a larger circle of supporters who are traditional in their observance yet not Orthodox, and a third circle of voters who are not observant themselves, but take pride in their ethnic traditions and identify with the mission of the party to restore traditional values, and may also receive a variety of services from the party.[106]

Much of the religious and political outreach of Shas is directed to winning over what Bick calls the second (traditional) and third (secular) circles. As we noted earlier, the movement's schools draw most of their students from Mizrahi families who do not share the ultra-Orthodoxy of their teachers. The hope of Shas's leadership is that these schools will bring the next generation and, even more importantly, their parents—as current voters—to teshuva. Shas's political leader, Aryeh Deri, described in a campaign speech the hoped-for process of increasing theological commitment as follows:

[A] child arrives at these schools at the age of four or five, he knows nothing besides curses and the ways of the street. After two weeks, you can see the difference.

He cleans himself up and begins to wear the clothes of *bnei torah*. He returns home from school with sacredness in his eyes, with sparks in his eyes—he answers his mother and father, yes, mother; yes, father. Later he returns home on Friday afternoon, he asks his mother to light the sabbath candles. And the mother who hasn't remembered to light the candles for who knows how long, remembers her righteous mother, and she lights the candles.... What Sephardi mother can stand against this force? She begins to cry and makes the blessings that she can return in *teshuva*, and that the older children will return as well.[107]

Once in the movement itself, Shas initiates face "cascading demarcations," beginning with minimal commitment and sacrifice but progressing to the point that "if they are to join fully then they must give up old jobs, old ties and eventually old family ..., develop a new quasi-family, and ... acquire a spouse who will meet with the approval of the religious authority."[108] The sacrifice required of Shas rabbis and leaders is even greater, involving an almost total commitment of time—evenings at work until late, long hours spent in meetings, and time away from family.[109] At this highest level of commitment, Shas, like the other movements we chronicle, resembles sociologist Lewis Coser's "greedy institutions," which demand all of the individual's loyalty, commitment, and time.[110]

BORROWING FROM MODERNITY

As does each of the movements whose stories we tell, Shas uses modern technology in its effort to sacralize Israeli society. The movement, which is in part a reaction against what it sees as the individualism and immorality of the secular Israeli society and state, was initially very suspicious of the internet. Nonetheless, carefully supervised websites disseminating religious texts, Haredi-sponsored internet discussion groups, and online consultations with religious authorities have helped bolster the sense of community among the ultra-Orthodox, and allowed them, in Rabbi Yosef's words, "to fight [non-Haredim] with their own tools."[111] Moreover, despite the fact that religious parties up until 1999 generally eschewed the use of the mass media,[112] Shas's electoral campaign that year was a high-tech, multimedia affair, with Rabbi Yosef dramatically transported by helicopter from one mass rally to another, full-page newspaper ads for Shas's candidates, lectures by Yosef and other Shas religious authorities broadcast on closed-circuit TV networks, tapes and videocassettes of campaign speeches distributed to voters, entertainment at mass assemblies provided by Mizrahi stars, and speeches given in the style of American televangelists.[113] Shas, like the other movements whose stories we tell, uses the tools of modernity to fight what it sees as its false values.

SURVIVING A LEADERSHIP SCANDAL

In 1990, an investigation was begun of charges that Aryeh Deri, Shas's party leader and Israel's minister of the interior, was illegally directing funds from his ministry to institutions affiliated with Shas, bullying mayors into giving more municipal resources to Shas institutions, pocketing some of the money intended for Shas institutions, and taking bribes and kickbacks. Three years later, in 1993, Deri was indicted on the charges connected to taking bribes.[114] Shas followers were able to reconcile the dissonance between their strict moral standards and their leader's alleged crimes by viewing the charges as a politically motivated attack on Mizrahim and the product of an Ashkenazi-controlled justice system—an example of Shas's successful framing of the matter by drawing upon existing resentments among its political supporters. Two years later, the announcement of Deri's sentence of four years in prison was carried live on TV and radio one week before the 1999 parliamentary elections, when it could have had a devastating effect on Shas's electoral chances. The spiritual leader of Shas, Rabbi Yosef, promptly proclaimed Deri innocent under halachic law, and Shas distributed over 200,000 video-cassettes with the title *J'accuse* (drawing on the anti-Semitic case against Alfred Dreyfus in late nineteenth to early twentieth-century France), which portrayed Deri as the victim of Ashkenazi persecution and complained that the only two comparably public announcements of verdicts were for Nazi war criminal Adolf Eichmann and accused war criminal John Demjanjuk. The videotape also contrasted Deri's modest apartment with the luxurious homes of the trial's prosecutors and judges and showed crowds of enthusiastic supporters carrying posters proclaiming Deri "Innocent and Blessed."[115] Some Mizrahi Haredim, who saw Israel's secular law as derived from "the teachings of gentile judges," felt that, even if Deri broke secular law by diverting government funds to Shas institutions, this served a higher good. As Israeli historian Noah Efron observes, for such people, "Deri is a hero, not despite breaking the law, but *because* he broke the law."[116] Regarding Deri's skimming money for himself from funds intended for Shas's welfare institutions, one Shas supporter said, "If you pour honey, no one can blame you for licking your fingers."[117]

One week after his conviction, Deri led his party to its greatest electoral victory to date, winning seventeen Knesset seats to make Shas the nation's third-largest party.[118] Deri was later forced to resign his seat in the Knesset in order to serve his prison sentence. Rabbi Yosef reluctantly ordered Deri's replacement as party leader by Eliyahu Yishai, the son of Tunisian immigrants, briefly precipitating an internal struggle in the movement between Deri's and Yishai's supporters. The conflict was eventually resolved in Yishai's favor, and he remains party leader of Shas (and deputy prime minister and minister of the interior). Although not as charismatic as Deri, Yishai was able to use Shas's critical membership in the Labor government of Ehud Barak to win repayment of debts accrued by Shas's educational network.[119] While scandals involving televangelists in the United States during the late 1980s temporarily undermined support for the "New Christian Right" among religiously orthodox Protestants,[120] the charges against Shas's leadership were taken by many of the movement's followers as resulting from political retaliation on the part of the state and specifically by the Ashkenazi establishment, rather than as indicative of genuine moral failings.

BACKLASH AND RECOVERY

Governments in Israel accepted Shas during its early years and helped fund its welfare network, partly in the hope that Shas would draw support away from the militantly Zionist and territorially expansionist Gush Emunim (Bloc of the Faithful) movement and from left-leaning, ultra-secular Mizrahi groups that were seen as a greater threat. Shas fulfilled its part of the bargain, and these groups diminished in support as Shas grew.[121] By the late 1990s, Shas had succeeded in building through its welfare and educational network an alternative civil society based on Mizrahi beliefs and practices. The movement was seen by the government as a competitor to the Israeli state in providing for needy citizens and as a direct challenge to the state's efforts to promote secular ideals. To counter this appeal, Ehud Barak of the Labor Party campaigned for prime minister in 1999, arguing that "A situation in which the Haredi public is exempt from serving in the army, but receives substantial benefits from the state, is unfair and must be changed."[122] In this framing battle with Shas, Barak drew on the importance and legitimacy of the military in a society where citizens see themselves as continually under attack from outside enemies and thus in need of a strong army. In counterpoint, Shas framed its (male) followers' full-time study of the Torah as providing as essential a service to the nation as military service. Barak planned to cut government funding of Shas-controlled welfare programs and substitute government-controlled programs. But after Barak won the prime ministry, Shas was able to use its own electoral success and its leverage as a member of his governing coalition to ensure continued generous support and autonomy for its welfare network.[123]

In 2003, the secular, anti-Haredi party Shinui (Change) arose, with the battle cry of "putting an end to the usurious exploitation of the State's coffers for religious purposes." Shinui was able to cut substantially into Shas's support, winning fifteen seats in the 2003 elections, compared to Shas's eleven seats.[124] For the first time in its history, Shas was shut out of the governing coalition and had to serve in opposition to Ariel Sharon's Likud (later Kadima) coalition. Without Shas's bargaining power, child allowances—which are critical to Shas supporters, many of whom have large families—were cut in half.[125] In the 2006 elections, Shas rebounded to become again Israel's third-largest party, garnering even more votes than Likud. The leadership of the militantly secular Shinui party had split and it received too few votes to earn even a single seat in the Knesset. Shas, again in the position of coalition-maker, joined Ehud Olmert's Kadima coalition.[126]

The most serious threat to Shas's continued role as kingmaker in Israeli politics—and to the considerable benefits and autonomy that accrue from this—was precipitated by the movement itself in 2008. With Prime Minister Ehud Olmert of Kadima under investigation for corruption, the future of his coalition was in doubt. Shas took the opportunity to make two demands for its continued participation in the coalition: (1)

an increase in child allowances of NIS30 (US$7.10) per child per month, which Shas spokesman Roi Lachmanovitch said would "lift a half million children above the poverty line,"[127] and (2) an agreement that the Israeli government would not divide Jerusalem in any peace settlement with the Palestinian Authority and would allow continued building of settlements in the occupied territories. With the ultra-Orthodox population growing rapidly due to high fertility rates, Shas party leader Eli Yishai took a harder stance on the question of the occupied territories than Rabbi Yosef's responsa (ruling) seemed to warrant in order to allow for the "natural growth" of the Haredi community. When Foreign Minister Tzipi Livni, the likely new party leader of Kadima, was unwilling to meet Shas's demands, Shas withdrew from the coalition, forcing Livni to call new elections to be held on February 10, 2009.[128]

The 2009 campaign took place as Israel invaded Gaza, claiming retaliation for Hamas's bombing of cities in the south of the country. Yisrael Beiteinu (Israel Is Our Home), a party that took a hard line on Israel's Muslim Arab population, threatened to take votes away from Shas. Yisrael Beiteinu's leader, Avigdor Lieberman, called for a mandatory "loyalty oath" that "would require all Israelis to vow allegiance to Israel as a Jewish, democratic state, to accept its symbols, flag, and anthem, and to commit to military service or some alternative service."[129] The loyalty oath was ostensibly directed at Israel's Muslim Arabs, who are exempt from military service and whose loyalty was especially being questioned in light of street demonstrations in support of Hamas by some Arabs in Israel. But the oath was undoubtedly also intended to raise doubts about the loyalty of Shas's Haredi supporters, who are exempt from military service if they are engaged in full-time yeshiva studies and who, like the Muslim Arabs in Israel, come from non-European origins. Five days before the election, Shas's founder, Rabbi Ovadya Yosef, responded by warning his followers that to vote for Yisrael Beiteinu, which he referred to only obliquely as "the Russian party" in an effort to stir the ethnic loyalty of Shas followers, would be to commit a "sin that will never be forgiven."[130]

While Yisrael Beiteinu, with fifteen Knesset seats, came in third in the election, Shas dropped by only one seat to eleven seats. Benjamin Netanyahu, whose Likud party, with twenty-seven seats, came in second by one seat to Livni's Kadima Party, appeared most likely to be able to form a government, and was asked to do so by President Shimon Peres. Kadima refused to join Netanyahu's coalition, which needed sixty-one seats to succeed, leaving Netanyahu to negotiate with Yisrael Beiteinu, Shas, and Labor (with thirteen seats) in forming a coalition that would give him sixty-six seats.[131] Shas leader Eliyahu Yishai, again in the position of kingmaker, successfully negotiated four ministries for Shas (with himself as minister of the interior and one of four deputy prime ministers), control of the ultra-Orthodox education network, the highest funding ever for Shas's yeshivas and women's seminaries, funds for constructing and renovating synagogues, and an increase in child allowances to the levels before they were cut in 2003.[132]

SHIFTING PRIORITIES TO PUT ECONOMIC CONCERNS FIRST

Creatively prioritizing and reprioritizing among their theological, cultural, and economic agendas can give religiously orthodox movements the flexibility to overcome the liability that their moral absolutism and multipronged agendas may present. As we saw in chapter 2, the Muslim Brotherhood's parliamentary members after the election of 2005 downplayed the movement's theological and cultural missions and added a new democracy plank to their platform. Shas has been no less flexible in adjusting its priorities to internal and external opportunities and crises. While there has long been a communitarian ethos of mutual support among the Haredim whereby they looked out for the community's poor, the economic need in the community has undoubtedly been exacerbated by the increasingly common practice among Haredi men of undertaking full-time religious studies, which prevents them from taking jobs to support their families. Economist Eli Berman estimates that while 41 percent of ultra-Orthodox men between the ages of twenty-five and fifty-four were in yeshiva studies rather than employment in 1980, fully 60 percent were by the end of the 1990s. The Haredi fertility rate during the same period rose from 6.5 children per woman to 7.5. Berman attributes both trends to the exemption from military service for men in full-time yeshiva study and to the generous child allowances that Shas has won for its constituency.[133] That more Haredi men are in religious studies, together with their larger family sizes in recent years, makes the movement's need for continued welfare subsidies, especially higher child allowances, even more pressing. This is a case, like the ones we will see that the Salvation Army also faced, where success on one of the movement's many agendas may jeopardize or preclude success on others. Shas's success in winning the military exemption for its yeshiva scholars—a religious goal—means a setback in its goal of advancing the economic standing of those in its community, and now necessitates making issues of economic well-being the movement's top priority.

The government funds that Shas won for its welfare network, coupled with the military exemption for full-time yeshiva students, have earned the movement much criticism for being, in the words of Uri Avneri, editor of a weekly politics magazine, "parasites sucking the blood of the nation."[134] Outraged by such characterizations, Shas founder Ovadya Yosef declared in 2003, "Whoever has wicked thoughts on 'yeshiva students' and calls them 'parasites' is a bastard, heretic . . . it is allowed to kill him."[135] As we noted earlier, an explicitly anti-Haredi party, Shinui, temporarily made gains in the 2003 Knesset elections at Shas's expense. In an effort to counter its opponents' framing of Shas as a free rider and to appeal to a broader constituency, Shas began to support legislation that would extend government social services to all Israeli citizens, not just Haredim or Mizrahim.[136]

Before the 2006 elections, in which Shas returned full force, the movement posted on the internet two jingles that it was trying to decide between for the upcoming campaign. The first emphasized religious/cultural themes:

Shas—for our Torah.
Shas—for our children.
Shas—for our future.
You're the only one who remained loyal to the nation and the country.

The second jingle reflected Shas's growing concern with the economic needs of its constituency:

We're sick of the promises / enough of speeches
We're sick of statements / Shas will sort it out
Shas is a party with security
Only Shas will keep its promises
It will bring social justice and equality
And help the needy

No more poor people / no more hungry people
We're sick of the games / only Shas will help the needy
This is a party with security / Shas keeps its promises
You will be blessed for this choice / the blessing of the righteous.[137]

The economic jingle was the one selected, although even this connects an appeal for economic justice with righteousness.

In the 2009 elections, Shas took a page from Barak Obama's 2008 U.S. presidential campaign, plastering its slogan "Yes We Can" ("Ken anachnu yecholim"), preceded in Shas's case by "God Willing," on billboards and busses. Again reflecting the economic justice themes of the 2006 campaign, Shas spokesman Roi Lachmanovitch said that "We are the Israeli Obama because we are fighting for those the establishment has ignored."[138] On its website, while Shas promoted strengthening religious education and increasing support for religious institutions, it especially highlighted the movement's economic justice concerns, calling for "reducing poverty by at least 1% per year until 2015," "a mandatory pension," "progressive taxation," "raising the minimum wage by 25%," and "providing every child, elderly, handicapped, and every family in need their basic welfare needs"—programs that are not specifically limited to Haredim or Mizrahim.[139]

Shas's response to its (as it turned out, temporary) decline in popularity after 2003 and the growing economic need of its constituents was thus to narrow its frame to focus more on economic matters but to begin to broaden the scope of its social welfare mission to include all Israeli citizens, much as sociologists Daniel Cornfield and

Bill Fletcher found that from 1881 to 1955, the American Federation of Labor, when faced with a loss of union bargaining power vis-à-vis employers, made its mission more inclusive of all working-class and poor Americans, not just labor union members.[140]

Yet controversy over Shas's position in Israeli politics and society refuses to go away. In June 2010, Israel's High Court of Justice decided to end monthly stipends to married yeshiva students because such stipends were no longer available to married university students. Fearing that Shas would withdraw from the coalition, Netanyahu's government did an end run around the high court and voted to reinstate the stipends of married yeshiva students with three or more children. The stipends will be available to the students for four years, after which they will be reduced in the fifth year to encourage a transition into the labor market, and cut completely after five years. Shas party leader Eli Yishai told university students protesting the reinstatement that he supported giving comparable stipends to married university students who had at least one child, but the Knesset has taken no action on this matter at the time of our writing.[141]

In December 2010, Chaim Amsellem, a Shas member of Knesset and an ultra-Orthodox rabbi, suggested publicly that only a small proportion of highly gifted Haredi men—those capable of becoming religious jurists or rabbis—should be engaged in full-time yeshiva studies. The rest, he said, "should go out and earn a living," perhaps combining this with studying the Torah in their spare time. The statement led Shas to expel Amsellem from the party, much as the Muslim Brotherhood has expelled members who depart from the party line. As we noted earlier, the ever-growing number of ultra-Orthodox men in full-time yeshiva study (now estimated at 60,000), together with their larger family sizes, is a key factor in the poverty of their families; an estimated 56 percent now live in poverty.[142] Given that the Haredi population is expected to increase from 9 percent of Jewish Israelis currently to 15 percent by 2025,[143] the *New York Times* reports that "Worry—and anger—is deepening about whether Israel can survive economically if it continues to encourage a culture of not working."[144] As Haredi radio host Kobi Arieli observes, "The Haredim have set up a state within a state and have a long conflict with the state of Israel, which is now on the eve of an explosion. There is no chance that this situation will continue."[145]

Shas's recent concern with protecting the interests of its Haredi constituents led Aryeh Dayan, a columnist for the *Jerusalem Post*, to argue that Shas "has stopped competing with Likud for the non-haredi Sephardi vote and, for all practical purposes, has given up trying to change Ashkenazi and secular society. Shas is once again a haredi party."[146] We would argue that it is too soon, based on a few recent incidents, to conclude that Shas has given up so easily on those Jews, especially Mizrahim, who are not yet in the fold. More pragmatically, Shas's extensive network of welfare and educational services depends in part on state funding derived from its lynchpin position in governing coalitions—a position it is unlikely to retain unless it continues to draw on a broader segment of the Israeli population than the Haredim.

CONCLUSIONS

Since it first entered parliamentary elections in 1984, Shas has grown to become the nation's largest religious party and, in two elections (1999 and 2006), the third-largest party in Israel. Throughout its more than quarter century in Israeli party politics, Shas has been a kingmaker, serving in governing coalitions of Labor, Likud, or Kadima in almost every year since the party first contested seats in the Knesset. Having survived in the late 1990s the most highly publicized leadership scandal ever faced by an Israeli party to that point, two attempts by opposition parties to seriously undercut its support, and feelings in some sectors of the Israeli population that Shas is a free-rider on the state, Shas continued its lynchpin role in the 2009 Knesset elections.

Shas is distinctive among the movements we chronicle in having been a political party, as well as a religious movement, from the start. The Muslim Brotherhood in Egypt saw politics as an outcome of its grassroots efforts to transform consciousness by building a network of alternative theological, cultural, and economic institutions that bypassed the state. Only after the network was firmly established did the Brotherhood enter Egyptian politics. Shas, in contrast, first entered party politics and then used its political clout to win government support for a nearly autonomous network of religion-imbued institutions, which allowed the movement to build a broader political base and win further resources and autonomy from the state. Shas thus represents the unusual case, possible in the context of Israel's multiparty system and "enclave" society, where a movement entered the state in order to sidestep it. Shas has built a network that is nearly as autonomous organizationally as the networks of the other three religiously orthodox movements we chronicle, but this resulted in part because the movement was able to use its critical role in governing coalitions to establish its own enclave in Israeli society. Shas penetrated the largely secular Israeli state in order to bypass it.

Shas is also unique among the movements whose histories we narrate in mobilizing not only the religiously orthodox but also an ethnic group—Mizrahi Jews of North African and Middle Eastern origins. It was Mizrahi class/economic disadvantage and ethnic subordination at the hands of more affluent and socially powerful Ashkenazi Jews that led to a specifically Mizrahi Haredim movement as opposed to a broader ultra-Orthodox movement. Shas's slogan, "Restoring the crown to its ancient glory," alludes to a greater Mizrahi past that needs to be reestablished, but like the multivocal slogan of the Muslim Brotherhood—"Islam is the solution"—its appeal is on multiple levels, in Shas's case to the ethnic, religious, and class interests of its potential constituents. Shas could have mobilized Mizrahim solely along class or economic lines, but it chose initially to emphasize religious and cultural themes centered on loss of faith and the breakdown of the family, with a focus on preserving conservative standards of sexual modesty and dress and traditional separation of the sexes. An economic justice agenda was soon added, reflecting the caring, economically communitarian side of religious orthodoxy. Most recently, this economic theme has come to the fore as the financial survival of the movement's Haredi core is threatened by larger family sizes, greater numbers of fathers who are in full-time yeshiva study and thus cannot work to support their families, and no doubt the world economic crisis as well.

Entering politics from the start meant that Shas immediately faced exceptional obstacles to success resulting from its broad agendas, ideological strictness, and reluctance to compromise—obstacles that, according to the social movement theory and research that we saw in chapter 1, are often fatal to a movement. To a casual observer, it would seem that Shas has been willing to pragmatically give up its ideological purity and compromise in working with parties of all ideological stripes—left, center, and right—in order to win resources for its constituency and promote its religious mission. Yet, as we noted above, the key issue distinguishing left and right in Israel—how much land should be returned to the Palestinians in exchange for peace—has not, until recently, been central to Shas's aims, while building an autonomous and religion-infused welfare and educational network has been. As a coalition partner, Shas has pushed for its own agendas, often to the point of threatening to pull out of a governing coalition if concessions are not made.

The extensive, grassroots network that Shas has established in Israel is much more than the elements comprising it that are funded by the Israel state. Shas's network depends as well on the private donations and volunteer labor of supporters, and encompasses organizations and programs that receive no state funding. Politically, the network has been critical to Shas in reaching, both religiously and politically, beyond its core of ultra-Orthodox or Haredi Mizrahim to traditional (partially observant) and even secular Mizrahim, and some Haredi Ashkenazim as well.[147] With Mizrahim making up only about half of Israel's Jews, and Haredim less than one tenth of Mizrahim, Shas undoubtedly would have failed within a few years of its founding without the support of this much larger constituency.

Shas won over many in this broader population not by compromising theologically but by permeating Israeli society with synagogues, schools, women's and youth clubs, rotating-credit societies, after-school programs, social work agencies, programs for farmers, childcare services, discount stores, and acts of kindness, many of which fulfill religious, cultural, and economic needs not being met by the state. As social scientists David Lehmann and Batia Siebzehner observe, "The diversity of their involvement in all sorts of nooks and crannies of Israeli society made Shasniks appear ubiquitous: . . . not only were they present between elections, they seemed to be everywhere, all the time, making their presence felt."[148] Much of Shas's support in elections among those Mizrahim who do not share the movement's ultra-Orthodox theology has been an expression of appreciation for this institutional presence among a community subject to ethnic subordination and class disadvantage. Of course, the fact that Shas's institutional outreach is partly funded by the state gives some precariousness to their network and necessitates their continued participation in governing coalitions.

Many of Shas's institutions grew out of the caring side of the movement's communitarianism—a deeply held belief in "equality, charity, compassion, and mutual support."[149] At the same time, as is true of all of the religiously orthodox movements we chronicle, these institutions often serve multiple purposes, representing, in the case of Shas, communitarian theological goals of bringing all Israelis to back to the faith; cultural goals of strictly regulating family life, sexuality, dress, and gender relations; and economic justice goals of looking out for those in need. Thus, for example, Shas's educational network, Ma'ayan Hahinuch Hatorani, seeks to bring not only its students but their parents as well to teshuva (repentance and return to faith), upholds strict norms of obedience and tightly scheduled timetables, and now offers courses that may help elevate its students' economic standing when they become adults. This has the utility of embodying the movement's ideals, advancing the cause simultaneously on multiple fronts in a single institution, and thus magnifying the effects of these schools.

Shas's continued survival and success is by no means guaranteed, although the movement has adeptly overcome serious challenges and challengers in the past. Still, it is difficult to imagine how Shas could ever be in a position of heading its own governing coalition, mainly because it has thus far failed to win the support of large numbers of voters who are neither Mizrahim nor Haredim. Nonetheless, apart from this apparent ceiling on its political aspirations, Shas has been able to garner enough votes to make the movement a kingmaker in election after election, thus ensuring its continued ability to build an alternative, religiously infused civil society, deliver resources to its constituency, and have an important voice in the future of Israeli society and politics.

COMUNIONE E LIBERAZIONE
Laying the Building Blocks of a Parallel
Christian Society in Italy

You cannot have a faith without a cultural expression and judgment on the
world. Faith has to do with life—politics, sport, everything we live—it encompasses all of life.
                                           —VOLUNTEER AT COMUNIONE E LIBERAZIONE'S
                         2008 MEETING OF FRIENDSHIP AMONG PEOPLES, RIMINI, ITALY

THE TACIT INDICTMENT THAT THE NETWORKS of the Muslim Brotherhood and Shas
make of government welfare efforts in their countries is in good part responsible for
their success in recruiting followers and garnering political support. Comunione e
Liberazione (CL) is a Catholic integrist (orthodox) movement that developed its religious, cultural, and economic institutions in Italy, which, unlike Egypt and Israel, has
a highly developed welfare state. Thus, a weak welfare state is not a necessary precondition for adopting the strategy of bypassing the state with a network of alternative
institutions. Quite the contrary, CL built its institutions to obviate the need for such
a strong state, an agenda that has been much shaped by its struggles against secular
communist and socialist parties.

Comunione e Liberazione is working to secure greater roles for the Church and
the pope in Italian society.[1] CL is today the "largest [Catholic] renewal movement in
contemporary Italy."[2] But since its founding in 1954, the movement has faced many
challenges to its survival, including the defection of most of its membership to radical
left movements in the late 1960s, the failure of efforts by its political wing to reverse
Italy's liberalized abortion and divorce laws in the 1970s and 1980s, the dramatic fall
in the midst of corruption scandals of Christian Democrat politicians associated with
the movement in the early 1990s, and the death of the movement's charismatic leader
in 2005.

Comunione e Liberazione survived these crises and continues to thrive in Italy
because it developed a society-wide network (rete) of over 1,100 faith-infused social
service, cultural, and educational institutions linked with tens of thousands of CL-

inspired or -affiliated businesses. The institutions include Solidarity Centers to connect unemployed young people with CL-affiliated businesses, a national Food Bank
Foundation that furnishes meals to needy individuals and families by using the excess
production of CL-affiliated farms and food companies, homes for recovering drug
addicts and the disabled, hospices for the terminally ill and patients with AIDS, organizations providing financial assistance to families in need, bookshops, consumer
cooperatives, and primary and secondary religious schools, among others.[3] Some of
the nonprofit organizations are partly funded by grants from the Italian government,
others are based on partnerships with CL-affiliated businesses, and many draw upon
the movement's "common fund," to which participating Catholics are encouraged to
give to monthly as "witness to a communal concept of personal property."[4]

As with the other movements whose stories we tell, CL's institution-building grew
out of a strongly communitarian theology that sees religious experience as fully realizable only in a community, emphasizes mutual responsibility, and encourages an active
presence in and engagement with the world. The strict side of this communitarianism
can be seen in Comunione e Liberazione's insistence on obedience to Church teachings
and the pope and in its efforts to bring Italian law into line with Church doctrine—for
example, on abortion and divorce. Its caring side is visible in the extensive services it
offers throughout Italy. Yet unlike the "state within a state" or "surrogate state" established by the Muslim Brotherhood and Shas, which are intended to prefigure a new
religion-infused state, the "parallel society"[5] that Comunione e Liberazione has built
under the slogan "More society, less state"[6] is intended to show that largely nonstate
social service agencies, schools, and for-profit enterprises can meet citizens' spiritual,
cultural, and material needs better than can the state.

CHARISM, COMMUNITARIANISM, AND MILITANCY

Father Luigi Giussani founded the movement that later became Comunione e
Liberazione in 1954. Giussani's orthodox theology begins with Christ's resurrection
as the "charism"[7] or "saving event of human history"[8]—an event made immediate and
contemporary through the individual's experience of a personal encounter with Christ.
This encounter, which Giussani called "bumping into" Christ,[9] is said to have two consequences: the communion and liberation referred to in the movement's name. The idea
that religious or spiritual life can only be lived in communion (*comunione*) with others
experiencing the same encounter with Christ is a foundational belief of CL, making the
movement, like the others we chronicle, strongly communitarian. As Giussani wrote in
his book *The Christian Event*, "The community, the company, where the meeting with
Christ occurs, is the place where our ego belongs, the place where it acquires the ultimate manner of perceiving and feeling things, of grasping them intellectually and judging them, of imagining, of planning, of deciding, of doing."[10] CL's theology condemns

individualism as "an age-old temptation to solve problems your own way . . . founded on a colossal error: thinking that happiness corresponds with accumulating things."[11]

The strict or obedient side of this communitarianism is expressed in the movement's idea of liberation (*liberazione*) or freedom, which, it argues, refers to the adherent's decision, freely made, to follow the authority of the community. As Giussani expressed this, "our point of view does not follow its own path, but submits to comparison and in comparison obeys the community."[12] Thus, CL recasts the modernist virtue of individual freedom to refer to the choice to submit to a higher authority and larger community; the language of modernism is used to subvert modernism. The strict side of CL's communitarianism can also be seen in the movement's political efforts to promote the Church's culturally conservative positions on divorce and abortion and its general stance that state law should be aligned with Church doctrine.[13]

The caring side of the movement's communitarianism is realized through the adherent's seeing his or her life as a calling or vocation to do work in service to others. This work, according to the movement's website, need not be formally institutionalized. It may involve "going into an oratory [youth club] or neighborhood to play with children, or to a nursing home to keep elderly persons company; helping younger children with their studies; sharing difficult situations like poverty, mental illness, or the last stages of a terminal illness; helping people find work, etc."[14] For Father Giussani, "Life must be total sharing, but disattention, fear, love of comfort, obstacles in the environment, malice—all empty life of the value of charity. To create a mentality of charity, the most humble and effective way is to begin to live some remnant of free time expressly, purposely as a sharing in the life of others."[15] In addition to inspiring much private volunteerism on the part of CL adherents, this caring side of the movement's communitarianism has been institutionalized in the extensive network of services that CL has established throughout Italy and in dozens of other countries.

Although Comunione e Liberazione does not call for the establishment of religious law in Italy, as do the Muslim Brotherhood in Egypt and Shas in Israel, it is pushing to bring state law, especially on cultural issues such as abortion and divorce, into line with Church doctrine. As Italian sociologist Mario Zadra observes, "CL boldly claims that the Church embodies authoritative truth that is binding on society at large. By claiming the presence of Christ, the Church also claims divine authority—a kind of inerrancy, not of the biblical text (as in Protestant fundamentalism), but of the Church. . . . The Church ought to be considered the living and legitimate paradigm of society."[16] For Giussani, the historical model for society is the Middle Ages, which he idealized "as a time of unity between faith and life. . . . [He rejected] entirely the Enlightenment, the French Revolution, and modern culture, as having interrupted that unity."[17] In this, he has allies in Shas, the Muslim Brotherhood, and the Salvation Army.

According to CL belief, the transformative encounter with Christ and immersion in a community of believers leads CL followers to see themselves as called to active engagement with the world. It is common for CL adherents to refer to themselves as *militanti* (activists)—"a visible and uncompromising Christian presence in a secularized society."[18] As the movement's website explains the activism of its adherents:

> Political action, in the conception of CL, is one of the fields in which a Christian is called with greater responsibility and ideal generosity . . . in the face of the problems posed by the life of society and institutions. God gave men power so that they could work in His creation through the commitment of their own talents, family, and society, to the point of that "demanding form of charity"—as Pope Paul VI called it—which is politics. It should thus not be surprising that out of CL have come people engaged on various levels, directly and on their own responsibility, in political action.[19]

CL's use of "charity" is very encompassing, transforming this into political action. In a slogan that would suit the Muslim Brotherhood and Shas as well, Comunione e Liberazione refers to "*senso religioso, opera politica*" (religious sense, political work), which sums up much of the institutional outreach of the movement.[20]

The label "integrist" has often been used by European academics to refer to CL's belief that religion is the solution to all of the problems of society—a belief similar to the Muslim Brotherhood's slogan "Islam is the solution." Italian poet and member of CL's central planning committee Davide Rondoni sees the label of integrism as "a negative epithet" which implies that CL offers an oversimplified, reductionist analysis and solution to complex problems in homes, workplaces, schools, and political life.[21] Critic of the movement Gordon Urquhart notes in his book *The Pope's Armada* that CL, while rejecting integrism as a label, "coined the term 'presentialism' (*presenzialismo*) for their approach. They asserted that . . . the movement should come up with a clear Christian answer to every problem, providing a visible alternative. This belief led them to found their own schools, cultural centers, magazines, businesses—even their own political party."[22] Thus, while the label "integrism" is rejected by CL because the movement feels this is used in a disparaging way by secular academics, the term describes CL belief well.

TAKEOFF AND CRASH: GIOVENTÙ STUDENTESCA

Comunione e Liberazione traces its origins to 1954, when Father Luigi Giussani, a thirty-two-year-old theology teacher at a seminary in Venegono in the Lombardy region, requested reassignment to teach religion at Milan's Berchet classical high school. At the school, Giussani was shocked by the lack of knowledge about or outright rejection of Christianity that he found among students: "Not long after becoming a religion teacher . . . I noticed a group of youngsters, always the same, who met on the stairs during class intervals and spoke with great intensity and animation. Once I asked them what they were talking about, and they responded: 'Communism'. I wondered why

Christianity was not capable of inspiring such fervor and unity among youth."[23] Giussani decided to found a group for high school students called Gioventù Studentesca
(Student Youth), or GS. As Giussani recalled his ambitious goals for the movement
in 1976, "In 1954 we did not go into the schools looking for an alternative project for
the school; we went in aware that we were bringing something that saves man . . . also
into the school, which makes man real and authenticates the search for truth, that is,
Christ in our unity. Our purpose was *presence*."[24]

Gioventù Studentesca was founded as a youth group under the auspices of Azione
Cattolica, the official lay Catholic movement in the country. GS attracted some suspicion on the part of Church authorities from the start because it was co-educational,
while all other groups in Azione Cattolica were sex segregated,[25] earning GS participants a reputation among the group's detractors as "Catholics of easy virtue,"[26] though
in fact its position on matters of sexual morality and reproductive rights was quite
strict. Moreover, in contrast to most branches or groups in Azione Cattolica, which
were based in parishes, Giussani's group was centered on what he called "the environment"—the high school—in order "to reach young people where they are most con-
ditioned by society . . . where their mentality and culture is formed."[27] This focus on
the environment of the school foreshadowed the movement's eschewing of the parish
as a primary center of activity and instead working to reach Italians where they were:
in the workplace, high school, university, or seminary.[28]

One former high school student, Mattia, gave the following testimony in 2006 in
the movement's magazine *Traces* on how she became involved in GS through contact
with members at her school:

> In June, I got to know the young people of GS when I went to sell my school
> books at [Gioventù Studentesca's] second-hand book market. I was struck by their
> happiness and the unity they expressed as they were working at the market. . . .
> I never expected Tommaso and Lorenzo, two boys older than me who I knew
> only slightly, to come looking for me during breaktime at school. . . . But that was
> the way I met Christ, through people who, without knowing me, bothered about
> me. . . . [I]t revolutionized my whole life and so I began to approach everyone
> in a new way. I wanted to do the same for someone . . . so that they, too, could
> have the chance that I had had, of finding in Christ the answer to my desire for
> happiness.[29]

Gioventù Studentesca had two pillars in its efforts to establish a Catholic presence
in high schools: the "ray" (*raggio*) and "initiatives" (*iniziative*). The ray was a weekly
meeting in which students involved in GS at the school and their invited friends participated in a discussion, coordinated by a leader, on their experiences in the movement, current events, elements of Giussani's theology, and other similar topics as "an
instrument by which the individual made a personal commitment to the proposal of

community."[30] Initiatives, or acts of service to others, were "an invitation to commit oneself and one's generosity to the ideal that had been encountered" in the ray.[31] The initiatives would later evolve into the institutional outreach or "works" (*opere*) of the movement.

While GS began as a primarily theological movement seeking to bring young Italians to a personal encounter with Christ, the economic outreach of the movement—an outcome of the initiatives—began as early as 1958, four years after its founding, when several hundred students each week went to the impoverished outskirts of Milan to "help families meet their needs."[32] In 1962 the students undertook a mission to Belo Horizonte in southeastern Brazil, which was led by four graduates of the movement who were now university students and was wholly funded by the students in GS. All but one of the university students, shocked by the deep and entrenched poverty they encountered in Brazil and their inability to respond effectively, left the movement by the end of the 1960s for leftist groups offering more radical solutions to the problems of poverty. The student who remained, Pigi Bernareggi, went on to become a priest in the local community and helped the movement establish a strong branch in Brazil that continues today.[33]

With the encouragement of the archbishop of Milan, Giovanni Battista Montini, who in 1963 would become Pope Paul VI, GS grew during the 1950s and early 1960s and spread to several other Italian cities.[34] Still, there was concern among the Milanese Church authorities that Giussani was establishing through GS a "shadow diocese" that was independent of the parishes.[35] Hierarchical organizations, such as the Roman Catholic Church, often try to prevent autonomous, grassroots movements from gaining a foothold. For example, in the parlance of labor unions, "breaking the chain"— union locals taking action that has not been approved by the national leadership—is strongly condemned.[36] Because Giussani was coming to be seen as too independent from the Church hierarchy, he was reassigned in 1964 by Milan's archbishop to a theology professorship at Milan's Università Cattolica del Sacro Cuore, and the leadership of the movement passed to others.[37] In 1966, GS was officially recognized by Cardinal Giovanni Colombo of Milan, but remained contained within Azione Cattolica, much to Giussani's dismay.[38] Moreover, Giussani's request that he be allowed to lead the students who had graduated from secondary school and moved on to university was turned down by Colombo in favor of incorporating these students into Azione Cattolica's university student association. Giussani was able to bypass the Church hierarchy's decisions by forming the Charles Péguy Center for university students in Milan, aptly named after a French poet who had converted from socialism to Catholicism.[39] Nonetheless, these decisions by the Church hierarchy, along with the increasingly divergent paths that Azione Cattolica and GS began taking in Italy during the student rebellions at the end of the turbulent 1960s, created a classic case of social movement organization (SMO) competition and division between two organizations with similar goals—a rift that has only recently begun to be resolved.

The sense of emotional communion among GS participants that Giussani had helped build kept Gioventù Studentesca together for fifteen years. Yet, ironically, Giussani's encouragement of "sharing" with the poor and disadvantaged, his defining "charity" very broadly to include political action, and his fostering the notion of a calling or vocation among his young followers led many of them to carry these ideals in a more radical left direction. Most of the students involved in GS left the movement after the student revolts of 1968, many of them joining Marxist student movements.[40]

RESTART AND EARLY POLITICAL ENGAGEMENT: COMUNIONE E LIBERAZIONE

In 1969 Giussani was able to pull together the few remaining members of GS under the banner of "unity and authority," the former referring to their desire to hold the movement together in the face of many desertions to the secular left and the latter to their submission to the movement and the pope.[41] The reconstituted movement was called Comunione e Liberazione, the name it goes by today.[42] Comunione e Liberazione especially appealed to high school students, university students, and young professionals, many of whom had grown disaffected with the extreme left. In 1971, the movement held its first national assembly and began expanding throughout Italy using the networks of GS members, now university students, who had remained loyal to Giussani.[43] Much as the activities of Gioventù Studentesca were centered on the "environment" of the high school rather than the parish, those of CL were organized into groups focusing on different nonparish environments: high schools, universities, and workplaces. This is, of course, similar to the Muslim Brotherhood's strategy of burrowing into professional syndicates and student unions. University students in Comunione e Liberazione were mobilized in CLU, workers in CLL, educators in CLE, seminarians in CLS, and high school students in GS.[44]

The scope of the CL's activities on the cultural front can be seen in several institutions that were established early on in the reconstituted movement's history. In 1972, CL founded its think-tank, Istituto di Studi per la Transizione (Institute of Studies for the Transition), with "working units" on philosophy, history, architecture, political theory, economics, and theology, among other disciplines, suggesting the movement's intent to formulate alternative solutions to a wide range of problems. CL's publishing house, Jaca Book, which would eventually become one of the leading publishers of religious books in Italy, was also founded in 1972.[45]

In 1980, CL held its first "Meeting for Friendship among Peoples" in Rimini on the Adriatic coast, which attracted tens of thousands of participants. The aim of what came to be called "Il Meeting" in the movement was to offer a Catholic alternative to the Feste de l'Unità (Unity Festivals) held by the Communist Party in cities throughout the country.[46] Although the nemesis of CL, the Italian Communist Party (PCI) provided the movement with examples of effective organizational strategies from which CL freely borrowed. By 1986, *Time* magazine reported that CL's Rimini meeting was attracting 600,000 followers.[47] Much as the other movements that we chronicle have been willing to use modern technology in proselytizing, Comunione e Liberazione, which rejects the secularism, individualism, and materialism of modernity and idealizes the Middle Ages as a high point of human history, has nonetheless been quick to use technology in getting the word out. CL's meeting at Rimini is now promoted on its state-of-the art website (www.meetingrimini.org/) as "the world's biggest summer festival of encounters, exhibitions, music and spectacle." Since the 2004 meeting celebrated the fiftieth anniversary of the movement and this coincided with the half century since Elvis Presley released his first album (*"la nascita del Rock"*), the event featured a "Good Rocking Tonight" exhibition, along with appearances by opera singer José Carreras, head of the Versace fashion empire Santo Versace, and an all-star lineup of Italian politicians. Now attracting some 800,000 CL supporters annually, the meeting has been called "Italy's largest public event."[48]

What was to become another cultural icon of the movement, the weekly magazine *Il Sabato*, began in the early 1980s. While *Il Sabato* was initially a well-researched current-affairs magazine, it eventually became more strident in its approach, battling what its writers saw as a massive anti-Catholic conspiracy of Freemasons, liberal Jesuits, communists, secular humanists, and Protestants.[49] Supposed adversaries of CL, including some within the Church, were tarred as "neo-Pelagians," referring to the fourth-century heresy of Pelagianism that denied Original Sin and insinuating that CL's opponents were not true Catholics.[50] Just as Muslim Brotherhood theoretician Sayyid Qutb condemned Egyptian President Nasser's regime as jahiliyyah (paganist), and as ultra-Orthodox members of Shas regard adherents of Conservative and Reform Judaism as inauthentic Jews, orthodox movements often see themselves as having a monopoly on truth. As sociologist Christian Smith points out about Evangelicals in the United States, orthodox movements tend to see themselves as embattled and they thrive in struggles to distinguish themselves from less orthodox or more modernist members of their faith.[51] *Il Sabato* eventually became so controversial that the Vatican distanced itself from it, leading Giussani to break CL's ties with the magazine in 1989.[52]

Much as the Muslim Brotherhood succeeded in taking over student unions throughout Egypt during the 1990s, CL created in 1975 a coalition of Catholic groups on university campuses, Cattolici Popolari (the People's Catholics), to challenge the dominance of university councils by leftist and secular student groups. The slates that Cattolici Popolari put forward for university councils were in many cases successful in defeating non-Catholic groups.[53] By 1986, *Time* magazine, in an article characterizing CL as "the pope's youthful 'New Jesuits,'" reported that "Italian student councils once dominated by radicals are now in the hands of CL adherents."[54]

Through CL's Cooperativa Universitaria Studio e Lavoro (CUSL), founded in 1977, the movement gained control of student dining halls and student housing. Just as the Muslim Brotherhood provides services to university students throughout Egypt, the CUSL in Italy would eventually offer a used-book purchasing service, a bookstore, and a card for student associates giving discounts at CL-affiliated businesses, favorable terms at banks associated with the movement, reduced photocopying prices, and so forth. Today, CUSL reports that it has fourteen branches with more than 50,000 student associates on university campuses in Milan alone.[55]

In another "environment" of the movement—the workplace—Comunione e Liberazione began to establish a Christian presence in the early 1970s as a direct challenge to secular labor unions. Members of CL's labor group, CLL, initiated the "liturgical way to liberation" whereby CL workers in a factory would conduct a service or Mass at the workplace before each workday began.[56] Thus, in contrast to labor unions and leftist movements that defined workplace liberation mainly in terms of workers' material (economic) gains in pay or benefits or workers' control of the workplace, CLL defined liberation spiritually.

CL's breakthrough into the Italian national scene came in 1974, only five years after its reorganization, when Pope Paul VI asked CL, rather than Azione Cattolica or other official Catholic organizations, to spearhead the Church's position in a national referendum on divorce.[57] Despite the movement's best efforts, the referendum, which would have turned back Italy's 1970 liberal law on divorce, won only 41 percent of the vote.[58] As Davide Rondoni of CL notes, "Catholics realized brusquely that in Italy they were a minority."[59] Since self-professed Catholics were certainly in a majority at the time of the referendum, Rondoni's observation implies that no "true" Catholic would allow divorce. The referendum campaign, although it failed, put CL in good stead with the pope and with many, although by no means all, bishops. It also helped motivate supporters of the movement and dramatically raised CL's profile on the national scene. As Italian sociologist Mario Zadra observes, "From that moment on, CL saw itself in the forefront of the battle between the friends and enemies of the Church."[60] The following year, in 1975, Pope Paul VI, in a private meeting with Father Giussani, gave his blessing to the movement, saying, "This is the path, go on like this."[61]

In 1975, CL took its new visibility in the national political arena to the next level by establishing a political arm, the Movimento Popolare (the People's Movement), connected to the movement only unofficially, as "an instrument for a presence in society, against the elimination of Christians from the public arena, in favor of a renewal of action on the part of the Catholic movement."[62] Although the Italian media immediately labeled the Movimento Popolare—and CL more broadly—a political party, it was not a party but a pressure group or "independent power broker"[63] which endorsed candidates for office at all levels. Just as the decision to participate in party politics was difficult for the Muslim Brotherhood—and earned the Brotherhood criticism from inside and outside the movement—Comunione e Liberazione undertook involvement in formal state politics with strong reservations. CL's founder, Father Giussani, viewed the secular Italian state as hostile: "The Christian," he warned, "[is] confronted with a state which is no less an enemy to him than the Roman Empire of the first centuries."[64]

An important frame of CL and the Movimento Popolare was "*Più società, meno Stato*" (More society, less state); thus, the movement sought to diminish the role of the state and expand the role of the Church in public life, rather than establish a theocracy.[65] As CL founder, Luigi Giussani, wrote, "I do not hold a 'confessional [religious] state' to be the political ideal, but rather a State which is guided by men surely religious. . . . Such an ideal situation would become more feasible if its reactivation were trusted . . . to a company of men profoundly religious: a true company of Jesus."[66]

The creation of the Movimento Popolare and CL's greater visibility in the 1970s generated considerable hostility from both the left and right. The movement reported numerous attacks during the early 1970s against its adherents, peaking in 1977 with 120 attacks on CL personnel and offices.[67] In 1975, a fascist group savagely beat two CL students who were posting placards. On the other side of the political spectrum, an internal document of the ultra-left Red Brigade proclaimed that "The men and the bases of CL must be targeted, struck and dispersed. In schools, in districts and wherever CL takes root it must find no room to maneuver either politically or physically."[68] Comunione e Liberazione is certainly not alone among the movements whose stories we tell in facing hostility; the Muslim Brotherhood has been subject to much state repression, Shas is considered to be a parasite on the state and society by many Israelis and has been the target of venomous caricatures, and as we will see, the Salvation Army's early street actions were often met with violence.

In 1981 Church authorities again turned to Comunione e Liberazione to present the Church's case—this time on a national referendum to overturn Italy's 1978 law legalizing abortion. CL's rival movement, Azione Cattolica, had taken the position, called the "religious choice," to accept religious pluralism in Italy and distance itself from the Christian Democrats (Democrazia Cristiana, DC) and their anti-abortion stance. The outcome of the referendum on abortion was even more disheartening for CL than its defeat in the 1974 referendum on divorce: Only 32 percent of the Italian electorate voted to outlaw abortion.[69] For those in the movement, according to CL activist Davide Rondoni, the failure to win the referendum "confirmed, if there had still been any need to do so, that the position of the Church and Catholic culture had by this point only marginal influence on people's conscience."[70] The battles over divorce and abortion are exemplary of sociologist Joseph Gusfield's notion of "symbolic politics," in that the electoral results can be experienced as an endorsement of a secular way of life, where individual conscience and rights reign, and hence a denigration of the honor and status of traditional, orthodox Catholics.[71]

CL's efforts to champion Church positions on sexuality, gender, and family issues and to sacralize Italian society by law, although unsuccessful, won the favor of Pope John Paul II, who gave Giussani the title of monsignor in 1983 and in a 1984 statement embracing the movement said, "We, as the Church, as Christians, as *Ciellini* [from the Italian letters for CL], must be visible in society."[72] One factor drawing John Paul II to CL was the movement's rejection of the Vatican II Council's principle of "collegiality," or the joint authority of the bishops and the pope, in favor of centralization of authority in the pope.[73] The pope's endorsement lent legitimacy to the movement. Yet CL's moral absolutism, militancy, and direct obedience to the pope, often bypassing the authority of the bishops, made the movement highly controversial, both within the Church and in the broader Italian society, earning CL a reputation as "the pope's Rambos," "Wojtyla's [Pope John Paul II] monks," and "the Stalinists of God" for "pitting the Pope's teachings against statements by certain (reform) Bishops," and for "using the Gospels as a 'bludgeon.'"[74] Giussani's own unquestioning fealty to the pope could be seen when he was asked by an interviewer in 1985 if he had ever doubted the pope's opinions. He responded, "I have never experienced that type of doubt. Why should I tire myself in such a manner, when it is so much easier to obey the Holy Father?"[75]

While the natural beneficiaries of the Movimento Popolare's support would seem to have been the (Catholic) Christian Democrats, CL viewed the Christian Democrats to be almost as accommodative to secular society as the left.[76] Rather than endorse all the candidates of the Christian Democrats, the Movimento Popolare supported with considerable success CL-affiliated Christian Democrat candidates for election to local and national office during the 1980s and early 1990s. One observer estimated that the Movimento Popolare delivered up to one third of the votes that the Christian Democrats received in some elections.[77]

HANDLING SCANDAL ARISING FROM BAD COMPANY

Comunione e Liberazione faced scandal from 1992 to 1994, when some Christian Democrat politicians associated with CL's political arm, the Movimento Popolare, were indicted in the Mani Pulite (Clean Hands) investigation for their questionable financial links with the business enterprises in CL's Compagnia delle Opere (CdO; Companionship of Works), the umbrella organization that encompasses all the movement's educational, cultural, and economic institutions. At the time, neither the Movimento Popolare nor the Compagnia delle Opere was officially connected to CL or to each other. Politicians backed by the Movimento Popolare were accused in the investigation of favoring legislation that would positively affect businesses in the CdO. The investigation resulted in the conviction of 582 Italian politicians, including some supported by the Movimento Popolare and associated with CL, and led to the collapse of the Christian Democrats in 1994.[78] CL's Rome branch involved itself heavily in defending seven-time former prime minister (and CL supporter) Giulio Andreotti against charges, also being investigated in Mani Pulite, that he had ordered the Mafia killing of an investigative journalist in 1979.[79] Andreotti was acquitted of these charges in 1999 to much celebration among the Ciellini,[80] only to have the verdict overturned in 2002, and then reversed again, with Italy's highest court declaring Andreotti innocent, in 2003.[81] Just as Shas founder Ovadya Yosef declared the movement's political leader Aryeh Deri innocent of charges brought against him by the Israeli state, CL founder Giussani, early on in the Mani Pulite investigations, condemned them as politically motivated.[82] For both Shas and CL, handling scandal involved appealing to a higher law than that of the state and suggesting that those critical of movement practices were enemies of God.

Much as U.S. Protestant fundamentalists withdrew from politics into personal piety for decades after their defeat in the Scopes evolution trial of 1925, Comunione e Liberazione, "drained by the ambiguities and harshness of the exhausting political struggle of those years," including its failed efforts to push the Church's cultural agenda on divorce and abortion and what it saw as politically motivated charges against its politicians, dissolved the Movimento Popolare in 1993.[83] At its 1996 Meeting of Friendship among Peoples in Rimini, the movement's leadership announced that it was "disillusioned" with involvement in politics and would instead concentrate on the spiritual development of its members and, through the Compagnia delle Opere, on its charitable and economic outreach.[84] Although the movement continued its involvement in politics—albeit more quietly—at the local (especially in Lombardy) and national levels, Comunione e Liberazione decided to shift much of its efforts to establish a Christian "presence" in Italian society from a top-down, formal politics approach to a bottom-up, institution-building strategy.

BUILDING A PARALLEL CHRISTIAN SOCIETY

Gioventù Studentesca, which spawned Comunione e Liberazione, began as a primarily theological movement but added an economic or charitable mission in 1958, only four years after its founding, in which students helped poor families in the outskirts of Milan.[85] CL's economic mission was not formally established until 1986, when the Compagnia delle Opere was begun. This largely economic mission has since thrived, while as we saw in the previous section, CL's cultural agenda has not. After 1993, CL abandoned the political pursuit of most of its culturally conservative mission, retaining only its campaign to win equal government support for religious and public schools. The Compagnia delle Opere gradually took the place of the Movimento Popolare in CL's effort to establish a Catholic presence in Italy.[86]

Even in relatively generous welfare states, religiously orthodox movements may feel that the state is not doing enough to meet the community's economic needs, to say nothing of its spiritual and cultural needs. As Italian sociologist Mario Zadra observes, "CL opposes the idea that the state is the necessary agent of human perfection. . . . They argue that the main cultural agent in society should be the Church. The state should exist only as an instrumental agent, adjunct to the Church and society."[87] Even more so than did the Movimento Popolare, the Compagnia delle Opere embodies the movement's slogan of "More society, less state." The CdO represents nothing less than an attempt to establish what CL envisions as a truly Christian society in Italy—an "example to the world of how Christianity in a pure and untrammeled form is the only solution to all its ills."[88]

CL's view of the proper positions of the state, society, and Church has been much shaped by its struggle with its Marxist opponents, which has preoccupied the movement from the beginning. To CL, communists and others on the secular left are godless materialists. That CL has established its extensive network of services in Italy, which has a well-funded welfare state, shows that a weak welfare state is not a necessary condition for a religiously orthodox movement to set up a network of alternative economic and social service institutions. Social spending in Italy, according to the most recent figures of the Organization for Economic Cooperation and Development (OECD), made up a sizable 24.9 percent of the nation's gross domestic product (GDP) in 2007, compared to 15.5 percent in Israel and 16.2 percent in the United States (no figures are available for Egypt).[89] Although CL applies for and receives some government funding for its charitable services, it views the CdO as demonstrating the ability of largely nonstate ventures of individuals, businesses, and social service organizations to bypass the state and directly meet human needs.[90]

Roberto Formigoni, a CL adherent and four-time president of the Lombardy region, expressed in 1975 the vision that CL has tried to bring to fruition through the CdO: "To live an experience of communion that involves every dimension of human life, that realizes an experience of concrete liberation, including the social possession of the means of production."[91] In many of Italy's larger cities, the CdO has created an institutional environment in which "It is possible for CL members to bank, shop, educate their children, receive health care, and take their holidays within structures provided by the movement."[92] The CdO has established in Italy what British journalist and CL critic Gordon Urquhart calls "a parallel society which serves all its members' needs."[93] Italian sociologist Mario Zadra prophetically wrote in 1991, only five years after the founding of the Compagnia delle Opere:

> If CL is going to be a way of living the Christian faith, the *Opere* provide . . . a way in which their vision of a renewed Church is fulfilled. According to CL, the *Opere* are the building blocks of a new Christian society, or the points of force

from which CL may push toward the advent of that new society, while also creating a setting in which individual economic, political, and cultural motivations are reshaped.[94]

Italian investigative journalist Ferruccio Pinotti, author of *La Lobby di Dio*, expresses alarm over the size and influence of CL and the CdO in Italy, especially in Lombardy in northern Italy, where the movement was founded. He warns that "bit by bit it has created a lobby that is political, religious, economic, and financial. . . . [It is] colonizing vast areas of the country like Calabria, Sicily, Lazio, and so many other areas of Italian life." Pinotti cites several investigations by the Italian courts of the business dealings of administrators of the CdO in some cities—none of which has resulted in convictions—as evidence of the power of "God's lobby" in Italy to sweep the allegations under the rug.[95]

Like the networks of the other movements whose stories we tell, the Compagnia delle Opere's operations are concentrated at the local level. CL bases its grassroots efforts on the principle of Catholic social teaching called "subsidiarity"—that initiatives should be undertaken on the level most immediate to those being served and should be given as much autonomy as possible. Subsidiarity, which was developed in Pope Leo XIII's 1891 encyclical *Rerum Novarum* and elaborated on in Pope Pius XI's 1931 encyclical *Quadragesimo Anno,* is an attempt to offer a middle course—a third way—between laissez faire capitalism and socialism. Father Andrew Murray summarizes subsidiarity as follows: "the principle states that a government should intervene in the affairs of citizens when help is necessary for the individual and common good but insists that all functions that can be done by individuals or by lower level organizations be left to them."[96] Former British prime minister Tony Blair, a recent convert to Catholicism, endorsed this "third way" in an address to attendees at CL's 2009 meeting in Rimini, saying that it represents "a balance between . . . an overmighty state and an untrammeled market."[97]

Following this "bottom-up," grassroots principle, the Compagnia delle Opere is diffuse and decentralized. The organization's website lists branches in forty Italian cities and regions, with dozens—in some cities, hundreds—of local social service organizations and CL-inspired or -affiliated businesses in each.[98] In contrast to the Muslim Brotherhood, Shas, and the Salvation Army, whose grassroots efforts are based in local mosques, synagogues, or churches, "CL borrowed from socialism the concept of operating through cells within the 'environment'"—the workplace, the high school, the university, and the seminary.[99] Yet, as with these other movements, CL's grassroots efforts allow local adherents to tailor the movement's broad agendas to local concerns. Working in local branches, CL militanti identify needs in the community and initiate, foster, and support entrepreneurial projects in both the private and public sectors that may eventually become part of the Compagnia delle Opere.[100]

CL's website explains that the Compagnia delle Opere

• promotes and spreads the culture of entrepreneurship and supports the establishment of new entrepreneurial initiatives, both in the profit and in the non-profit sectors, working to favor employment at all levels.

• spreads and maintains constant relationships with Italian and international institutions, in order to examine and submit proposals for the solution of specific economic and social issues. A particular attention is given to solidarity with the poorest, to volunteer services in the non-profit organizations, to the collaboration between the NGOs and the countries where they operate, and to the growth of employment through the development of micro-businesses.[101]

The CdO's entrepreneurial efforts are intended to empower those involved in them: "As the young members of CL identify specific needs in the community and act on them, they are thrown into society with a real measure of responsibility and made to believe that the religious tradition and the community are entrusted to them."[102] The aim of these grassroots activities, according to the movement, is to create "pieces of new society" or "units of transition, entities in other words where an analysis and a political and social project in the wider environment are run on the basis of the new experience of Christian life."[103] They prefigure in a countercultural way a future Christian society—a "true company of Jesus" in Giussani's terms.[104]

Today, CL's Compagnia delle Opere is a massive operation in Italy. The CdO's "Executive Summary" reports that it is a nonprofit umbrella organization of 35,000 CL-inspired or -affiliated businesses in Italy, linked in a complex network with 1,100 non-profit social service organizations. As we noted earlier, CL applies for and accepts government funding for its programs, but the movement prefers that private individuals and businesses meet local needs. In the paragraphs that follow we discuss some of the larger associations in the nonprofit sector of the Compagnia delle Opere, in which the CdO reports some 120,000 people work in Italy,[105] in order to give a sense of the scope and diversity of its operations and the manner in which these have been initiated.

The Associazione Volontari per il Servizio Internazionale (Association of Volunteers for International Service, AVSI) was founded in 1972, fourteen years before the CdO was created, but is now part of this larger organization. Present in thirty-nine countries in Latin America, Africa, the Caribbean, Eastern Europe, the Middle East, and Asia, the AVSI's mission is "to support human development in developing countries with special attention to education and the global dignity of every person, according to the Social Teaching of the Catholic Church."[106] The work of AVSI includes more than 100 long-term projects and numerous short-term ones in the areas of health, sanitation, education and vocational training, agriculture, and emergency relief. The AVSI, in the entrepreneurial spirit of the Compagnia delle Opere, also promotes the initiation by citizens of income-generating activities and microbusinesses as a means of creating jobs, sometimes funding these efforts using microcredit.[107] AVSI's methodology of intervention is bottom up because "A top-down project is either violent, since not shared, or ineffective and unsustainable, since assistance-oriented. AVSI's approach to project planning and implementation consists in . . . starting from the relationship with the people to whom the project is targeted and building with them."[108]

An example of the projects that AVSI has initiated can be seen in Betim, a city on the outskirts of Belo Horizonte, Brazil, with some 350,000 inhabitants. AVSI developed a partnership with Fiat, the Italian car maker, which has a manufacturing plant in the city. Since more than a quarter of the residents of Betim are living in poverty, Fiat initiated several projects with AVSI in the spirit of corporate social responsibility. In addition to a literacy program, ABC+, which has reached some 9,800 students, AVSI and Fiat developed the Ávore da Vida (Trees of Life) project. Ávore da Vida has an apprentice program through which youth fifteen years old and older are offered hands-on work experience under close mentorship, followed by professional training in such areas as computer repair and technical support, photography, and publishing—all offered by local businesses. After the training, these young people are helped in their job search by the Work Reference Center. Youth who wish to launch a small business using the skills acquired in the training program may be offered microcredit. Some graduates of the program have set up a cooperative business, Cooperávore, which supplies goods to Fiat and other local businesses.[109]

Another major element in the CdO is Famiglie per l'Accoglienza (Families for Welcoming), an association of families who are available to host in their homes children, young people in trouble, adults with problems, unwed mothers, and students. It was founded in Milan in 1982 by, among others, Lia Sanicola, a CL activist and professor of social work at Università degli Studi di Parma. The motivation behind this association, according to its website, is a more communal notion of family:

> Every human being needs to feel welcomed and loved in order to grow, and the family is the first natural place where this happens. Our Western culture tends to consider family life as a private entity to be guarded jealously and lived in a closed manner. This influences the structure of the family and proposes individualistic models which are very different from . . . traditional models. The main purpose of the Association is to support families and individuals to live the value of the family as an essential place for the growth and embrace of the person. It also seeks to develop the cultural significance of the family and promote its social role.[110]

Famiglie per l'Accoglienza, which is now present in eighty-five provinces in Italy and eight nations, thus provides a social service while also promoting an inclusive notion of the family as an institution. Like the other movements whose stories we tell, CL rejects the privatization of life associated with modernity.

Also founded in 1982 and now part of the Compagnia delle Opere is Solidarietà Cooperativa Sociale (Social Solidarity Cooperative), which offers training, rehabilitation, and employment counseling to the homeless and down-and-out and tries to place them in jobs with CL-affiliated businesses. One of the CdO's most successful nonprofit ventures, the Foundazione Banco Alimentare (Food Bank Foundation), was founded seven years later, in 1989. This foundation distributes excess food production to some one million Italians annually.[111] The Foundazione Banco Alimentare, according to its website,

> gathers food surplus and redistributes it to institutions and organizations that in Italy take care of assisting and helping the poor and the marginalized. For this reason it is at the service, on the one hand, of the sector's enterprises [that] have stock and surplus problems of perfectly edible products; on the other hand, it is at the service of associations and welfare institutions that continuously distribute to the people they assist meals or foodstuff. The Food Bank network is then the ideal means to transform possible "waste" of the food industry into riches for the welfare institutions, which every day, with effort and dedication, host the poorest among us.[112]

The CdO's Food Bank thus embodies the movement's efforts to link CL's nonprofit service organizations and for-profit business affiliates in what is seen as a third way, between capitalism and socialism, to meet human needs, especially those of the most marginalized of community members.

Just as the Muslim Brotherhood and Shas—but not, as we will see, the Salvation Army—established religious schools to pass their message on to the next generation, the CdO's Federazione Opere Educative, which was founded in 1996, is an association of operators of 520 religious kindergartens, primary and secondary schools, and vocational training institutions that are run by religious bodies, foundations, and parental cooperatives associated with CL. These schools have served some 49,000 students throughout Italy.[113] Oftentimes CL schools were established in the school buildings of existing religious orders that no longer had the monks or nuns to staff them. One of the movement's largest schools, Istituto Sacro Cuore in Milan, has over 1,000 students.[114] Years after her attendance at Sacred Heart, Michele wrote the following testament in CL's magazine, *Traces*, to the effect that the school and Father Giussani had on her:

> My first contact with the Movement was in middle school, at the Sacred Heart Institute. I remember well that the school trips, more than the day-to-day life at school, were organized in a way that was full of love. The songs, the games, hearing people like Fr. Giorgio or other teachers speak about the problems of life and how the love for Jesus should be the center of everything marked me in the best way, and unconsciously the seed Fr. Giussani had given to everyone who joined the Movement had taken root in me.[115]

The desire of CL followers to educate their children in an environment that supports the teachings of CL has also led the CdO's Federazione Opere Educative to campaign, thus far unsuccessfully, for equal funding of public and religious schools by the Italian state.[116]

One of the most recent associations to be created in the Compagnia delle Opere is the Banco Farmaceutico Associazione, which was established in 2000 in collaboration with the Pharmacy Owners' Association to collect and distribute pharmaceuticals to people in need.[117] On February 12, 2011, the Banco Farmaceutico organized its eleventh National Drug Collection Day to "Give a drug to those in need." Organizers report that the drive brought in 365,000 pharmaceuticals, from nearly 3,200 Italian pharmacies, which were donated to 1,390 agencies for distribution to those who needed these medicines.[118]

In offering nonprofit social, educational, and religious services, the CdO relies on its network of some 35,000 CL-inspired or -affiliated businesses, none of which is owned by the CdO or CL. CL reports that the businesses in its network have a total capitalization of €45 billion (US$59.6 billion) and some 420,000 employees. Most of the businesses are small or medium-sized; nearly half (47 percent) have fewer than five employees and only 2.5 percent have more than 100. Nonetheless, the CdO's network of companies includes some major multinational corporations, such as Fiat, Renault, and Best Western, and others that are less familiar internationally but are well known in Italy.[119] In addition to their involvement in the delivery of the social services discussed earlier, the businesses in the network offer services at reduced rates to other CL-affiliated businesses and to individuals associated with the movement, drawing on "the tradition of mutual solidarity" and working to establish "the presence of Italian Catholics in society."[120] For individuals and businesses, the CdO is a major purchasing group, offering discount prices, lower interest rates on loans, favorable credit arrangements, less expensive telecommunications, lower fares on airlines and rental cars, and so on. More specialized services, technological assistance, and business consultation and mentorship are also offered gratis or at a discount by and to CL-affiliated businesses.[121]

Sergio Marchionne, the chief executive officer of Fiat, told attendees at CL's Rimini meeting in 2010, "We are no longer in the 60s, we should abandon the mode of thought that sees a struggle between capital and labor and between employers and employees."[122] Rather than analyzing relationships at work in terms of class, CL and the CdO prefer to think of these relationships as having the potential to be mutually beneficial "alliances" that serve the needs of employees, employers, and the larger society. Bernard Scholz, president of the CdO, said in a 2009 speech delivered at Columbia University:

> What gives meaning to the employment relationship is . . . a kind of "alliance" . . . between one who offers his skills on the one hand, and one who represents the purposes of the organization on the other. To conceive the partnership as an

"alliance" strengthens the trust in a realistic way, because it . . . indicates the content of the reciprocity in a transparent manner, thus avoiding undeclared interests or secondary purposes. . . . [A]sking [employees] to take responsibility is therefore the greatest value that can be done in the world of work. It is about giving value to the entrepreneurial skills which reside within each of us.[123]

Thus, the movement's analysis is that if employees are brought into companies in such a way that they understand the higher purposes of the organization and their role in this, and if they are given the responsibility to express themselves creatively and entrepreneurially within the organization, the desires of employees and employers, as well as the needs of the larger society, will be met. Critics would regard CL's analysis of workplace relations as masking the class interests of workers and employers, ignoring the greater power of employers, and turning the underlying logic of capitalist enterprises—profit-making—into a higher purpose.

While much of Comunione e Liberazione's cultural, educational, economic, and religious outreach is organized through the Compagnia delle Opere or has eventually become incorporated in the CdO, some of the movement's entrepreneurial efforts are less formally organized. For example, in the maximum security Due Palazzi prison in Padua, a group of prisoners influenced by Monsignor Giussani's teachings formed one of CL's Scuole di Comunità—weekly discussion groups following in the tradition of the "rays" of Gioventù Studentesca. In the same way that many of the entrepreneurial projects of the CdO originated at the grassroots level, the prisoners decided to initiate several businesses: a *patisserie* or pastry shop, a call center, a shop making tailors' dummies for the fashion industry, a paper factory, and a luggage workshop—all within the confines of the prison. The patisserie is highly regarded by Paduans. Says Allessandro, the bakery's master pastry chef, "The production is entirely for the outside. During the Christmas period, we make over 200 *panettoni* [Christmas breads] a day, as well as 100–120 pounds of cakes and pastries."[124] While the recidivism rate for the rest of Italy's prisons is around 80 percent, CL says that this has dropped to 15 percent at the Padua prison. The empowering effect of working in these self-established local enterprises is evident in the words of Alberto, one of the prisoners:

When you work, you take up responsibilities. In the [tailors'] dummy workshop we managed to get recognition at the European level and, apart from the gratification, it helps you to come out of the de-personalization that prison life causes. You are no longer a number, but a worker, at the same level as someone outside. You feel a part of the world and not a piece of prison wall.[125]

Proud of their work, the prisoners at Padua petitioned for and received special permission to attend CL's 2008 Meeting for Friendship among Peoples in Rimini to present an exhibition of their businesses, along with a photography exhibit on prison life in the past and today. It was the most popular exhibition at that year's meeting.[126]

PROVIDING GRADUATED MEMBERSHIP LEVELS

The Muslim Brotherhood, Shas, and, as we will see, the Salvation Army allow new recruits to enter at comfortable levels of commitment to the movement's ideology and with modest demands for sacrifice. Comunione e Liberazione similarly offers a range of levels of theological adherence and commitment, from mere attendance at the annual Meeting for Friendship among Peoples in Rimini (an estimated 800,000 people attended in 2011) or volunteering at the Meeting (roughly 4,000 people);[127] through involvement in CL's Compagnia delle Opere; participation in "vacations" (retreats); involvement in the weekly catechism and discussions of the local Scuole di Comunità (roughly 50,000 people[128]); to participation for a self-specified period of time in La Fraternità de Comunione e Liberazione (about 50,000 participants), which involves a commitment "to a way of life that supports the path to holiness" and requires "personal *ascesis* [self-denial], participation in spiritual formation meetings . . . , and commitment to support . . . charitable, missionary, and cultural initiatives promoted or supported by the Fraternity."[129] As sociologist Mario Zadra noted of the flexibility afforded by these various levels of participation in 1991, when many of the movement's participants were young:

> The movement . . . has developed structures of membership that are well adapted to the particular demographic group to which it appeals. . . . Because a significant proportion of CL's participants are men and women at the beginning of their adult and professional lives, there is an inherent instability in the CL population. CL has responded to this by creating flexible forms of membership that allow for such coming and going.[130]

At the highest level of commitment and sacrifice—membership in Memores Domini (Those Who Remember the Lord), which originated in 1964 at the time of Gioventù Studentesca—the individual commits for life to vows of poverty, celibacy, and obedience. The lay people who take these vows live in separate homes for men and women but otherwise live a life in the world.[131] Like the highest levels of commitment and sacrifice expected by the Muslim Brotherhood, Shas, and the Salvation Army, CL's Memores Domini can be seen as a "greedy institution" that demands all of the individual's time, effort, and loyalty.[132] While only CL requires celibacy of those at this highest level of commitment, the other movements whose stories we tell tightly regulate dyadic relationships at the highest levels of membership, requiring that spouses also be movement members and/or approved by the movement.

RECONCILIATION, SUCCESSION, AND SURVIVAL

Comunione e Liberazione is today "a massive phenomenon in Italy."[133] From its humble beginnings at a Milan high school, it has grown to become "the highest-profile

Catholic pressure group in Italy,"[134] as well as a transnational movement, reporting branches in sixty-one countries and strong organizations and websites in Argentina, Brazil, Chile, Kenya, Mexico, Spain, Switzerland, Uganda, and the United States.[135] Recently, the movement has reached out to members of other faith traditions. An extension of the 2010 annual Rimini meeting, held in Cairo, Egypt, at the suggestion of Wael Farouq, a Muslim professor at the University of Cairo, drew nearly 1,000 people to hold a Christian–Muslim dialogue.[136]

While CL remains controversial in the Church and broader Italian society, the movement has taken steps to lessen some of the tensions it has with its opponents, especially its decades-long clash with Azione Cattolica. Gioventù Studentesca, the movement that spawned Comunione e Liberazione, never accepted the decision by Church authorities to put the movement under the control of Azione Cattolica. And after Azione Cattolica made what was called the "religious choice" to take a more pluralistic, apolitical approach, while CL became actively involved in politics as the Church's champion in opposition to divorce and abortion, "the debate," in the words of veteran Vatican correspondent John Allen, "turned so bitter that some spoke of 'mutual excommunications.'"[137] Yet Paola Bignardi, the president of Azione Cattolica, unexpectedly appeared at the August 2004 Rimini meeting of CL and invited CL to join with Azione Cattolica in a greeting to Pope John Paul II at the Shrine of the Holy Family in Loreto, Italy, the following month—a gesture that was widely reported as an effort to reconcile the rift between the two movements.[138] While the motivations behind this rapprochement are not entirely clear, it is the case that many movements have failed by not attending to competition from other social movement organizations in the same field or, if not failed, then lost their original focus on refashioning the world and instead became locked in battle with rivals in the same cause. CL seems to have addressed this problem with Azione Cattolica, thus allowing the movement to continue to focus on sacralizing the larger Italian society.

Less than a year later, on February 22, 2005, CL's founder, Monsignor Luigi Giussani, died in Milan. Giussani's funeral, which drew tens of thousands, was broadcast live on television as if it were a state funeral, and the Italian parliament adjourned early that day so that the prime minister and members of parliament could attend the service.[139] Monsignor Giussani's longtime friend, Cardinal Joseph Ratzinger, asked to deliver the homily at the funeral. With the death of Pope John Paul II only four weeks later, Cardinal Ratzinger was elected in a papal enclave to become Pope Benedict XVI. Vatican correspondent John Allen reported in 2005 that Ratzinger was "closer to the ciellini [CL] than to any other movement in the Catholic Church."[140]

Many movements fail to survive the loss of their charismatic founder. The Muslim Brotherhood, the Salvation Army, and Comunione e Liberazione, each of which faced problems of succession after the loss of their founder, all managed to move on from this crisis. We suggest that their elaborate institutional structures, especially their massive, society-wide networks within which many people serve and on which many people depend, helped hold these movements together in the face of loss of their leaders. Beyond this, the reasons for survival may be unique to each movement. Hasan al-Banna's assassination at the hands of the Egyptian state made him a martyr to members of the Muslim Brotherhood and likely made them even more determined to pursue his goals. Two decades before his death at the age of eighty-three, the Reverend William Booth of the Salvation Army named his son, Bramwell, as his successor to ensure the movement's continuity. Monsignor Giussani, whose death at age eighty-two could not have been unexpected, was succeeded by his right-hand man, Spanish priest Father Julián Carrón. Carrón had moved to Milan the year before at Giussani's request to assume joint leadership of the movement, thus ensuring a gradual transition in leadership.[141]

By all indications CL continues to thrive under Carrón's direction, although CL followers clearly revere his predecessor. On March 24, 2007, the twenty-fifth anniversary of Pope John Paul II's recognition of Comunione e Liberazione as an Association of Pontifical Right, an estimated 130,000 followers braved the pouring rain in St. Peter's Square to hear Pope Benedict XVI repeat Pope John Paul II's words to the movement: "Go forth into the world and bring the message of truth, beauty and peace which is found in Christ the Redeemer."[142] Three years later, in 2010, Pope Benedict XVI took the advice that Monsignor Giussani had given to Pope John Paul II in the early 1980s to create a new dicastery (department within the Vatican) to reawaken faith in secularized Europe and the United States, calling it the Pontifical Council for the New Evangelization.[143] CL thus continues to enjoy the legitimacy that a pope's blessing confers, and the movement's moral resources, like its institutional network and financial assets, continue to grow.[144] In August 2011, some 800,000 people attended CL's annual meeting in Rimini.[145]

CONCLUSIONS

Comunione e Liberazione is today the most powerful religiously orthodox movement in Italy and has now established an international foothold in scores of countries. Just as each of the movements we chronicle had to overcome obstacles in its efforts to sacralize its society, CL faced the defection of most of its members to the secular left in the late 1960s, the failure of its political wing to win victories for the Church in referenda on divorce and abortion in the 1970s and 1980s, an embarrassing investigation of corruption among political candidates it supported in the 1990s, and the death of its leader in 2005. What held the movement together, in addition to the charisma of its founder, Monsignor Luigi Giussani, was a strongly communitarian theology that saw the religious life as only fully realizable in communion with fellow believers, in the subordination of individual will to the will of the community and Church, and in institutional outreach to those in need.

We argue that it was this theological communitarianism that led the followers of Giussani to feel a calling to establish a Christian "presence" in the larger Italian society and the world. In the movement's early years, this took the form of efforts to put into law the Church's positions on divorce and abortion—efforts that embodied the strict or authoritarian side of the movement's communitarianism. This strict side also led the movement to a tenacious loyalty to the pope that generated much condemnation from secularists in the larger Italian society, as well as from those within the Church who wanted a less papal-dominated leadership.

Yet the caring side of Comunione e Liberazione's communitarianism has produced its most remarkable accomplishment: a huge institutional effort to bypass the state. CL's Compagnia delle Opere and the "parallel society" that it is establishing through this are unique among the institution-building efforts of the movements we chronicle in several respects. First, CL's Compagnia delle Opere makes far greater use of for-profit companies in offering services to the poor, homeless, unemployed, and sick, as well as to the movement's followers, than do the networks of the other movements. While the Muslim Brotherhood and the Salvation Army have also incorporated businesses in their networks, CL's 35,000 affiliated businesses are thirty-two times more numerous than its 1,100 nonprofit social service organizations. This unusually heavy reliance on corporate social responsibility in CL's institutional outreach derives in part from the staunch anticommunist and antistatist positions that have characterized the movement from the start and that may now encourage downplaying class tensions in Italian society. While the Muslim Brotherhood, Shas, and the Salvation Army have also taken secular communism or socialism as a foil at some point, communist and socialist movements offered relatively weak competition in Egypt, Israel, and the United States. In Italy the communist party (PCI) has historically been strong, and defections to Marxist movements during the 1960s decimated CL's precursor, Gioventù Studentesca.

Second, in contrast to the Muslim Brotherhood and Shas, which seek to take over the state, CL's efforts are intended to show that a strong state is unnecessary. The message of CL's Compagnia delle Opere is that private citizens and entrepreneurs, called by faith, can better address human needs and can do so at a level more immediate to the community and individual than can a distant state and in a way that addresses both spiritual and material needs. While some will see this message as motivated by compassion and faith in humanity, others will regard it as an attempt to weaken the state to the point that all that prevents corporate owners from pursuing purely self-interested goals is the community-mindedness or corporate social responsibility that faith is believed to bring.

Third, the form that communitarianism takes in Comunione e Liberazione with respect to economic matters is different from that of Shas, the Muslim Brotherhood, and as we will see, the Salvation Army. In its economic outreach, CL makes frequent reference to charity as a Catholic virtue, a form of "total sharing," and a basis of political activism, but rarely refers to social or economic justice. The Muslim Brotherhood, Shas, and the Salvation Army are far more likely to frame economic concerns as matters of justice than is CL. The different foci of these movements have implications for how they address inequality. While the Muslim Brotherhood and Shas have both pushed the state for greater equalization of incomes, a higher minimum wage, and progressive taxation, and while the Salvation Army, in its more limited political role, has lobbied for more government spending on homelessness, poverty, and hunger, CL has generally not engaged in legislative lobbying on these matters, preferring instead to emphasize Christian charity and corporate social responsibility, together with religiously inspired public and private entrepreneurship, as the solution to these problems. At the same time, the herculean effort that CL has put into building its network of state-like institutions to meet the needs of the marginalized is far beyond what could be characterized as laissez faire individualism or as holding the poor, homeless, and sick as responsible for solving their own problems.

Fourth, unlike the Muslim Brotherhood, Shas, and the Salvation Army, which situate their activities around local centers of worship that they have built or control, thus gaining legitimacy from these long-standing bases of civil society, Comunione e Liberazione prefers to center its operations on "the environment"—the high school, university, seminary, and workplace. CL is the only religiously orthodox movement among the four we consider that does not have its own places of worship. The goal of establishing a Catholic presence in these nonparish environments is what motivates CL's outreach. Interestingly, the Reverend William Booth of the Salvation Army (who began his ministry by going beyond church walls and preaching to the poor in the streets of East London), Hasan al Banna of the Muslim Brotherhood (who took his message to coffee houses and other settings of everyday life in Egypt), and Rabbi Ovadya Yosef of Shas (who rejected a life of pious retreat and took his teachings to the Israeli public) had similar approaches, although their movements' efforts quickly became centered on places of worship.

At the same time, Comunione e Liberazione has much in common with the other movements: a focus on the local community, a membership structure that allows individuals to join at comfortable levels of ideological adherence and commitment and then subsequently move to higher levels, and a willingness to reprioritize agendas as internal and external circumstances change. Moreover, CL's vast social service network serves much the same purpose as the networks of the other movements in helping it overcome what social movement theory would say are three strikes against it—a morally absolutist ideology; extraordinarily broad agendas on theological, cultural, and economic fronts; and strong reluctance to compromise in bringing in other groups.

The parallel Christian society of state-like institutions that CL is working to establish gives skeptics about the movement a taste of what their lives might be like if the movement succeeded in bringing about what it sees as "a true company of Jesus"[146] in

Italy. It allows local followers of the movement to identify unmet needs in their communities that can then be institutionally addressed through nonprofit or for-profit enterprises in the Compagnia delle Opere, thus allowing the movement's theology and broad agendas to be implemented where they are most needed and appreciated. And it empowers these local followers as they innovate entrepreneurially in creating ways of addressing spiritual and material needs and come to feel a sense of accomplishment in laying what they see as the "building blocks" of a new Christian society.

THE SALVATION ARMY USA
Doing Good to Hasten the Second Coming

Action, action! Religion in action, this is what the world needs—religion
alive, religion living among the people, religion going about doing good as
well as singing hymns.
—EVANGELINE BOOTH, NATIONAL COMMANDER,
SALVATION ARMY USA (1908)

THE SALVATION ARMY USA TAKES ITS name literally and, like the Muslim Brotherhood, Shas, and Comunione e Liberazione, sees itself as battling secularism and modernity. It differs from the other three movements in having become known to most
Americans more for its economic mission than for its theological or cultural agendas.
The Salvation Army USA is also distinctive in that it has never formed a political party
or pressure group. While its purpose has been broadly political, the Army has limited its direct political engagement to moving the state in what it sees as a Christian
direction through behind-the-scenes lobbying on Capitol Hill. And the Army differs
from the Muslim Brotherhood and Shas in that its social service network has generally not been seen by the public as putting the state's modest efforts to help the poor
to shame, in part because many Americans have minimal expectations of the social
welfare functions of government. In its early years in the United States, the Salvation
Army bypassed the state by establishing institutions that offered faith-infused services
to the poor, unemployed, homeless, and sick that were not provided by the state. In
more recent decades, the Army has sidestepped the state in that its institutions complement or fill holes in the service delivery of the weak U.S. welfare state. Throughout its
history, the movement has regarded its efforts in building a vast network of religion-
based institutions as having the critically important theological purpose of paving the
way for the Second Coming of Christ.

The Salvation Army USA is the nation's largest charitable organization, faith-based
or secular,[1] with assets of $8.76 billion according to the Army's 2010 *Annual Report*.[2]
When most Americans today think of the Salvation Army, they likely think of the Army's thrift shops and its annual Red Kettle Drive at Christmastime. Yet less than 15
percent of the Salvation Army's revenue comes from these activities,[3] and the Army's
extensive network of faith-based social services in the United States goes far beyond

thrift shops. The Salvation Army USA's *2010 Annual Report* states that the Army offers assistance of $3.1 billion to 29.4 million Americans—almost one in ten Americans— through 7,821 centers of operation, including worship centers; hostels for the homeless; group homes for needy children, the elderly, and single mothers and their babies; hospices for HIV patients; day care facilities; addiction dependency programs; missing persons location services; domestic violence shelters; disaster assistance programs; outreach programs for released prisoners; summer camps for children; career counseling centers; and medical facilities; among others.[4]

The Salvation Army USA began as, and continues to be, a religious movement. Today, it has 1,241 churches, called "corps," offering regular religious services; 400,055 Americans call the Salvation Army their church.[5] The Salvation Army—an evangelical Protestant movement—began in 1865 with the preaching of the Rev. William Booth to the poor and downtrodden in London. The American branch—our focus here—was founded fifteen years later in 1880.[6] This makes the Salvation Army USA the longest surviving movement of the four whose stories we tell. To give a sense of how remarkable it is for an organization to achieve this longevity, a recent national commander of the Salvation Army USA, Robert Watson, reported the following: "Of the firms listed among the original Dow Jones industrials in 1896, only one—General Electric—is still in business."[7] Marketing specialist Peter Ducker, interviewed by *Forbes,* called the Salvation Army USA "by far the most effective organization in the United States." "No one," he continued, "even comes close . . . in respect to clarity of mission, ability to innovate, measurable results, dedication, and putting money to maximum use."[8]

The longevity of the Salvation Army USA is all the more noteworthy when what the movement had to overcome is considered. In the first decades that the Army was in the United States, Salvationists—or "Sallies" as they were called—faced angry and sometimes violent mobs, resulting in the deaths of five Salvationists. The movement had to survive two major schisms, one of them initiated by the founder's son and daughter-in-law. In 1890, twenty-five years after the movement began and only ten years after the founding of the American branch, the Salvation Army made the most dramatic reprioritization of agendas of any of the movements we chronicle. And in 1912, the Army, still headed by its charismatic founder William Booth, had to survive his death.

The Army's persistence, despite these crises, owes much to its deeply rooted communitarianism. This led Booth and his followers to "share the keys to the Kingdom" with others and bring them into a "sacred community" of believers.[9] It gave the Army a strict side that required its "soldiers" and "officers" to forswear alcohol, drugs, pornography, profanity, and gambling, and led to a culturally conservative agenda on abortion, homosexuality, marriage, and pornography that is unknown to most Americans. Yet this theological communitarianism also had a more visible caring side that is reflected in the Army's building of an extensive network of religion-based social services. For the Army, establishing religious and economic institutions was intended not to prefigure a state governed according to religious law as is the case for the Muslim Brotherhood and Shas, or to lessen the need for an extensive welfare state as for Comunione e Liberazione, but to advance what it saw as the Kingdom of God on Earth and hasten the Second Coming of Christ.

EVANGELICALISM, COMMUNITARIANISM, AND RELIGION IN ACTION

The Rev. William Booth, who in 1865 founded in England the movement that would later become the Salvation Army, grounded his preaching in the evangelical theologies of John Wesley (the founder of Methodism) and the Holiness Church.[10] The broader evangelical Protestant movement had begun, in part, as a reaction against the individualism of the Enlightenment and early industrial capitalism. As sociologist John Hazzard observes of the ideologies prevailing in Victorian England when the Army was founded, "Enlightenment ideas about the importance of the individual over and against social institutions, mixed with liberal [laissez faire] economic ideology and democratic political notions, undermined the political and religious hierarchies, leaving individual judgment as the touchstone to truth."[11] At the time of the movement's founding, "Evangelicals were known for a desire to save the souls of themselves and others, a pious moral existence that sometimes included total abstinence from alcohol . . . and a strong social conscience."[12]

Just as the founders of the Muslim Brotherhood, Shas, and Comunione e Liberazione saw the sacred texts and teachings of their faith as inerrant, Booth believed the Bible to be divinely inspired and he held to a literal reading of it.[13] The eleven doctrinal positions of the Army, which were established by 1874[14] and are now posted on the website of the Salvation Army USA, begin with the statement, "We believe that the Scriptures of the Old and New Testaments were given by inspiration of God, and that they only constitute the Divine rule of Christian faith and practice."[15] Booth's preaching and all of the theological, cultural, and economic agendas of the movement he founded have been justified by citing Scripture.

Sociologist Rebecca Anne Allahyari, in her ethnography of how two social service organizations, the Salvation Army USA and Loaves and Fishes (the latter inspired by the Catholic Worker movement of Dorothy Day), relate to the people they serve in Sacramento, California, sees the Army as having an essentially conservative, individualistic moral rhetoric that emphasizes hard work, responsibility for families, and sobriety.[16] While there are elements of individualism in the Army's theology, there is a strongly communitarian or caring aspect to the efforts of Salvationists to bring others to the faith—to "share the keys to the Kingdom of heaven."[17] In his preaching, William Booth stressed Jesus's communalist exhortation to "Love our neighbor as ourselves"

(Matthew 22:39),[18] and this Scripture is today used to justify the movement's work for "economic justice" on the website of the Salvation Army USA.[19] Booth sought to build a sacred community in which the "saved" would join the cause and work to save others. Historian and Salvationist Edward H. McKinley observes that

> After salvation, converts were urged to dedicate their hearts to Christ without reservation, so that His love would pour in and purge all selfishness and pride. The "sanctified" soldiers could then spread the love of God abroad in an ever more brightly burning desire to save souls, to share love, and to provide some kind of physical or emotional comfort to the miserable and desperate people they daily encountered. . . . [F]or the Salvationist, the work of grace was never purely individual; there was always a communal dimension.[20]

As Robert Watson, former national commander of the Salvation Army USA, sums up the importance of community in Salvationist theology: "The idea of community is crucial to our 'theology of service.' Humans are linked in a family with God. We are truly brothers and sisters, equal in our eligibility for grace and transformation. When we heed the call of reconciliation in that family, we can see the links that connect us more clearly and can begin to honor and strengthen the bonds."[21]

The community that the Salvation Army seeks to build is not solely spiritual. As historian Lillian Taiz writes about those involved in the early years of the movement in the United States, "For these men and women, Salvationism was more than a religion; it provided them with a sacred community within which they created new definitions of manhood and womanhood, gained meaningful careers, found marriage partners, and accrued moral and administrative authority."[22] Allahyari herself reaches the unanticipated conclusion in her contemporary ethnography that while the middle-class volunteers in Loaves and Fishes (the Catholic Worker group) maintained a distance from their clients, "At the Salvation Army men of diverse ethnicities shared caring friendships based on mutual support and expressiveness. The moral code of sociability at The Salvation Army fostered solidarity and, to a lesser extent, generosity as moral ideals."[23]

William Booth's book, *In Darkest England and the Way Out*, took a collectivist approach to alleviating poverty that was heavily influenced by the American Social Gospel movement. This movement, which was prominent among progressive Protestant groups from 1870 to 1920, applied Christian social ethics to the social problems of industrialization, urbanization, and immigration, pushing for child labor laws, poverty relief by government, better wages and improved working conditions in factories, reduced racial tensions, greater economic equality, educational opportunity, and other such efforts. As we discuss later in this chapter, Booth acknowledged in his book structural causes of poverty and joblessness, condemned laissez faire capitalism as "anti-Christian," and offered a utopian "way out" that involved building a complex set of institutions—city, farm, and overseas colonies—to move people out of poverty.[24] Former national commander of the Salvation Army USA Robert Watson writes, "[T]he Scriptures are explicit about our responsibilities to one another: We are to feed the hungry, give drink to the thirsty, clothe the naked, and visit the sick and imprisoned as if we were attending the needs of Jesus himself: 'Inasmuch as ye have done it unto one of the least of these my brethren, ye have done it unto me' (Matthew 25:40, KJV [King James Version])."[25]

Finally, we note that each of the other movements we chronicle shares with the Salvation Army the notion that individual conversion must precede the effort to sacralize society. For the Muslim Brotherhood, the individual must first be brought to a new understanding of Islam, and the effects of this are seen as proceeding in ever-widening circles to the believer's family, community, society, and state. For Comunione e Liberazione, the individual's "encounter with Christ" occurs first, but spirituality is only fully realized in a community of believers and in a vocation to transform society. And Shas's calling of less-observant Jews to teshuva assumes that first individuals will be brought to this, then their families and communities, and ultimately the larger society and state. It is difficult to imagine how a proselytizing movement—"evangelistic" in the broader sense of the word, which encompasses all of the movements whose stories we tell—could sacralize the world without first bringing individuals to a new understanding of faith. We do not take this as a sign of an individualist ethos undergirding the Salvation Army or the other three movements. Rather, we see all four movements as grounded in a strong communitarian logic.

For the Salvation Army, as for the other movements whose histories we have narrated, the duty of the faithful does not stop with self-conversion or even with leading other individuals to the faith; it entails an obligation to remake the community and larger society. Focusing on both material and spiritual transformation, William Booth wrote toward the end of his life, "While women weep, as they do now, I'll fight; while little children go hungry, as they do now, I'll fight; while men go to prison, in and out, in and out, as they do now, I'll fight; while there is a drunkard left, while there is a poor lost girl upon the streets, while there remains one dark soul without the light of God, I'll fight—I'll fight to the very end!"[26]

This commitment to go beyond the individual in sacralizing the broader society is rooted in the "postmillennialism" of the Army's Holiness theology. Postmillennialism "holds that the millennium will come first, usually 'as the fruit of present Christian agencies now at work in the world,' and that the Second Coming [of Christ] . . . will occur at the end of the process."[27] For postmillennialists, Christians "should take a major social and political role in reshaping the world to advance God's Kingdom on earth,"[28] and for Booth, this meant working for social justice for the most marginalized members of society. Premillennialists, in contrast, believe that since God will first destroy and then remake the world, there is no need for Christians to work to transform the world or the material condition of humankind.[29] As postmillennialists, Booth and the Salvationists saw themselves as "God's vanguard"[30] in "transform[ing] the secular world into the Kingdom of God" on Earth.[31] Much as the Muslim Brotherhood, Shas, and Comunione e Liberazione generally held deeds to be more important than words, Evangeline Booth, daughter of the founder and national commander of the Salvation Army USA from 1904 to 1934, called for "Action, action! Religion in action, this is what the world needs—religion alive, religion living among the people, religion going about doing good as well as singing hymns."[32]

The theologically communitarian Christianity of the Salvation Army is also evident in the cultural agendas it has pursued since its establishment in the United States in 1880 to the present day. For the Army, individuals are not seen as having the right to reach their own moral decisions about abortion, homosexuality, sex outside marriage, pornography, and so forth as modernists would expect them to, but are instead required to follow a strict set of what the movement views as divinely ordained communal standards. The Army's positions on cultural issues, while unknown to most Americans, are almost always conservative. Since its founding, the Salvation Army has lobbied for prohibition of alcohol and against pornography and sex trafficking. The movement's website today posts strict position statements on a wide array of cultural issues, all supported by references to Scripture:

> The Salvation Army believes in the sanctity of all human life and considers each person to be of infinite value and each life a gift from God to be cherished, nurtured and redeemed. Human life is sacred because it is made in the image of God and has an eternal destiny (Genesis 1:27). . . . [The Army] is opposed to abortion as a means of birth control, family planning, sex selection or for any reason of mere convenience to avoid the responsibility for conception.[33]

> [The Army] affirms the New Testament standard of marriage, which is the loving union for life of one man and one woman to the exclusion of all others. Marriage is the first institution ordained by God (Genesis 2:24), and His Word establishes its significance (Matthew 19:4–6). . . . Marriage is the only proper context for sexual intimacy. Scripture demands abstinence before, and faithfulness within, marriage. . . . Marriage reflects the relationship of Christ and His Church. It is a loving, mutually respectful union intended for life (Ephesians 5:21–33). . . . Marriage provides the optimal environment for the welfare of children and contributes to the stability of society.[34]

The Army's cultural positions on issues of sexuality and gender are not entirely static. In 1985 the Army regarded homosexuality as a condition to be "treated,"[35] while today its position statement does not mention treatment, noting instead that:

> Whatever the causes may be, to deny its reality or to marginalize those of a same-sex orientation have not been helpful. . . . [Nonetheless,] Scripture forbids sexual

intimacy between members of the same sex. The Salvation Army believes, therefore, that Christians whose sexual orientation is primarily or exclusively same-sex are called upon to embrace celibacy as a way of life.[36]

Yet in contrast to the Muslim Brotherhood, Shas, and Comunione e Liberazione, the Salvation Army has, throughout much of its history, incorporated women into high leadership positions. The Army's position on women has often been conveyed through the personae of the women who led or co-led the U.S. movement, most of whom in the early years were daughters or daughters-in-law of founder William Booth. For example, Booth's daughter-in-law Maud Booth, who along with her husband, Ballington, headed the Army in the United States from 1887 to 1896, tried to embody the ideal of the "advanced woman" or "woman warrior," who "combined Victorian womanliness with a sense of mission that empowered her to act boldly in the public sphere."[37] None of the Army's position statements today prescribe different roles for women and men.

Far better known to most Americans today than these cultural positions is the Army's caring side or economic mission,[38] embodied in its massive network of social services, which like its culturally conservative agenda, grew out of its biblically based theological communitarianism. Initially, William Booth's ministry to the downtrodden was strictly to evangelize them, not to ameliorate the conditions under which they lived.[39] This was not because Booth lacked firsthand experience with the debilitating effects of poverty. His father was a nail manufacturer and homebuilder, which gave William a comfortable life when he was young. All this changed abruptly when William was thirteen and the family was plunged into poverty by his father's business mistakes. William was removed from school by his family and apprenticed to a pawnbroker, where he daily met people who were even more impoverished than himself.[40] Despite this background, however, when he began preaching, Booth saw his mission as saving souls, not improving the living conditions of the destitute to whom he preached.

By 1890, William Booth had come to see capitalist economies—specifically their high rates of unemployment and low wages—as responsible for poverty, drunkenness, and immorality. He rejected laissez faire economics as "anti-Christian," attacking its Social Darwinist premise that "it is an offense against the doctrine of the survival of the fittest to try to save the weakest from going to the wall."[41] Leaders of the Army's U.S. branch vigorously defended Booth's anticapitalist stances against their many American critics.[42] And in contrast to many competing social service organizations, the Salvation Army USA refused to draw the individualistic distinction between the "worthy" and "unworthy" poor that was (and is) so popular with Americans.[43] The Salvation Army USA today continues to recognize structural causes of poverty and inequality, noting in its position statement on "economic justice"—a "justice" frame with which the Muslim Brotherhood and Shas, but probably not Comunione e Liberazione, would be comfortable—that "certain social structures can perpetuate economic injustice and [the Army] is committed to seek constructive changes in those structures wherever they exist."[44]

FOUNDING, BRANCHING OUT, AND
OVERCOMING SCHISMS

The Salvation Army traces its origins to Sunday, July 2, 1865, when the Rev. William Booth began preaching in an old tent erected in a Quaker graveyard in London's East End to what he called "the heathen."[45] Much as, in sacralizing their societies, Muslim Brotherhood founder Hasan al-Banna would later take his preaching out of the mosque and into the coffee houses and everyday locales where people lived, as Father Luigi Giussani of Comunione e Liberazione would seek to establish a Christian presence in nonchurch "environments" (high schools, workplaces, universities, and seminaries) beyond the local parish, and as Rabbi Ovadya Yosef of Shas would eschew the pious withdrawal of many Haredi religious scholars and take his teachings to ordinary men and women, William Booth "abandon[ed] the conventional concept of a church and pulpit . . . to preach the gospel of Jesus Christ to the poor, the homeless, the hungry and the destitute."[46] Salvationist and historian Roger Green describes the area where Booth launched what he called the Christian Mission, as "a place of horror, a community of poverty, disease and crime unmatched in the nineteenth century. Anyone walking through the East End at that time would witness the bleakest of living conditions and the utter disregard for human life and human values."[47] While Booth's ministry to the downtrodden was primarily aimed at evangelizing them, Booth created in 1870 the Food-for-the-Millions program, which provided meals to the poor at discount prices. Four years later, Booth abandoned the program, feeling that it was a financial and emotional drain on his ministry.[48]

Booth often used war metaphors to describe his evangelizing and in 1878 seized on the name by which the movement goes today, naming himself as the new Salvation Army's first general.[49] Today on its website, the Salvation Army USA reports that "The word *army* indicates that the organization is a fighting force constantly at war with the powers of evil."[50] This bellicose language reflects the Army's "good vs. evil" moral absolutism and "us vs. them" approach to its sacralizing efforts, features that can be seen in each of the orthodox movements we chronicle.

The U.S. branch of the Salvation Army was founded in New York City in 1880 by Commissioner George Scott Railton and seven "Hallelujah lassies," as Army women were called. The American founders wasted no time in attracting attention to their arrival from England: They disembarked from the ship *Australia,* waving the Army's red, blue, and yellow "Blood and Fire" flag, and "[i]nvoking Christopher Columbus's legendary arrival some four centuries earlier, . . . knelt on the cold, damp ground, planted their flag, and claimed America for God."[51] The "blood" in the Army's slogan referred to the "atoning work of Christ" and the "fire" to the "fiery baptism of the Holy Spirit."[52]

While responding to similar modernizing forces that created its parent movement, the Army in the United States initially focused its energies on the consumerist culture of materialism that it saw as taking over American life.[53] Drawing on a largely working-class membership, combining "the culture of the saloon and music hall with a frontier camp-meeting,"[54] and using tactics that might today be called "street" or "guerrilla theater" (marching, singing, public testimonials, morality plays, etc.), the Army sought to "spiritualize the world and, in the process, sacralize public space. The crusade to hallow the city—its buildings, public squares, and streets—was part of the Army's attempt to establish the Kingdom of God."[55] In a statement that applies well to all of the movements we study, an 1896 editorial in the Army's newspaper, the *American War Cry*, reflected on this sacralizing spirit:

> The genius of the Army has been from the first that it has secularized religion, or rather that it has religionized secular things. . . . On the one hand it has brought religion out of the clouds into everyday life, and has taught the world that we may and ought to be as religious about our eatings and drinkings and dressings as we are about our prayings. On the other hand it has taught us that . . . [a] house or a store or a factory can be just as holy a place as a church; hence we have commonly preferred to engage a secular place for our meetings. . . . [O]ur greatest triumphs have been witnessed in theaters, music halls, rinks, breweries, saloons, stores, and similar places.[56]

As historian Lillian Taiz describes the communitarianism that these spiritualizing efforts embodied, "Saving souls and promoting the Army's sacred community expressed an ethic of mutuality common to working-class families and neighborhoods. In contrast to the market values that ruled most social relations of the era, the Salvation Army revival meeting could be regarded as a place of *spiritual* 'mutual aid.'"[57]

Nothing better symbolizes the Salvation Army's sacralizing, evangelical agenda in the United States of the late nineteenth century than its notion of the figurative "cathedral of the open air," which historian Diane Winston says "signified a sacred space large enough to encompass the entire city and also, by evoking the holy sites of medieval Christianity, signaled the belief that God was the hub of all life, the center of all meaning, and the base for human activity."[58]

All of the movements whose stories we narrate rely on modern technology, social science, mass media, economic innovations, and so forth to accomplish their theological, cultural, and economic agendas. The Salvation Army of the late nineteenth century reacted against the consumerist culture of American capitalism that "hallowed acquisition as the key to happiness, the new as superior to the old, and money as the measure of all value,"[59] while at the same time using advertising, entertainment, publicity, and other tools of the marketplace to challenge the dominant culture and sell instead its own version of salvation. Even as it condemned popular entertainment like amusement parks, baseball, and the theater as directing attention away from God, the Army offered its own parades, concerts, and street theater to draw the public's attention back to Christian virtue. Salvationists initially dismissed the bicycle as an unseemly popular fad, only to later adopt the "Bicycle Brigade as 'the very latest' strategy for soul-saving."[60] The Army's concern with efficiency in the delivery of its services, its pioneering use of magic lanterns (slide projectors) and motion pictures to get out its message, and its adoption of professional social work methods reflect a willingness to borrow liberally from secular society in order to challenge what the Army regarded as its evils.[61]

Not surprisingly, there was much resistance to the Salvation Army's early tactics. The Army's guerrilla theater tactics in American cities provoked strongly negative and sometimes violent reactions from the general public. The movement's saloon takeovers, street parades, and loud bands were met by angry mobs delivering "a shower of insults, mud, and garbage" on the Sallies.[62] Salvationist historian Edward McKinley reports that mobs killed Salvationists in five different cities during the 1880s and 1890s.[63] Because city officials viewed street evangelism as disruptive of the peace and often shared the same opinion of the Salvationists as the crowds that attacked them, they rarely provided police protection. Yet the persecution that the Sallies endured seemed only to make them more committed to their mission, seeing themselves as martyrs to the cause much like the early Christians.[64] Making the Army even more controversial in its early years in the United States, the American branch took a strong stand against racial segregation—a position that at the time even progressive labor unions, most of which had a "whites only" policy, refused to take.[65]

Unfortunately for the movement, George Railton proved to be a poor leader. He opened a dozen corps in the United States but failed to stabilize them. Sensing that there was nonetheless a mission for the Salvation Army in the United States, William Booth relieved Railton of his command in 1881 and replaced him with Major Thomas Moore, who had spent eleven years in the United States, amassed a fortune, and converted to Holiness theology and the Salvation Army. Moore immediately consolidated the twelve corps into five. When these were well established, he expanded the movement to other cities and towns across the country. Moore used the movement's newspaper, the *American War Cry*, to establish connections among the Salvationists, promote loyalty to himself, and advertise the Army's mission in the United States.[66]

As the American movement began to purchase or build permanent worship halls, the question of who owned the Army's property arose. General William Booth saw the Salvation Army as an international movement, of which the U.S. branch was only one part, and felt that any property, regardless of where it was, should be held in his name on behalf of the Army. Because states in the United States had different rules about whether foreigners could own property, Moore appealed to Booth to allow him to incorporate the American offshoot so that it could own the U.S. assets. Fearing that he would lose control of the American branch, Booth rejected this idea. Moore then suggested a compromise where he, himself, as an American citizen, would hold title to the assets on the Army's behalf. Booth rejected this too. Facing the loss of the movement's assets in some states, Moore went ahead and incorporated the U.S. movement, putting its property, insignia, and the *American War Cry* under the control of an American board of trustees. Irritated by Booth's unwillingness to resolve the property issue and grant any autonomy to the American branch, Moore cut all ties to the parent movement and declared himself general of the renamed Salvation Army of America (as distinguished from the Salvation Army *in* America). He announced in the *American War Cry* that "'THE SALVATION ARMY OF AMERICA' is an American institution . . . in no way connected with *The English Salvation Army,* under the Rev. W. Booth, of London, England."[67]

Sociologist Lewis Coser distinguishes several types of breakaway efforts that may occur in social movements. The "dissident" stays in the movement while raising questions about its ideology and goals, a dangerous situation that allows the dissident daily contact with members and the opportunity to affect their thinking and undermine their loyalty to the movement. The "renegade" founds a rival organization or movement that has similar goals, but rejects some aspect of the movement's ideology or tactics. This is what we saw when jihadist groups endorsing the use of violence split off from the Egyptian Muslim Brotherhood in the mid-1960s. Finally, the "heretic" goes to the other side, as when many young followers of Gioventù Studentesca in Italy left the movement that would later become Comunione e Liberazione at the end of the 1960s to join Marxist movements. Heretics are the easiest for a movement to dismiss as traitors or as misguided all along.[68] Major Thomas Moore's actions were those of a "renegade." He founded a new movement—or, more accurately, took control of a branch of an established movement—over the issue of national autonomy.

Booth did not take the defection of the U.S. branch lightly. He immediately dispatched Major Frank Smith, as national commander of the Worldwide Salvation Army in the United States, to try to win back the rebels. Smith worked to establish the Worldwide Army in cities and towns where it did not have to compete with Moore's organization. William Booth himself made a visit to the United States in 1886 to stake his claim to the American branch. When Smith was unable to resolve the conflict with Moore's group, Booth appointed his son and daughter-in-law, Ballington and Maud Booth, to head the American branch in 1887. To counter charges that the Army was an English (that is, foreign) organization, Ballington and Maud adopted American symbols, adding an eagle to the movement's flag and displaying the American flag alongside the Army's flag at all of the movement's revival meetings. When Moore's mismanagement endangered the financial solvency of his rival Salvation Army of America, the board of trustees replaced him with Colonel Richard Holz, who in 1889 reconciled the renegade group with the original U.S. branch in a tearful public ceremony.[69]

The secession crisis was over. Ballington and Maud Booth continued to Americanize the movement with their selective use of symbols. When William Booth revisited the United States in 1894, he found—much to his disappointment—red, white, and blue bunting adorning the branch's headquarters and the home of his son and daughter-in-law. A special commemorative medallion in honor of Booth's visit showed him flanked on both sides with American flags. Alarmed by what he derisively began to call "Yankee Doodleism," Booth briefly considered merging the Army's U.S. and Canadian branches to counter American nationalism. Booth may also have resented the success of Ballington and Maud in raising funds from rich donors and feared that the American branch would eclipse his English operations.[70] When Ballington and Maud were summarily relieved of their command by Booth and ordered home in 1896, they decided to leave the Salvation Army, fearing that William Booth would not allow subsequent national commanders to tailor the movement to American sensibilities.[71] Less than a year later, the couple founded their own movement, Volunteers of America, an evangelical ministry of service which continues to this day (http://www.voa.org/). A few officers and most of the musicians in the Army's Staff Band followed Ballington and Maud to their new movement.[72] A furious William Booth regarded the actions of his son and daughter-in-law as traitorous.[73] Yet while, like Thomas Moore, they had established a separate renegade movement, this was less threatening to the international Salvation Army because it left the original American branch largely intact.

ADDING A SECOND, INSTITUTION-BUILDING MISSION: THE SOCIAL WING

Since none of the movements we chronicle experienced a steady progression of membership and success in achieving its goals, we are interested in how their agendas and framing responded to internal crises, such as loss of membership or mission failure, as well as changing political opportunity structures.[74] Prior sociological research on how movements shift agendas and framing has not uncovered a single pattern. Joseph Gusfield finds that after Prohibition had been repealed in 1933, the Women's Christian Temperance Movement (WCTU) in the United States shifted its focus from militant activism in support of a total ban on alcohol to a broader, more widely acceptable, reformist agenda focusing on "narcotics prevention, chronic alcoholism, juvenile delinquency, censorship of obscene literature, and religious devotions."[75] In contrast, historian Leila Rupp and sociologist Verta Taylor find that leaders of the National Women's Party in the United States, to retain the loyalty of the movement's core during a period of abeyance between the first and second waves of feminism, held fast to their ideological principles, rather than water these down or broaden their agenda to attract mass support.[76] Sociologists Sam Marullo, Ron Pagnucco, and Jackie Smith's study of the U.S. peace movement during a period of contraction from 1988 to 1992 finds that the movement adopted a "retention frame" that was both wider in scope in order to "appeal to a broader segment of a shrinking potential constituency" and more radical (structuralist in its explanations) to retain the movement's core, who had increasingly come to recognize the connections between societal structures and the problems they were addressing.[77] Finally, sociologists Daniel Cornfield and Bill Fletcher find that from 1881 to 1955, the American Federation of Labor, in response to employers' lesser dependence on unions for labor, used "frame extension" to broaden its agenda from pro-union labor legislation to legislation that would improve the conditions of all workers through the provision of social welfare and greater regulation of private-sector workplace conditions.[78]

As we saw in the previous chapters, each of the movements whose stories we tell benefitted from the flexibility with which it pursued its broad agendas. The Salvation Army, like these other religiously orthodox movements, focused on its religious mission and did not have an economic agenda when it began. Beyond this, there is no single pattern by which these movements reprioritized their agendas in response to internal or external crises and opportunities. The Muslim Brotherhood—in parliament, if not in its "state within a state" network—broadened and radicalized its agenda after the turn of the twenty-first century by adding a democracy platform—a confrontational stance in view of Egyptian president Mubarak's authoritarian rule—while also downplaying its strict religious and cultural agendas. Comunione e Liberazione in the 1990s and Shas since the 2003 elections narrowed their agenda sets to concentrate primarily on their theological and economic missions, although Shas also began to broaden the scope of its economic outreach to include all Israelis. Shifting the priorities assigned to agendas allowed these movements to retain their ideological principles while deciding that not all goals were equally important to pursue or likely to succeed at the moment.

Robert Watson, national commander of the Salvation Army USA from 1996 to 1999, attributes part of the Army's success to its clear, unchanging mission—"offer[ing] our 'customers' the same dual 'product' of salvation and service as we did more than a century ago."[79] Yet by all other accounts, including those of insiders to the movement, when William Booth began preaching to the downtrodden in East London in 1865, his goal was to evangelize them, not to ameliorate their material life conditions.[80] Nonetheless, by 1890, under prodding from his wife and fellow evangelist, Catherine, and from Frank Smith, the former commander of the American branch, William Booth had come to believe, "[W]hat is the use of preaching the Gospel to men whose whole attention is concentrated upon a mad, desperate struggle to keep themselves alive?"[81]

Historian Norman Murdoch argues that one factor pushing Booth to accepting an economic mission was that his mission to evangelize London's poor had failed and the Army's membership was falling. Using Booth's own membership statistics, Murdoch shows that Booth's proselytizing mission never caught on in London's slums, mainly because "the dominant Irish Roman Catholic casual workers had instituted cultural norms to shield them against assimilation into English culture. . . . [T]hey particularly opposed Protestant revivalists."[82] By 1877, Booth himself acknowledged that his evangelizing efforts in East London were "stagnating," adding that "if anybody would like to try their hand with London, come along."[83] The Salvationists' evangelical work in New York was faring no better.[84]

Facing failure of the movement's primary mission, Booth sought to renew it through adoption of a second ministry[85]—an economic agenda that we would argue was an expression of his theological communitarianism and that reflected a growing recognition on his part that spiritual poverty and material poverty were intricately connected. Much as sociologist Sam Marullo and his colleagues found that the U.S. peace movement, facing decline from 1988 to 1992, broadened and radicalized (structuralized) its framing,[86] the Army's new social mission can be seen as both broadening its agenda to include an economic ministry and radicalizing it because, as we noted earlier, Booth had come to recognize structural causes of poverty, arguing that the poor were not shiftless but wanted to work, declaring laissez faire capitalism to be "anti-Christian," and offering a detailed social program, the "Darkest England Scheme," to combat poverty.[87]

Booth laid out his ambitious, utopian plan in his book, *In Darkest England and the Way Out,* published in 1890 to raise funds for the movement's new economic mission. The book quickly became a best-seller in both England and the United States.[88] While Booth was listed as the book's sole author, by all accounts Frank Smith, a follower of the progressive Social Gospel movement who had been national commander in the United States after the defection of Thomas Moore, was the architect of the plan.[89]

The Darkest England plan involved instituting three types of "colonies": city, farm, and overseas. The city colony program had, for the most part, already been established by Smith in the United States and consisted of rescue homes, shelters, food depots, workshops, and salvage brigades. The salvage brigades, which had only recently been initiated and which later became the movement's thrift shops, involved taking in used furniture, clothing, books, and similar items that were then repaired by unemployed men and women and sold at low prices to people who could not afford them new. Thus, the brigade provided both work for the unemployed and affordable secondhand merchandise for the poor and working class.

The farm colony would move poor and unemployed people from the city to small, three- to five-acre farms and train them in small-scale farming, as well as teach them how to make bricks, furniture, and clothing. The program would be self-sufficient: Farm colonists would borrow money from the Army and eventually repay the loans with interest.[90]

The overseas colony would resettle England's poor to plots of land donated by British colonial and postcolonial governments. When no land was forthcoming from these countries, Booth moved people anyway, and by 1938 some 250,000 people had emigrated from England to British colonies or former colonies, especially to Canada, where the government helped them find jobs.[91]

While, as we noted earlier, Booth recognized the structural causes of poverty, joblessness, and homelessness, the Darkest England plan was, for the most part, directed at the meso (institutional) or micro (individual) level and not at the macro (societal) level. As Booth wrote in *In Darkest England and the Way Out*, "I make no attempt in this book to deal with society as a whole."[92] In the plan, Booth did not seek a fundamental restructuring of society or takeover of the state; rather he sought to build a set of institutions that would move the poor out of poverty. Salvation Army member and sociologist Ann Woodall contrasts Booth's reaction to the prevailing method of manufacturing safety matches in Britain with that of Karl Marx. Marx wrote in *Capital*, volume 1, on the match-making industry:

> The manufacture of matches dates from 1833, from the discovery of the method of applying phosphorous to the match itself. . . . The manufacture of matches, on account of its unhealthiness and unpleasantness, has such a bad reputation that only the most miserable part of the working class, half-starved widows and so forth, deliver up their children to it. . . . With a working day ranging from 12 to 14 or 15 hours, night labour, irregular meal-times, and meals mostly taken in the workrooms themselves, pestilent with phosphorous, Dante would have found the worst horrors in his Inferno surpassed in this industry.[93]

Marx used conditions in the match-making industry to highlight the need for a workers' revolution to overthrow capitalism.

Booth's approach to such dire working conditions was at the meso level. As an element of his city colony, Booth proposed to establish match factories paying better-than-prevailing wages. He wrote in *In Darkest England:* "[W]e propose at once to commence manufacturing match boxes, for which we shall aim at giving nearly treble the amount at present paid to the poor starving creatures engaged in this work."[94] While Marx's discussion of the match-making industry is clearly part of a larger effort to overturn capitalism, Booth offered instead what Woodall calls "a practical solution to a specific problem."[95] In 1891, Booth founded a factory producing "Lights in Darkest England" matches. The factory paid higher wages and eliminated unhealthy yellow phosphorous from the production process. The cover of the matchbox noted that they were manufactured by the Army's Social Wing and should be bought because they were intended "to raise the wages of the matchmakers, to fight against sweating [sweatshop labor], and to help the poor to help themselves by labour." Over the next decade, competition from Booth's factory forced other match manufacturers to raise their wages and stop using yellow phosphorous, whereupon Booth closed his factory.[96] In establishing his match factory, Booth was also modeling—to employers and workers alike—what a decent workplace should look like.

Despite its reliance on meso- and micro-level solutions, Booth's Darkest England plan won the respect of Marx's co-author and socialist compatriot, Fredrick Engels, who wrote in 1892, "[T]he Salvation Army, which revives the propaganda of early

Christianity, appeals to the poor as the elect, fights capitalism in a religious way, and thus fosters an element of early Christian class antagonism, which one day may become troublesome to the well-to-do people who now find the ready money for it."[97]

To spearhead the Army's new institution-building strategy, in 1890 William Booth appointed Frank Smith as head of the newly created "Social Wing" of the international movement.[98] In the United States, where Ballington and Maud Booth were working in the 1890s to establish an Americanized version of the movement, little progress was made in carrying out Booth's economic program, except for establishing "The Lighthouse" rescue shelters in several cities beginning in 1891.[99] Work on the Darkest England plan began in earnest in the United States with the 1897 appointment of Frederick Booth-Tucker, Booth's son-in-law, as national commander of the Army in the United States. Booth-Tucker framed the Army's new social mission for an American audience, proclaiming that to "nail poverty to a cross of shame and treat it as a crime [is] contrary to the spirit of our American institutions."[100] In contrast to competing social movement organizations, especially the Charity Organization Society, the Salvation Army never drew the individualistic distinction, popular in the United States, between the "deserving" and "undeserving" poor, which placed the responsibility for poverty not on structural conditions or on the nature of capitalism but on the poor themselves.[101]

Booth-Tucker, upon his arrival in the United States in 1897, quickly went to work establishing rescue homes, shelters, hotels, and salvage brigades as elements of Booth's city colony. An 1898 report issued by the U.S. movement stated that the number of the Army's social service institutions had gone from twenty-eight to eighty-five in a single year.[102] Booth-Tucker especially embraced the idea of the farm colony, which he liked to tout to potential donors as a means of linking "the landless man to the manless land."[103] Booth-Tucker was alarmed at what he called "domicide"—"the annihilation of home and family life" in cities, and saw the farm colonies as allowing the relocation, along with their families, of city men, who were often forced to leave their families to look for work. Booth-Tucker also saw the rural setting of the farm colonies as a more positive environment for raising children than the crowded cities. He created three such colonies, and in the military parlance of the Army, called them forts, situating them near Cleveland, Ohio, in eastern Colorado, and in northern California. All failed, mainly because the urban poor sent to them lacked farming skills, a situation repeated in many rural communes of the 1960s. Booth-Tucker, who still had faith in the idea, helped draft a congressional bill to resettle impoverished urban residents on 100,000 acres of irrigated western land. The bill received much media attention, newspaper endorsements, and public support but, due to opposition from western states, never was reported to the congressional floor. Despite Booth-Tucker's efforts, only the institutions that comprised the city colony persist to this day.[104]

The economic mission of the Salvation Army was to become much more extensive in the United States than in Great Britain. This is likely because the British government began providing social insurance covering workers' compensation and retirement pensions as early as 1911, while in the United States the government safety net offered to citizens was much later in arriving and far less comprehensive. Historian Lillian Taiz writes that the very different welfare states in the two countries pushed the Army's missions in different directions: "While the growth of the welfare state enabled the Salvation Army in Britain to deemphasize its social welfare work and reemphasize its working-class religious and temperance role, in the American *semi*-welfare state the Army's social and emergency rescue work continue to serve an important public function."[105] In the context of a weak welfare state, the American branch of the Army constructed religion-infused institutions that bypassed the state: in its early years by providing a safety net for Americans that was not offered by the government and in its later years by complementing the modest efforts of the U.S. state.

Much as the Muslim Brotherhood established businesses to provide services and funding for other units in its network and Comunione e Liberazione made for-profit businesses a large and integral part of its network, Booth-Tucker got the Army involved in several businesses. The American Trade Department, established in the 1880s, sold a wide array of goods, including books, uniforms, musical instruments, flags, lanterns, and stoves. The Army also founded stores selling shoes, tailored goods, dresses, and bonnets, and offering bookbinding services—all based on labor required of clients of the Army's social services. Two companies for which the Army sold stock but held for itself enough common stock to retain control included the Reliance Trading Company, which in 1902 took over all of the Army's merchandising and printing operations, including the production of the *American War Cry*, and the Salvation Army Industrial Homes Company, founded in 1903 to purchase buildings and extend the Army's salvage work, shelters, and food kitchens.[106] Fund-raising for the Army's social mission was aided when an Army captain in San Francisco initiated the first Red Kettle Drive in 1891, which spread nationwide by 1897.[107]

In these enterprises and activities, and in the delivery of social services, Booth-Tucker used the latest business practices to increase the efficiency of the Army's operations,[108] an orientation that can be seen in the observation of one of his successors, National Commander Robert Watson, who served from 1996 to 1999:

> The Salvation Army hasn't grown and prospered for more than a century, eclipsing the life spans of most other enterprises, by ignoring practical business considerations. . . . In strictly business terms, our service recipients are our customers and our supporters are investors. Like any other company, the Army has employees to recruit, train, and retain. It has property to manage. It has revenue streams to monitor and costs to control. It has a brand to protect. And it is as determined

as any business to generate more money than it spends in order to expand its programs and reach an ever-wider "market" of needy people.[109]

Clearly, business acumen, strategic flexibility, and an entrepreneurial bent are key elements of the success story—not just of the Salvation Army but of all of the movements whose stories we tell.

The Army's institution-building economic mission, captured well in the movement's slogan, "Heart to God, hand to man," drew recruits to the movement and quickly won public approval in both the United States and Britain that had been largely withheld from its evangelical mission. Yet the new agenda did not initially sit well with all the movement's core members, many of whom had been attracted to the Army largely for religious reasons. In Britain and the United States, the adoption of a dual mission initially caused conflict between officers promoting evangelical work and those supporting efforts to empower and give assistance to the poor, threatening to split the movement.[110]

In the United States, the Salvation Army began gradually cutting back on its evangelizing street performances to the point that, in Lillian Taiz's words, "Salvationism evolved from a camp-meeting style religion, using the vernacular of urban working-class leisure culture, to a much more decorous religion that combined carefully scripted or choreographed Salvationist rituals, judicious uses of the emerging technologies of middle-class commercial culture, the 'refinement of spectacle,' and restraint of the audience."[111] The shift in strategy was prompted in part by the arrest in 1897 of Fredrick Booth-Tucker for keeping "an ill-governed and disorderly house," following a boisterous all-night revival meeting at his home in New York City.[112] Despite his lawyer's argument that New York was a noisy city anyway and that the Army's meetings were much like earlier forms of revivalist worship, Booth-Tucker was found guilty. Realizing that this kind of publicity could hurt the Army's efforts to raise funds among the wealthy for the movement's economic mission, the Army decided to tamp down its boisterous street tactics. Increasingly, the Army in the United States "focused its spiritual energies inward, toward preserving its own membership, rather than outward, [toward] advertising salvation to the masses."[113]

On August 20, 1912, William Booth, the founder and only general of the international Salvation Army, died in London. As we noted with regard to the death of the founders of the Muslim Brotherhood and Comunione e Liberazione, the death of a movement's charismatic leader can be devastating to a movement. Twenty-two years before Booth was "promoted to Glory," he had ensured his succession by naming his son Bramwell to take over upon his death. The Salvation Army USA had by that point been led by several national commanders, many of them Booth's sons or daughters, so it was used to leadership transitions. Sociologist and fifth president of the American Sociological Association, Edward Allsworth Ross, had written prophetically in 1897 that the Salvation Army was like the Catholic Franciscan order in that: "With age, the vitality of an order comes to reside [not in the] ascendant personality of its founder, but in its models or ideals"[114] or in Max Weber's terms, the source of the movement's legitimacy became less charismatic and more routinized and bureaucratic.[115] Both the parent movement and its American branch continued to thrive.

William Booth's daughter, Evangeline Booth, was Booth-Tucker's successor as national commander of the Army in the United States (1903–1934). She made economic outreach to the disadvantaged and marginalized the Army's top priority. In 1933, at the height of the Great Depression, the Army's economic mission and the need for it had grown to the point that a report of the National Conference of Social Work estimated that 20 percent of the nation's homeless and transient population were being cared for in Salvation Army facilities.[116] Sixty years later in 1993, when sociologist John Hazzard conducted a survey of 252 of the Army's officers, half of them believed that the Army's evangelical and economic missions should be equally important, while the rest were evenly divided on which mission should have priority, suggesting that by then the movement's core saw economic outreach to the poor as a central goal of the movement.[117]

In 2005, the Army unveiled an update to its traditional red shield, adding a non-particularistic, desacralized slogan, "Doing the Most Good," beneath the shield.[118] Yet, today, the Salvation Army still trumpets both its theological and its economic missions on its website. At the time of our writing, the home page of the Army's website prominently proclaims, "We combat natural disasters with acts of God."[119] The Army also highlights its evangelical mission in its fund-raising. For example, an August 14, 2010, solicitation that we received from the Salvation Army Indiana Division featured on the front page of the *County Line Newsletter* an article on the Hidden Falls Camp in Bedford, Indiana, titled "Life Changing Summer," where the experience of one camper, Jerry, is recounted:

> Jerry arrived at camp questioning the very existence of God. He was a smart kid who spent a lot of time watching the History Channel and he had his rebuttal of all things biblical. You see, Jerry was convinced that prayer didn't work. He shared that he used to pray all the time, pleading that God would keep his parents together, even though his dad hit his mom. But, his parents divorced, so God must not listen. Jerry is the kind of kid that Hidden Falls was created to reach. For a brief week or so of each year, kids who would otherwise spend their summer days at home alone while a parent works or wandering streets and neighborhoods find a place to belong at The Salvation Army's Hidden Falls Camp near Bedford. And something special is waiting for each of the nearly 800 campers who choose Hidden Falls, the life-changing message of Jesus Christ.

A HIDDEN CULTURAL MISSION

While the caring side of the Salvation Army's communitarian mission is known to most Americans, few are aware of the movement's cultural agenda. This strict agenda, as we noted earlier, can be seen in the culturally conservative stances the Army has taken in position statements on abortion, homosexuality, marriage, and pornography, among other issues.[120] This agenda is not only a matter of theology; it also has implications for the funding of the Army's economic programs. In 1998, the Human Rights Commission in San Francisco ordered the local branch of the Army either to extend work-related benefits to same-sex partners or to forfeit the $3.5 million that the city annually provided for the Army's social service agencies. The Army's Western Corporation (one of its four national corporations) initially agreed to provide these benefits. Yet in response to an outcry from the Army's officers and a campaign by conservative Christian groups such as Focus on the Family, the Army's national leadership reversed the policy, thus forfeiting the local funding. Said Commissioner Lawrence R. Moretz after the decision, "We must stand united in the battle that will undoubtedly follow from those who would now challenge our biblical and traditional position. . . . We will not sign any government contract or any other funding contracts that contain domestic partner benefit requirements."[121]

In 2002, the Army was again forced to choose between compromising on its cultural agenda of condemning homosexuality or its economic mission of serving the poor in responding to a Portland, Maine, city ordinance requiring that organizations receiving city funding provide health care benefits for domestic partners of employees. The Salvation Army of Portland had been receiving $60,000 annually from the city to deliver meals to the elderly and operate a senior center. The Army decided to turn down the funding rather than provide benefits for same-sex partners.[122] Thus, while the Army's cultural platform is known to few Americans, it sometimes trumps the movement's economic agenda. Such are the dilemmas that multiple-agenda movements like the ones we study have had to address. The Army's decision in these cases to prioritize its cultural agenda over its economic mission may have had its costs beyond the loss of city funds. A campaign by gay, lesbian, bisexual, and transgendered organizations to boycott giving to the Salvation Army may have been responsible for a decline in donations in some cities.[123]

BUILDING FROM THE GROUND UP

Each of the orthodox movements considered here has developed organizational features that allow it to recruit and retain individuals with different issue concerns in different locales. Building grassroots organizational structures, as we have seen with the Muslim Brotherhood, Shas, and Comunione e Liberazione, allows local members to address elements of the movement's ideology and agendas to local understandings and sensibilities and thus recruit a broader swath of constituents, avoid schisms, and tackle a wider array of movement concerns, even if these are not all addressed in all localities at the same time.

The Salvation Army USA, despite the top-down pyramidal structure that "Army" implies, is decentralized, with four corporations or territories in the United States, then further split into divisions, and finally into local "corps" or churches, whose "functions . . . include religious and social services which are adapted to local needs."[124] In its *2010 Annual Report*, the Army reports that it has 1,241 corps (churches) and 6,580 social service centers connected with these.[125] Both the evangelizing and social welfare missions of the Army have always been directed at the grassroots level, with volunteers and staff sometimes drawn from among the recipients of the Army's services. In her ethnography of the Salvation Army Shelter Services Center for the poor and homeless in Sacramento, sociologist Rebecca Anne Allahyari finds that "the social category of 'homeless' often began to fray at the edges with the selective incorporation of the client population into volunteers and then sometimes into staff."[126]

The Army raises funds regionally and locally, not nationally, reflecting its desire to target fund-raising to address local concerns and sensibilities. The movement's *2008 Annual Report* notes that "[N]ew ministry efforts are often launched when local leaders approach us with an idea—or more likely a problem that needs addressing."[127] In Chattanooga, Tennessee, for example, Major Jim Lawrence, drawing on Isaiah 61:4 ("And they shall rebuild the old ruins, they shall raise up the former desolations, and they shall repair the ruined cities"), had an idea for how to use a large space in the old Salvation Army Corps building that had been left vacant after the church was moved to another location. Once the space had been renovated, he put in the ReCreate Café for the homeless. Then Major Lawrence got the idea of incorporating the arts into the space by putting the work of local artists on the walls. He wanted to create a place where the homeless and local artists who need a home or space to work could mix. Says Salvation Army volunteer Tenika Dye, "This is reaching out in a different way. We want to have artists willing to come in and erase those lines between the homeless community and the rest of us." Dye, who had arranged for the musical "Behold the Lamb of God" to be performed on the small stage in the space, says "The idea is that the arts are for everybody. Too many people perceive the homeless as 'drunks or druggies' or otherwise have a negative connotation about them."[128]

Another local effort was initiated in St. Joseph, Missouri, by Emily Cox, the Salvation Army's community center director. Five new programs for children, including Youth Nights, Mission: Literacy, Kid's Club Cooking Class, Brass Music Lessons, and Open Gym Time—all of which are free—were introduced. Hoping to initiate other arts programs for children during the summer months, Cox says, "Different arts, like painting and sculpting, are some of the first things cut from school when they have to cut programs."[129] Here, the Salvation Army is stepping in to provide what the state no longer does.

A surprising example of how much the Army's activities "reflect the unique aspirations and needs of [each] community"[130] is the Ray and Joan Kroc Corps Community Center in San Diego, which was funded by the late Joan Kroc, widow of the founder of McDonald's. In addition to an Army corps (church), the 12.4-acre center has an aquatic complex with three swimming pools, ice arena, rock climbing tower, indoor skateboard park, 600-seat theater for the performing arts, library, gymnasium, computer labs, sports fields, and a Family Enhancement Center that offers parenting and money management classes.[131]

More typically, in inner cities, local Army corps service units direct their efforts in much more modest facilities to meet the needs of a less-affluent clientele through, for example, the fifteen centers that professor of social work Beth Lewis documents in Philadelphia. These include:

> three emergency housing shelters; three transitional housing programs; one tem-
> porary residence for youth awaiting longer-term residential treatment, foster or
> group home placement; one program for developmentally disabled adults; one
> foster care program administering services to 50 foster families and 75 children;
> two residential treatment programs for adults recovering from drug and alcohol
> addiction; one childcare program consisting of nine day care and after-school
> programs; and one program providing supportive services to surrogate families
> and children of incarcerated adults.[132]

In our own locale of rural Indiana, a January 2, 2008, mailing from the Salvation Army Putnam County Service Unit contained the following communitarian appeal to local sensibilities:

> In rural areas like ours, "neighbor helping neighbor" isn't just a turn of phrase.
> It's a way of life. It's the old-fashioned concern for others that provides a safety
> net for each and every one of us when times are rough. In many communities,
> The Salvation Army is the neighbor you can't see. We don't have a community
> center like in the big cities. Instead, we serve those in need through a network of
> volunteers. These could be folks like the fire chief, a police officer or your local
> banker. They're just ordinary people who care about their neighbors. Our volun-
> teers form a community safety net that helps families who are facing hard times
> and have nowhere else to turn.

The appeal to communitarianism, small-town values, and local responsibility for those in need comes through strongly in this Salvation Army fund-raising campaign. Lest one forget the religious purpose behind all of these grassroots activities, the Army's *2008 Annual Report* notes, "though our work usually begins with meeting immediate needs, it rarely ends there, because spiritual transformation is essential for lasting change. Central to our mission is holistic ministry moving beyond the moment's crisis to address deeper spiritual hunger. We call it, 'serving a person into wholeness.'"[133]

Yet studies of the effectiveness of the material and spiritual efforts of the Salvation Army have yielded mixed results. Sociologists David Snow and Leon Anderson con-cluded, based on their ethnographic study of a Salvation Army shelter for the homeless in Austin, Texas, from 1984 to 1986 and in-depth interviews with a subsample of its residents, that the shelter—albeit the only housing for the homeless in the city—was an "accommodative" facility that "help[s] the homeless endure life on the streets rather than escape it."[134] These authors noted, however, that a new Army facility with five full-time social workers and better counseling services was built in Austin in 1988.[135] Sociologist Rebecca Anne Allahyari found through her ethnographic research at the Salvation Army center in Sacramento, California, from 1991 to 1993, that the Army "valued rehabilitation over handouts" and "adhered to a more complex individual and systemic understanding of homelessness that defied simple classification as victim blaming."[136] More recently in 2000, social worker Beth Lewis conducted interviews and focus group sessions with clients of services offered by the Salvation Army in Philadelphia, and concluded that "Service consumers were mostly unaware of the Salvation Army of Greater Philadelphia's religious auspice" and that they most appreciated the Army's "message of inclusion, respect, hope and belief in one's ability to change."[137] These very different reactions to the services offered by the Army may reflect the wide range of years in which the studies were done, the local control of these centers, the differential resource base of local Salvation Army centers, or how much demand for services outstrips the Army's ability to provide them.

PROVIDING GRADUATED LEVELS OF MEMBERSHIP

The Salvation Army, like each of the other movements we chronicle, provides membership structures that allow people to be incorporated into the movement at minimal levels of ideological adherence and commitment and then progress to successively greater levels of these. In its *2010 Annual Report*, the Salvation Army USA lists as personnel 3.4 million volunteers, 400,055 members or "adherents," 107,393 "soldiers," 283 "cadets," and 3,557 "officers."[138] Minimal familiarity with and commitment to the movement's ideology is required of people who contribute to the Army's Christmas Red Kettle Drive or who volunteer occasionally. Adherents consider the Army to be their church, but have not taken the oath of soldiers. Soldiers take vows (called the "Articles of War") pledging their lifelong commitment to the Army's religious doctrine, obedience to its leaders, and abstinence from alcohol, drugs, pornography, profanity, and gambling. After six months, soldiers are eligible to become cadets, whereupon they undertake two years of study at one of the Army's four regional colleges before becoming officers.

In addition to the commitments required of soldiers, officers are expected to marry either another officer or someone who has agreed to enter training to become an officer.[139] The Army takes this rule seriously: In 2008, Captain Johnny Harsh, head of the Army's Oshkosh, Wisconsin, chapter, became engaged to a nurse he had met through an online Christian dating service, after his wife, also a captain in the Army, had died of a heart attack. Because his bride-to-be was not a Salvationist, the Army terminated Harsh, ended his salary, and asked him to move out of the house that the Army provided him.[140] Beyond living by these strict Army regulations, the sacrifice required of officers is reflected in their relatively low pay. National Commander Israel L. Gaither received $241,941 in total compensation (including housing) in 2009, compared to an average of $2,201,540 for the CEOs of the next five largest (by assets) charitable organizations and the $624,225 average salary for the CEOs of the 200 largest charitable organizations in the United States.[141] In addition to relatively frugal salaries, officers and soldiers wear a uniform, which signifies that they are "all cut from the same cloth"[142] and helps to establish a communal identity apart from the larger society.

BYPASSING THE STATE TO ADVANCE THE KINGDOM OF GOD AND HASTEN THE SECOND COMING

As we have seen in the cases of the Muslim Brotherhood, Shas, and Comunione e Liberazione, one of the first decisions that social movement organizations, including religiously orthodox ones, face is whether to work to take over or directly challenge the state or at a minimum participate in government in the hope of making their agendas state policy. The Brotherhood decided in recent years to participate in Egyptian party politics, despite the founder's initial objection to political parties, as well as criticism both within and outside the movement that their participation was legitimizing a state that is not Islamic. Shas, in entering party politics from the start, had to overcome the historical ultra-Orthodox position that, because the Israeli state is governed by secular Zionist principles, Haredim should not serve as ministers in it. And Comunione e Liberazione got involved in party politics in Italy through its Movimento Popolare despite seeing the secular state as overwhelmingly hostile to Christians and as far too large. From its early days in Britain, the position of the Salvation Army was to eschew party politics. Writing in the *War Cry* in 1886, William Booth declared: "[W]e cannot as a religious organization mix ourselves up with one or [an]other political party."[143] As historian and Salvationist Edward McKinley describes it, "The Army's . . . view was that Christ alone was its Candidate, who alone could solve the problems of the world."[144]

Booth's prohibition against engagement in party politics alone would not necessarily have prevented the movement from later deciding that it was advantageous to become a party. As we saw in chapter 2, the Muslim Brotherhood's founder Hasan al-Banna was opposed to the Brotherhood's entering the political arena, but his successors took this step anyway. Yet two characteristics of the political structure in the United States put the Salvation Army in a unique position among these four movements. First, in contrast to the multiparty coalition systems in Egypt, Israel, and Italy that—at least in theory—allow even small parties to affect public policy through their participation in coalitions, the winner-takes-all, two-party system in the United States makes it nearly impossible for small parties to affect policy.[145] Thus, even if the Army had wanted to organize as a political party, as did Shas and the Muslim Brotherhood, it likely would have had little success in affecting legislation.

Second, as sociologists John McCarthy, David Britt, and Mark Wolfson point out, the U.S. tax code grants tax-exempt status to religious organizations and not-for-profit charitable organizations on the condition that such groups refrain from "engaging in any partisan campaign activities and from most other political activities."[146] This is especially the case since the enactment of the Internal Revenue Code of 1959, which specifically forbad such organizations to "participate in, or intervene in (including the publishing or distributing of statements), any political campaign on behalf of any candidate for public office."[147] In the United States, institutional channeling by the state of religious and charitable organizations through the tax code attempts—although not always successfully—to neuter them politically.[148] Had the Army wanted to form a political pressure group, as did Comunione e Liberazione with its Movimento Popolare, tax code would have precluded this. While the tax law in this respect is the same for religious and charitable organizations, the Army insists on registering itself for tax purposes as a church, not a charitable organization. It does this, according to historian and Salvationist Edward McKinley, to highlight its "fundamentalist Christian principles."[149]

For these reasons, bypassing the state for the Salvation Army USA took a different form than it did for the other movements whose stories we tell. In its early years from 1890 through the mid-1930s, the Army implemented social service functions that could well have been performed by the state, but were not, by providing much-needed services to the homeless, unemployed, poor, and sick—services imbued with evangelical Christianity. And in its last six or seven decades, the Army's faith-based services complemented the modest efforts of the nation's welfare state.

Yet despite the limitations that the American political context put on what the Army could do politically and despite the fact that the movement rarely directly challenged the state, the movement's purpose throughout much of its history has been, broadly speaking, political. Writing about the temperance and abolitionist movements as the first national, "life politics" movements in the United States, sociologist Michael Young argues that national social movements

> are collective struggles that attempt to impact a (national) community's patterns of obligations, interactions and identifications, and that trigger resistance. . . . [P]rotests that challenge influential institutions are political in the broad sense of the word even if they do not specifically target state institutions. . . . The forms, purposes, and sources of these movements are not exclusively, or even primarily, tied to interactions with the state, but they are no less political or contentious because of this.[150]

The Salvation Army, in the early years of its guerrilla theater tactics, was political in this broader sense of confronting and challenging mainstream secular and religious institutions and Americans' moral priorities, materialism, and often-condemning attitudes toward the less fortunate. And sociologists Elizabeth Armstrong and Mary Bernstein would argue from the "multi-institutional politics approach" to social movements that movements targeting societal institutions are as much political as those targeting the state.[151]

Moreover, despite its official nonpartisan stance, the Army has advanced its agendas in the political arena throughout its history. On the cultural front, a pressing political issue for the Army from the late nineteenth century to the early twentieth century was prohibiting the sale and consumption of alcohol. The Army's anti-alcohol position stemmed from the belief that using alcohol is a sin and can lead to joblessness, poverty, and immorality.[152] While the Army did not actively support the Prohibition Party in the 1880s, it lobbied hard against repeal of the Eighteenth Amendment (Prohibition) in the 1920s and according to historian and Salvationist Edward McKinley, for the only time in its history, endorsed a presidential candidate, Herbert Hoover, in 1928 because he favored continuing Prohibition.[153] More recently, in 1990, the Army, along with other groups in the Religious Alliance against Pornography, lobbied the White House against "child pornography and illegal obscenity."[154] In 2001, Salvationists secretly lobbied the White House for an exemption from requirements that faith-based service providers not discriminate in hiring on the basis of sexual orientation in order to receive locally distributed federal funds. In return, the Army promised to spend $100,000 a month lobbying on behalf of President George W. Bush's charitable choice initiative, which promoted faith-based service provision. When these discussions with the White House were leaked to the press, the Bush administration backed off its plan to exempt faith-based providers from local antidiscrimination laws and the Army decided not to lobby for the Bush charitable choice initiative.[155]

While the Army officially has taken a neutral position on labor issues, in 1894 it collected and distributed food for starving railroad strikers in the Pullman strike, winning praise from the strike's socialist leader, Eugene V. Debs, as "Christianity in action."[156] The Army's newspaper, the *American War Cry*, often carried stories on the deplorable conditions in the nation's slums, factories, and sweatshops.[157] An article published in 1897, for example, was no less condemning of sweatshop production in the United States than was Karl Marx of match production in England. The article editorialized: "It is difficult, in some respects, to see what advantage the sweatshop system . . . has over the serfdom of Russia. The vision dims in contemplation of its damning effects, and one is led to wonder at the glaring falsity of commercial ethics which permits the sacrifice of human flesh and blood for the sake of producing ultra-cheap articles of clothing."[158] As we mentioned above, Fredrick Booth-Tucker helped draft a bill at the turn of the last century that would have opened up acreage in the West to settlement by the urban poor. On another front, the Army in 1895 condemned in the strongest terms lynching in the United States; in the same year, two Salvationists tried unsuccessfully to stop the lynching of an African American man in Frederick, Maryland.[159]

More recently, the social justice focus of the Salvation Army comes across in a 2008 report in the Army's magazine, *Caring*, entitled "What Would Jesus Do?" The report notes "We are—and we remain—actively engaged in politically oriented lobbying on Capitol Hill," citing as the basis for this activity Proverbs 31:9—"Speak up for the poor and see that they get justice."[160] The Army employs "legally trained lobbyists" for this purpose and is allowed by U.S. tax code to spend up to 5 percent of its annual revenue on lobbying or up to $125 million, based on its (nongovernmental) revenue of $2.5 billion, as reported in the Army's *2010 Annual Report*.[161] Although the actual amount spent on lobbying is probably well below this figure, the Army gives no separate listing for lobbying in its annual reports. The *Caring* article notes that the Army has recently lobbied the government for "more funds to combat homelessness issues, hunger and poverty," in support of "charitable giving [tax] incentives," and against religious persecution in Sudan, human trafficking worldwide, elder abuse in nursing homes, and prison rape.[162] In lobbying on these issues, the Army promotes a communitarian notion, common in many West European welfare states, of citizenship as including social rights—in the Army's words, "All people have a right to secure the basic necessities of life (e.g., food, clothing, shelter, housing, education, health care, safe environment, economic security)"—a view that goes beyond the common American perception of citizenship as limited to civil and political rights.[163] This may explain why it is more palatable to many citizens and local governments to contract out social services to private charitable organizations like the Salvation Army rather than provide these services directly. In pushing the state to expand its efforts to meet the basic needs of citizens, any leverage or credibility that the Salvation Army has is undoubtedly due to the massive size and critical importance of its institutional network, not to the small number of worshippers (400,055) who consider the Army to be their church.[164]

The Salvation Army seeks, through its faith-based institution-building, to advance what it sees as the Kingdom of God on Earth and hasten the Second Coming of Christ.[165] Unlike the Muslim Brotherhood and Shas, the Army does not explicitly advocate making religious law the legal foundation of society. Its lobbying on behalf of laws and policies that are in accord with elements of its theology are akin to Comunione e Liberazione's Movimento Popolare that spearheaded the Catholic Church's efforts to end abortion and divorce in Italy, although CL's efforts were far more visible than those of the Salvation Army and focus on cultural, not economic issues.

In the context of the minimalist welfare state in the United States, the Salvation Army's extensive economic network appears today to be viewed by the movement, the state, and the public as complementing rather than challenging or competing with the efforts of federal, state, and city governments vis-à-vis the poor. President George W. Bush welcomed the involvement of voluntaristic, especially faith-based, organizations in the delivery of social services,[166] and his successor, Barak Obama, has established his own Office of Faith-Based and Neighborhood Partnerships.[167] We noted in chapter 2 that the immediate and highly successful response of the doctors of the Muslim

Brotherhood to the 1992 earthquake in Cairo served as a tacit indictment of the Egyptian state's ability to look out for its citizens. The Salvation Army's response in helping those affected by Hurricane Katrina in 2005 was praised by the *Wall Street Journal* "for its swift arrival in the most distressed areas and clearly winning the hearts of desperate residents." The effectiveness of the Army's response was attributed to its years of work with poor and homeless people in the area and its "military-style structure, which is designed for rapid mobilization and which puts a premium on training people in advance to deal with disasters."[168] Although there was much criticism of the U.S. government's delayed and ineffectual response to Katrina, this did not lead most Americans to press for a larger role of government in the handling of disasters or in ameliorating the poverty that was revealed by the hurricane. In disaster relief as in poverty relief, while many Americans expect government to play a role, they seem to prefer that such matters be handled primarily by nongovernmental agencies, funded by charitable donations, and carried out by volunteers.[169] Thus, the Salvation Army is seen as filling an important niche rather than as competing with the U.S. government or putting the state's modest efforts to shame.

In a characterization we dispute, sociologist Rebecca Anne Allahyari situates the Salvation Army today in what geographer Jennifer Wolch calls the "'shadow state'—a para-state apparatus comprised of multiple voluntary sector organizations . . . charged with major collective service responsibilities previously shouldered by the public sector, yet remaining within the purview of state control."[170] We argue it is incorrect to describe the Salvation Army as a "nonprofit for hire"[171] or as "street-level bureaucrats"[172] within the shadow state, as does Allahyari.[173] First, this assumes that the Salvation Army would not pursue its economic mission if state funding were unavailable—an assumption belied by the fact that the Army began its social service mission decades before it accepted state funding. Second, this characterization assumes that state funding hamstrings much of the activities of the Army, when only 14 percent of the Army's annual revenue comes from the government.[174] Even for state-funded services, the Army still has its name, the *Salvation* Army, on these services and is able to put its unique stamp on them. Clients of state-funded services may choose to participate as well in the Army's faith-based programs or attend the Army's church services, typically located in a nearby corps. Third, while the Army's tax status as a church limits its participation in party politics, this clearly has not prevented the movement from lobbying the president and Congress on behalf of its cultural and economic agendas. Finally, the Army has shown no reluctance to assert its independence from the state when the Army feels that state funding comes at the cost of its theological principles and cultural agendas. As we discussed, the Army has been willing to turn down state funding on principle when it has been required to accept the equivalence of same-sex domestic partners and heterosexual spouses, thus ensuring for itself some autonomy from the state.

The Salvation Army has built its extensive network of alternative institutions, not to replace the state with one governed by religious law, as the Muslim Brotherhood and Shas intend, nor to build a parallel Christian society that could eventually assume many of the functions of the state, as Comunione e Liberazione hopes, but to permeate American society with Christian-inspired institutions in the hope of advancing what it sees as the Kingdom of God on Earth and the Second Coming of Christ.

CONCLUSIONS

The evangelical Protestant Salvation Army USA bypassed the state by building a vast network of religion-based economic institutions that have today made it the nation's largest charitable organization. While many Americans are unaware of the religious basis of the Army's economic outreach, for the movement's core—and, no doubt, for some of the Army's clients—these services are infused with a spiritual purpose. The Army shares with the other movements whose stories we have told a theological communitarianism that emphasizes divinely ordained strict rules on cultural matters, as well as caring, mutual responsibility, and spiritual equality as the bases for action on economic matters. Like these other movements, the Salvation Army puts words into deeds by building institutions to sacralize individuals, families, communities, and society. Like the Muslim Brotherhood and Shas, but unlike Comunione e Liberazione, the Army centers its outreach on local centers of worship—corps. And like the other movements, the Army benefits from a grassroots organizational structure that allows local members to identify and work on issues of concern to their communities, thus bringing in a diverse range of people with different local concerns and sensibilities, and accomplishing different elements of the movement's agenda in cities, towns, and rural communities throughout the country.

Just as each of the movements we chronicle is unique in its own way, the Salvation Army USA has its distinctive elements. First, the Army lacks a key feature that the three other movements share—a religious schooling system that socializes the next generation into the movement's theological precepts. The Army has created four two-year colleges to train its cadets and has established schools in countries of the Global South, but to our knowledge has never considered establishing its own schools for children in the United States.

Second, William Booth's decision to eschew party politics, together with the American winner-takes-all, two-party system and restrictions on engaging in partisan electoral politics imposed upon tax-exempt religious organizations, have meant that the Army has not entered the arena of party politics as the other movements have. Nonetheless, the Army is clearly political in a broader sense and lobbies Congress and the president behind the scenes for its theological, cultural, and economic agendas. The Army bypassed the state in its early years by constructing a broad network of autonomous institutions that provided social services for the most marginalized of Americans that were not offered by the government. In its later years, the Army's network has continued to bypass the state by filling gaps in the weak U.S. welfare state's delivery of services to the poor, homeless, unemployed, and sick with its own faith-infused institutions.

Third, although all of these movements would see their primary objective as sacralizing society, the Army's theological aim in bypassing the state by building a massive network of faith-inspired alternative institutions—hastening the Second Coming—differs from the motivation behind the institution-building of the other three movements. The Brotherhood and Shas seek more direct control over the state and then establishment of religious law as state law, while Comunione e Liberazione is working to build a parallel Christian society that would partly replace the state but is not explicitly aimed at bringing about the Kingdom of God on Earth.

Peter Drucker's homage to the Salvation Army USA as "the most effective organization in the U.S."[175] could well be true of the Army's efforts in building a vast network of economic outreach to the dispossessed. Yet, despite the word "Salvation" in its name, TV advertisements that cite Scripture and explicitly mention the religious basis of its services, mail-order solicitations that include prayer cards, and copies of its clearly evangelical *War Cry* available at the movement's thrift stores and other institutions, the Salvation Army USA has been less successful in getting across its religious message than in accomplishing its economic goals. Perhaps because references to God, prayer, and blessings so permeate popular and political culture in the United States, many Americans today are unaware that the Salvation Army is as much a religious movement as it is an organization helping those in need.[176] In moving away from the boisterous, guerrilla theater evangelizing of its early years to become a more "respectable" movement with a multipronged agenda, the Salvation Army USA may have toned down its religious message to the point where many Americans cannot hear it.

CONCLUSION

By telling the stories of the Muslim Brotherhood in Egypt, the Sephardi To-rah Guardians or Shas in Israel, Comunione e Liberazione in Italy, and the Salvation Army in the United States, we have shown that the focus today in much scholarship and the media on the most violent of "fundamentalist" religious movements misses the fact that many of the most prominent, enduring, and effective religiously orthodox movements in the world today are pursuing a patient, gradualist, low-profile strategy, not one of suicide bombings and armed struggle. This strategy bypasses the state by setting up vast, nationwide networks of alternative institutions aimed at infusing civil society, and in some cases the state, with a renewed religious sensibility. Of the four movements whose stories we tell, only one, the Muslim Brotherhood, used violence at any point in its history, and this was in the context of a highly repressive Egyptian state that arrested, tortured, and killed many of the movement's members and disbanded the movement twice. During the Brotherhood's early years, its paramilitary Secret Apparatus used armed struggle, but since the late 1960s, the Brotherhood has disavowed violence. And from the start, the primary strategy of the Brotherhood's founder, Hasan al-Banna, was to build alternative institutions that would Islamicize and empower the Egyptian people in the hope of eventually winning enough popular support to estab-lish an Islamic order with the shari'a as the law of the land.

The facile dismissal of the participants in religiously orthodox movements as ir-rational, perhaps because they are not pursuing individualistic economic interests, fails to understand their underlying communitarian logic. The communitarian "watching over" of members of their community and society pushes religiously orthodox move-ments to make what they see as divinely inspired laws the legal foundation of society and to impose strict, authoritarian standards on sexuality, family, and gender but also to establish institutions to meet the needs of poor and disadvantaged fellow citizens. As we have shown for the four movements we chronicle, the communitarian theology of orthodox movements is internally consistent and logical, but conventional one-dimensional models of political space that array political stances on a single left–right continuum fail to capture it, making these movements appear irrational or inconsis-tent in their ideology and agendas.

The strict, authoritarian, punitive side of these movements in seeking to impose religious law on citizens, to limit sexual expression, to narrow the roles available to men and women, to forbid or limit divorce, and to restrict reproductive rights is certainly a concern to us and others who are working toward gender equality and the rights of sexual and religious minorities. Nonetheless, the failure to acknowledge what we have called the caring side of such movements, which leads them to build medical clinics, employment agencies, social welfare programs, hospices, and businesses paying better-than-average wages, is a serious shortcoming of much scholarship and media commentary on the religiously orthodox. Even when the economic outreach of orthodox movements is recognized, it is often dismissed as mere charity.[1] Yet, as we have shown, it is from this caring side or "egalitarian face" that much of the institution-building of these movements stems, to which they owe their continuity through crises of disbandment, mission failure, and leadership scandals or succession, and from which comes much of their popular support.

Bypassing the state to set up a vast network of alternative religious, cultural, and economic institutions is the strategy-in-common of the four movements whose stories we tell in this book. Because the attention of scholars of politics and social movements has often been directed to efforts that directly challenge or at the least engage the state—demonstrations, boycotts, building takeovers, general strikes, and armed struggle—the possibility of less visible, more patient, seemingly nonpolitical strategies that might accomplish the same ends has rarely been understood. Yet the commonality of this strategy among four of the most prominent and effective religiously orthodox movements in four different Abrahamic faith traditions and four different national settings suggests that it merits serious consideration.

As our cases well illustrate, bypassing the state can take a variety of forms, no doubt including ones not represented by the four movements whose stories we chronicle. The Muslim Brotherhood and Shas have worked to sacralize their societies by establishing states within states in their countries in the hope of ultimately controlling the state. The aim of Comunione e Liberazione is different: It is opposed to a strong state and seeks to build a parallel Christian society in Italy whereby spiritual, cultural, and material needs are met at the most immediate local level by individuals, social service organizations, and affiliated businesses, thus obviating the need for an extensive state. The Salvation Army USA bypassed the state in its early years by offering services that were not provided to the marginalized by the government. In more recent decades, the Army has circumvented the state by working to fill gaping holes in the safety net offered by the weak U.S. welfare state.

How bypassing the state relates to involvement in the formal political arena also differs for these four movements. For the Muslim Brotherhood, circumventing the repressive Egyptian state was both an end in itself and a prelude to involvement in politics; the hope was that the Islamization of society brought about through the movement's social and economic outreach and control of institutions in civil society (professional associations, student unions, schools, mosques, etc.) would help establish a solid base of popular support that would ultimately propel the Brotherhood to power electorally. Shas has a paradoxical relationship with the Israeli state: directly participating in the state in order to bypass it. Shas entered electoral politics from the start and discovered it could use its lynchpin position in governing coalitions to secure funding for what ultimately became a nearly autonomous surrogate state providing a wealth of educational, social, and economic services. It then used these services to garner the support of larger segments of Mizrahi voters, the majority of whom are not ultra-Orthodox, and to make further demands on the state for resources. In Italy, the involvement of Comunione e Liberazione in party politics occurred prior to much of the movement's institution-building, and the aim of this was not to wrest resources from the state but to enact into law the movement's strict cultural agendas on abortion and divorce. Only after its efforts in the formal political realm failed did CL seize on the strategy of bypassing the state to set up a parallel Christian society. Unlike Shas or the Muslim Brotherhood, CL distrusts a powerful state; it idealizes the weak state/strong church model of medieval Europe. The Salvation Army, although political in a broader sense and in its engagement of the state through behind-the-scenes lobbying, eschewed involvement in electoral politics from the start. Even if the Army had wanted to establish a political party, it would have been prevented from doing so in the United States by the politically neutering effects of U.S. tax policy for churches and by the extreme difficulty of establishing a new party in a two-party political system. Today the Army limits its political engagement to lobbying for its culturally strict and economically caring agendas.

While all of these movements seek to obey and please God with their missions, their ultimate aims differ. The Muslim Brotherhood and Shas seek to establish states governed solely by divine law. Comunione e Liberazione is working to bring about a Christian society that will constitute a "true company of Jesus" and will demonstrate that there is no need for as extensive a state as currently exists in Italy. The Salvation Army's aim—the postmillennial goal of hastening the Second Coming—is not state takeover, as it is for the Brotherhood and Shas; it is something more like the objective of Comunione e Liberazione in establishing a Christian society. For the Salvation Army, however, the aim is to reshape the world via faith-infused service institutions and thus prepare the way for the return of Christ.

Viewed from the perspective of civil society, each of these movements is working to permeate civil society with religiously imbued institutions, symbols, and narratives—in effect, to capture civil society. This can involve the building of new religious, cultural, educational, and economic institutions. It can also entail "burrowing into" existing organizations through the electoral takeover of professional associations and student unions, moving into neighborhoods, seizing unoccupied building sites, and permeating the airwaves with pirate radio stations. From Elizabeth Armstrong and Mary Bernstein's "multi-institutional politics approach," these movements are targeting not just the state, as the political opportunity structure (POS) approach would assume, but many institutions, with different underlying logics, using different strategies (building, burrowing) to effect institutional takeover.[2]

Through their efforts to penetrate the institutions of society, these movements have established vast networks of organizations, associations, clubs, agencies, schools, businesses, and places of worship. Certainly, none of these movements has fully "captured" civil society, but to varying degrees they have been able to gain a solid foothold. In a sense, the networks that these movements are establishing within their countries have "holes" in them, where some geographical areas and populations are not being reached, some needs are not being addressed, and some movement agendas are only incompletely accomplished. Yet as the network of worship centers, schools, social service agencies, affiliated businesses, and informal outreach is gradually filled in and becomes more and more dense, the movements are that much closer to installing their brand of religion at the center of society. A Gramscian analysis of the civil societies being established by these movements might view them as a form of resistance to the state since the members of most of these movements certainly consider themselves to be oppressed (or "embattled" in Christian Smith's terms[3]) by the secular state. The faith-imbued institutional networks they establish, with the possible exception of that of the Salvation Army, are resisting and/or contesting the state.

Bypassing the state helps religiously orthodox movements overcome what scholars of social movements have identified as three serious obstacles to movement success: (1) ideological rigidity or moral absolutism, (2) broad, multipronged agendas, and (3) a strong reluctance to compromise with other groups and individuals. Sidestepping the state helps overcome the obstacle of moral absolutism by allowing skeptics to "try on" the movements' alternative worship centers, schools, hospitals, businesses, and social service agencies in order to see what life might be like if the movements' ideology were put into practice society-wide. Grassroots structures help overcome the obstacle that this moral absolutism might present by allowing local members to build institutions from the ground up: identifying local needs, focusing on specific elements of the movement's ideology that could be used to address these needs, and working with others in the community to build institutions that turn the movement's words into deeds.[4] Bypassing the state in a decentralized, grassroots manner helps overcome the obstacle that ambitious multipronged agendas pose by dispersing the agendas across the country to be accomplished through bottom-up efforts in local communities and associations, rather than tackling them all at once through a top-down, nationwide effort. This allows the many agendas to be worked on, even if this is done piecemeal, here and there. And bypassing the state helps overcome the obstacle that reluctance to compromise presents to orthodox movements. Their decentralized institution-building allows groups and individuals across the country with different interests and concerns to be incorporated and empowered as they work on local matters without the movement having to compromise in bringing them in.

In the course of studying these four orthodox movements, we uncovered two other strategies that they share. First, each of these movements allows initiates to enter the movement without having to accept the movement's ideology and program "whole cloth." At the lowest levels of participation, many of those involved are not religiously orthodox. Each of the movements we study provides membership categories or forms of participation representing successively greater sacrifice and ideological commitment, to the point that at the highest level, they are "greedy institutions"[5] demanding nearly all of the participants' time, effort, and loyalty. At this highest level, individuals take vows of obedience to the movement's principles and leaders, devote their lives to the study of its theology/ideology, give up family ties, and remain celibate or marry only someone who is making similar commitments. It is at this highest level that the movement's ideology and behavioral prescriptions—rigid as they are—are accepted at their fullest, allowing those with lower levels of commitment to be incorporated "where they are." It is also at this highest level that the movement's ideology continues in its purest form, surviving whatever local tailoring is needed where the movement has its feet on the ground.

Second, each of the four movements creatively shifted among its agendas in response to external and internal crises and opportunities. None of the movements began with all of the agendas that it later developed. In each case, an economic agenda was added—usually early on—to what were originally theological and cultural platforms. Nor was there a consistent pattern of agenda reprioritizing and/or reframing that was used by all of the movements to survive crises of membership, mission failure, or changing political opportunity structures.

The Salvation Army initially broadened and radicalized its agenda to include an economic mission and recognition of structural causes of poverty, then downplayed its religious and culturally conservative agendas with the public. The Muslim Brotherhood, in the electoral realm if not in its state-within-a-state network, broadened and radicalized its agenda by adding a democracy platform but also downplayed its religious and conservative cultural agendas in the Egyptian Parliament. Comunione e Liberazione and Shas narrowed their agenda sets somewhat to concentrate more on their religious and economic agendas, although Shas also began to broaden the scope of its economic mission to include all Israelis, not just Mizrahi Jews. Maintaining flexibility of agendas—"bending with the wind" as sociologist Debra Minkoff aptly calls this[6]—appears to be the lesson here. While otherwise there was no common pattern of rebalancing agendas among the four movements, the practice of prioritizing and reprioritizing agendas gave these movements the flexibility that their strict, absolutist ideologies and reluctance to compromise with other political actors did not, allowing them to downplay goals that failed or were unlikely to be achieved without destroying the entire movement, add new agendas to capture new constituents when the political opportunity structure allowed, deemphasize an agenda with the general public while it continued with core members, and/or rebalance the agendas so that they had the broadest appeal. In contrast, when most single-issue movements fail at getting their agenda implemented, they decline or dissolve.[7]

The four movements chronicled here show that comprehensive agendas, ideological strictness, and reluctance to negotiate can be handled with strategy. Yet we suspect that generally these features *are* disadvantageous for movements. We note, however, an exception that could be explored in future research—the possibility that combinations of these liabilities may in fact be advantageous. Our research suggests that if a movement is ideologically strict or if it finds compromise extremely difficult, it may be beneficial for it to also have a broad, multi-issue agenda. Comprehensive agendas allow such movements to deploy two strategies—addressing different agendas to different local constituencies and reprioritizing agendas—giving them leeway that single-issue movements lack.

The religiously orthodox movements whose stories we have told are pursuing agendas that are communitarian both culturally (seeking strict regulation of sexuality, family life, and gender) and economically (seeking greater intervention by the community and/or state into the economy to help people in need). Of course, as we mentioned in the introduction, not all orthodox movements pursue communitarian agendas on both the cultural and economic fronts, and some pursue different combinations of these agendas. Do these other sorts of orthodox movements also use the strategy of bypassing the state? One of the most prominent charismatic Protestant movements in the United States today is the New Apostolic Reformation (NAR, http://www .newapostolicchurch.org), which combines a culturally strict agenda on homosexuality and abortion with support of laissez faire, individualistic economic policy. The NAR has used institution-building in establishing churches, but its primary strategy is similar to the "burrowing into" strategy used by the Muslim Brotherhood and Comunione e Liberazione in winning control of professional syndicates and/or student unions. The movement believes that the key institutions in society—the "seven mountains" of the arts, business, education, family, government, media, and religion—are now controlled by demons. The aim of the movement is to take dominion or control over these institutions by casting out the demons and replacing them with "Kingdom-minded" believers ("apostles") as a means of establishing the Kingdom of God on Earth.[8] This explicitly "multi-institutional politics approach"[9] is akin to those used by the Muslim Brotherhood, Shas, Comunione e Liberazione, and the Salvation Army USA to transform their societies.

Could it be that the religious orthodoxy of the movements we have chronicled, and not their artful strategy, allowed them to thrive? Each of these movements benefitted from being situated within a national context in which its faith tradition was dominant, allowing it to draw on religious narratives, resources, and symbols that have strong cultural resonance, although they also challenged existing interpretations of theology, religious institutions, and clerical authorities as having compromised with secular modernity. The Salvation Army, the Muslim Brotherhood, and Shas centered their religious, cultural, and economic institutions on local churches, mosques, or synagogues that they constructed or controlled, thus allowing them to build on one of the predominant and long-standing bases of civil society in their societies, while Comunione e Liberazione instead built its institutions around the "environment"—the high schools, universities, and workplaces where people live much of their lives. Believing that a divine force enjoins them to carry out their missions almost certainly gave the leaders and followers of these movements exceptional motivation and certainty,[10] although as sociologist James Jasper argues, participants in secular movements who see their mission(s) as having a moral imperative and/or historical inevitability may also be highly motivated.[11] Undoubtedly, the religious nature and context of these movements is partly responsible for their success, but their religious orthodoxy also gave them extraordinarily ambitious and difficult-to-achieve goals, limited their ability to maneuver ideologically, and hamstrung them in political give-and-take with those who might have been won over to their cause, requiring strategic innovation in overcoming these obstacles.

Is bypassing the state unique to movements of the orthodox? The strategy itself is not specifically religious and has been used by secular movements to overcome similar obstacles. Sidestepping the state, coupled with militant, confrontational tactics, was used by the Black Panther Party in the United States of the 1960s. The Panthers set up "survival programs" centered on local branches in inner cities, offering free breakfasts for children; employment services; medical clinics; distribution of free clothing, shoes, and food; cooperative housing programs; security services for the elderly; pest control services; police-alert patrols; ambulance services; and alternative "liberation schools."[12] The Black Panther Party used the discourse of a state within a state when it organized itself into ministries (finance, culture, health, and so on). Panther programs embodied the movement's frame of black self-determination, modeled community control, and empowered African Americans on the local level,[13] much as the four movements we chronicled empower their followers. Rejecting the notion that the Panther programs were merely reformist, the movement's co-founder Huey Newton observed, "We called them survival programs pending revolution. . . . They were designed to help the people survive until their consciousness is raised; which is only the first step in the revolution to produce a new America."[14]

The feminist movement in the United States is another largely secular movement that established nonprofit community services (for example, women's health clinics, shelters for abused women, rape crisis centers, reproductive health centers, feminist bookstores, and music festivals) aimed at prefiguring a world of gender justice.[15] The peace and conflict resolution movements in South Africa, Northern Ireland, Israel, and Palestine are other movements that established NGOs (such as human rights organizations, peace education centers, conflict-tracking organizations, trauma clinics for victims, cross-community dialogue groups, and research institutes) that portended the kind of world they desired.[16] Bypassing the state is clearly not unique to religiously orthodox movements.

Regardless of whether one subscribes to the aims of the four movements whose stories we have told, there is much to appreciate about them as movements. They have overcome schisms; failure of key missions; disbandment; government repression; violence directed at them by the state, other groups, or the general public; leadership scandals; and/or the deaths of their founders. They have developed a highly innovative movement strategy—bypassing the state—to overcome the substantial obstacles that their ideological strictness; highly ambitious, multipronged agendas; and reluctance to compromise present. They have been extraordinarily flexible in responding to changing political opportunity structures in their societies and to internal opportunities and crises. They have shown a strong entrepreneurial spirit in building effective social service agencies, medical facilities, schools, and businesses that often put the state's efforts to shame. For three of the movements—the Muslim Brotherhood, Comunione e Liberazione, and the Salvation Army—they have had not only a society-wide impact in their respective countries but also an effect in scores of countries across the world. While they are not the Christian militias, al-Qaeda cells, or Jewish extremist groups whose terrorism has directly confronted states around the world and has of late attracted much scholarly and media attention, the Muslim Brotherhood, Shas, Comunione e Liberazione, and the Salvation Army USA, with their patient, entrepreneurial, under-the-radar strategy of rebuilding society, one institution at a time, from the ground up, may well prove more successful in sacralizing their societies than movements that use violence.

NOTES

INTRODUCTION

1. While some social movement scholars distinguish between broad movements (e.g., the feminist movement) and the social movement organizations (SMOs) that comprise them (e.g., the National Organization for Women), we adopt the more conventional parlance of referring to both of these as movements.

2. See, e.g., Mark Juergensmeyer, *Terror in the Mind of God: The Global Rise of Religious Violence*, 3rd ed. (Berkeley: University of California Press, 2003); Jessica Stern, *Terror in the Name of God: Why Religious Militants Kill* (New York: Harper Perennial, 2004); Bruce Hoffman, *Inside Terrorism* (New York: Columbia University Press, 2006); "God's Warriors: Jewish Warriors, Muslim Warriors, Christian Warriors," *CNN*, reported by Christiane Amanpour, August 21–23, 2007.

3. See David A. Snow and Scott C. Byrd, "Ideology, Framing Processes, and Islamic Terrorist Movements," *Mobilization* 12 (2007): 119–136; Marc Sageman, *Understanding Terror Networks* (Philadelphia: University of Pennsylvania Press, 2004).

4. See, e.g., Frank Shaeffer, *Crazy for God: How I Grew Up as One of the Elect, Helped Found the Religious Right, and Lived to Take All (or Almost All) of It Back* (New York: Carroll and Graf, 2007). For a critique of the irrationality argument, see Rhys H. Williams, "Movement Dynamics and Social Change: Transforming Fundamentalist Ideology and Organization," in *Accounting for Fundamentalisms: The Dynamic Character of Movements*, ed. Martin E. Marty and R. Scott Appleby, 785–833 (Chicago: University of Chicago Press, 1994).

5. See, e.g., Sara Diamond, *Spiritual Warfare: The Politics of the Christian Right* (Montreal: Black Rose Books, 1990); Gordon Urquhart, *The Pope's Armada: Unlocking the Secrets of Mysterious and Powerful New Sects in the Church* (Amherst, N.Y.: Prometheus Books, 1999).

6. Nancy J. Davis and Robert V. Robinson, "The Egalitarian Face of Islamic Orthodoxy: Support for Islamic Law and Economic Justice in Seven Muslim-Majority Nations," *American Sociological Review* 71 (2006): 167–190.

7. Islamists (often called Islamic fundamentalists) seek the creation of an Islamic political order run according to Islamic law (the shari'a).

8. Noah J. Efron, *Real Jews: Secular vs. Ultra-Orthodox and the Struggle for Jewish Identity in Israel* (New York: Basic, 2003), 54.

9. Mario B. Mignone, *Italy Today: Facing the Challenges of the New Millennium* (New York: Peter Lang, 2008), 289.

10. William P. Barrett, "America's 200 Largest Charities," *Forbes.com*, November 17, 2010, http://www.forbes.com/2010/11/16/forbes-charity-200-personal-finance-philanthropy -200-largest-charities-charity-10-intro.html (accessed March 13, 2011).

11. See, e.g., Roberta Ash, *Social Movements in America* (Chicago: Markham, 1972); William Gamson, *The Strategy of Social Protest*, 2nd ed. (Belmont, Calif.: Wadsworth, 1990); Richard L. Wood, "Religious Culture and Political Action," *Sociological Theory* 17 (1999): 307–332; Vernon L. Bates, "The Decline of a New Christian Right Social Movement Organization: Opportunities and Constraints," *Review of Religious Research* 42 (2000): 19–40; Neil Fligstein, "Social Skill and the Theory of Fields," *Sociological Theory* 19 (2001): 105–125; Ellen Reese and Garnett Newcombe, "Income Rights, Mothers' Rights, or Workers' Rights? Collective Action Frames, Organizational Ideologies, and the American Welfare Rights Movement," *Social Problems* 50 (2003): 294–318; Marshall Ganz, "Why David Sometimes Wins: Strategic Capacity in Social Movements," in *The Psychology of Leadership: New Perspectives and Research: New Perspectives and Research*, ed. David M. Messick and Roderick M. Kramer, 209–238 (Mahwah, N.J.: Lawrence Erlbaum, 2005).

12. Scott Wilson, "Hamas Sweeps Palestinian Elections," *Washington Post*, January 27, 2006.

13. Adam Entous, "U.S.-Backed Campaign against Hamas Expands to Charities," Reuters, August 20, 2007, http://www.reuters.com/article/worldNews/idUSL2027514420070820 (accessed April 15, 2011).

14. Michael Slackman, "Mohamed Sayed Tantawi, Top Cleric, Dies at 81," *New York Times*, March 10, 2010; John L. Esposito, *The Oxford Dictionary of Islam* (New York: Oxford University Press, 2003), 32.

15. Marco G. Giugni, "Was It Worth the Effort? The Outcomes and Consequences of Social Movements," *Annual Review of Sociology* 98 (1998): 371–393.

16. Gabriel A. Almond, R. Scott Appleby, and Emmanuel Sivan, *Strong Religion: The Rise of Fundamentalisms around the World* (Chicago: University of Chicago Press, 2003), 146.

17. Daniel M. Cress and David A. Snow, "The Outcomes of Homeless Mobilization: The Influence of Organization, Disruption, Political Mediation, and Framing," *American Journal of Sociology* 105 (2000): 1096.

18. Cress and Snow, "The Outcomes of Homeless Mobilization," 1066.

19. For the languages we do not know (Arabic and Hebrew), we used translators to translate documents from the original language.

20. John L. Esposito, "Islam and Civil Society," in *Modernizing Islam: Religion in the Public Sphere in the Middle East and Europe*, ed. John L. Esposito and Francois Burgat, 71 (New Brunswick, N.J.: Rutgers University Press, 2003).

21. Rebecca Kook, Michael Harris, and Gideon Doron, "In the Name of G-D and Our Rabbi: The Politics of the Ultra-Orthodox in Israel," *Israel Affairs* August (1998): 16; Larry Derfner, "Social Concern," *Jerusalem Post Internet Edition*, May 24, 2000, http:// www.jpost.com/Editions/2000/03/19/Features/Features.4223.html (accessed August 22, 2007); Ben Lynfield, "The Shas of Israel Rise to Prominence," *Christian Science Monitor*, April 4, 2000.

22. Urquhart, *The Pope's Armada*, 330.

1. CONTESTING THE STATE BY BYPASSING IT

1. Strictly speaking, "fundamentalist" refers to early twentieth-century Protestants who resisted modernist trends within their denominations; however, of late, it has been applied to orthodox religionists in a variety of religious traditions, including Catholicism, Islam, Judaism, and Hinduism—traditions to which the term did not originally apply.

2. See, for example, Mona El-Ghobashy, "The Metamorphosis of the Egyptian Muslim Brothers," *International Journal of Middle East Studies* 37 (2005): 377; Robert S. Leiken and Steven Brooke, "The Moderate Muslim Brotherhood," *Foreign Affairs* 86 (2007): 112.

3. We use "modernist" for this ideal type because it avoids the political connotation attached to Hunter's term "progressive," a connotation that we have shown to be incorrect for their views on economic issues.

4. James Davison Hunter, *Culture Wars: The Struggle to Define America* (New York: Basic Books, 1991), 49.

5. Nancy J. Davis and Robert V. Robinson, "Are the Rumors of War Exaggerated? Religious Orthodoxy and Moral Progressivism in the United States," *American Journal of Sociology* 102 (1996): 756–787.

6. Davis and Robinson, "Are the Rumors of War Exaggerated?"; Nancy J. Davis and Robert V. Robinson, "Their Brothers' Keepers? Orthodox Religionists, Modernists and Economic Justice in Europe," *American Journal of Sociology* 104 (1999): 1631–1665; Nancy J. Davis and Robert V. Robinson, "Religious Cosmologies, Individualism, and Politics in Italy," *Journal for the Scientific Study of Religion* 38 (1999): 339–353; Nancy J. Davis and Robert V. Robinson, "Theological Modernism, Cultural Libertarianism, and Laissez-Faire Economics in Contemporary European Societies," *Sociology of Religion* 62 (2001): 23–50; Nancy J. Davis and Robert V. Robinson, "The Egalitarian Face of Islamic Orthodoxy: Support for Islamic Law and Economic Justice in Seven Muslim-Majority Nations," *American Sociological Review* 71 (2006): 167–190.

7. Nancy J. Davis and Robert V. Robinson, "Egalitarian Face of Islamic Orthodoxy."

8. Winston L. King, "Eastern Religions: A New Interest and Influence," *Annals of the American Academy of Political and Social Science* 381 (1970): 66–76.

9. Gabriel A. Almond, R. Scott Appleby, and Emmanuel Sivan, *Strong Religion: The Rise of Fundamentalisms around the World* (Chicago: University of Chicago Press, 2003), 37.

10. We can only speculate as to why the strict side of the orthodox cosmology focuses specifically on sexuality, reproduction, family, and gender roles. It may be that since the Abrahamic faith traditions originated in patriarchal societies in which men held vastly more power than women, religious laws sought to uphold men's power by regulating women's sexuality, reproductive options, and economic and family roles.

11. A study of Americans found that the religiously orthodox report more compassionate feelings toward others than modernists and that this leads them to support government efforts to help the poor. David Blouin and Robert V. Robinson, "Are Religious People More Compassionate?" Paper presented at the joint annual meetings of the Midwest Sociological Society and the North Central Sociological Association, Chicago, April 2007.

12. Corroborating the communitarianism of the orthodox, a study of Americans found that orthodoxy is the single most important factor promoting feelings of community across a wide range of sources of community (neighbors, friends, fellow congregants, co-workers or fellow students, and ethnic group members). Robyn R. Ryle and Robert V. Robinson, "Ideology, Moral Cosmology, and Community in the United States," *City & Community* 5 (2006): 53–69.

13. Davis and Robinson, "Are the Rumors of War Exaggerated?"; Brian Starks and Robert V. Robinson, "Moral Cosmology, Religion, and Adult Values for Children," *Journal for the Scientific Study of Religion* 46 (2007): 17–35; Brian Starks and Robert V. Robinson, "Two Approaches to Religion and Politics: Moral Cosmology and Subcultural Identity," *Journal for the Scientific Study of Religion* 48 (2009): 650–669; Blouin and Robinson, "Are Religious People More Compassionate?"

14. Modernists in the United States are more likely than the orthodox to prefer that children "think for themselves" over "obey," corroborating their individualism. Starks and Robinson, "Moral Cosmology, Religion, and Adult Values for Children."

15. Davis and Robinson, "Are the Rumors of War Exaggerated?"; Davis and Robinson, "Their Brothers' Keepers"; Davis and Robinson, "Religious Cosmologies, Individualism, and Politics in Italy"; Davis and Robinson, "Theological Modernism, Cultural Libertarianism and Laissez-Faire Economics"; Davis and Robinson, "Egalitarian Face of Islamic Orthodoxy."

16. Seymour Martin Lipset, *Political Man* (New York: Free Press, 1981). Italian political philosopher Norberto Bobbio, in his review of the concepts of "left" and "right," concluded that "the criterion most frequently used to distinguish the political left from the right is the attitude . . . to the ideal of equality"—what we have called the economic dimension. Nonetheless, to locate individuals in political space, Bobbio argues that another dimension—"liberty/authoritarianism"—is needed. Although he does not apply this second dimension specifically to cultural issues, as we do here, it extends easily to such issues. U.S. sociologist Fred Kniss advances another two-dimensional model, with one dimension concerning whether the locus of moral authority lies in a collective tradition or in individual reasoning and the other dimension concerning whether the moral project is maximization of the public good or individual utility. Kniss's first dimension corresponds roughly to our cultural communitarianism vs. individualism and his second to our economic communitarianism vs. individualism. Norberto Bobbio, *Left and Right: The Significance of a Political Distinction* (Destra e sinistra: Regioni e significati di una distinzione politica), translated by Allan Cameron (Chicago: University of Chicago Press, 1996); Fred Kniss, "Culture Wars: Remapping the Battleground," in *Cultural Wars in American Politics: Critical Reviews of a Popular Myth*, ed. Rhys H. Williams, 331–347 (New York: Aldine de Gruyter, 1997). See also Rebecca Klatch, "Complexities of Conservatism: How Conservatives Understand the World," in *America at Century's End*, ed. Alan Wolfe (Berkeley: University of California Press, 1992); Anthony Giddens, *Beyond Left and Right: The Future of Radical Politics* (Cambridge: Polity Press, 1994).

17. Davis and Robinson, "Are the Rumors of War Exaggerated?"; Davis and Robinson, "Their Brothers' Keepers"; Davis and Robinson, "Religious Cosmologies, Individualism, and Politics in Italy"; Davis and Robinson, "Theological Modernism, Cultural Libertarianism and Laissez-Faire Economics"; Davis and Robinson, "Egalitarian Face of

Islamic Orthodoxy"; Ted Jelen, "Religious Belief and Attitude Constraint," *Journal for the Scientific Study of Religion* 29 (1990): 118–125; Azamat Junisbai, "Understanding Economic Justice Attitudes in Two Countries: Kazakhstan and Kyrgyzstan," *Social Forces* 88 (2010): 1677–1702; Mark Regnerus, Christian Smith, and David Sikkink, "Who Gives to the Poor? The Influence of Religious Tradition and Political Location on the Personal Generosity of Americans toward the Poor," *Journal for the Scientific Study of Religion* 37 (1998): 481–493; Starks and Robinson, "Two Approaches to Religion and Politics"; Joseph B. Tamney, Ronald Burton, and Stephen D. Johnson, "Fundamentalism and Economic Restructuring," in *Religion and Political Behavior in the United States,* ed. Ted G. Jelen (New York: Praeger, 1989).

18. Stephen Hart, *What Does the Lord Require? How American Christians Think about Economic Justice* (New York: Oxford University Press, 1992); Heidi Rolland Unruh and Ronald J. Sider, *Saving Souls, Serving Society: Understanding the Faith Factor in Church-Based Social Ministry* (Oxford: Oxford University Press, 2005).

19. We do not argue that all communitarian sentiments and movements originate from a religiously orthodox cosmology. The Communitarian Network in the United States (http://www2.gwu.edu/~ccps/) has elements of the economic and cultural communitarianism that we have identified as characteristic of the religiously orthodox but was founded primarily by academicians who did not ground the movement in a specific moral cosmology.

20. Davis and Robinson, "Egalitarian Face of Islamic Orthodoxy."

21. Almond, Appleby, and Sivan, *Strong Religion.*

22. José Casanova, *Public Religions in the Modern World* (Chicago: University of Chicago Press, 1994); Rhys H. Williams, "Public Religion and Hegemony: Contesting the Language of the Common Good," in *The Power of Religious Publics: Staking Claims in American Society,* ed. William H. Swatos Jr. and James K. Wellman Jr. (Westport, Conn.: Praeger, 1999).

23. Rhys H. Williams, "Movement Dynamics and Social Change: Transforming Fundamentalist Ideology and Organizations," in *Accounting for Fundamentalisms: The Dynamic Character of Movements,* ed. Martin E. Marty and R. Scott Appleby, 820 (Chicago: University of Chicago Press, 1994).

24. See, for example, Roberta Ash, *Social Movements in America* (Chicago: Markham, 1972); William Gamson, *The Strategy of Social Protest,* 2nd ed. (Belmont, Calif.: Wadsworth, 1990); Richard L. Wood, "Religious Culture and Political Action," *Sociological Theory* 17 (1999): 307–332; Vernon L. Bates, "The Decline of a New Christian Right Social Movement Organization: Opportunities and Constraints," *Review of Religious Research* 42 (2000): 19–40; Neil Fligstein, "Social Skill and the Theory of Fields," *Sociological Theory* 19 (2001): 105–125; Ellen Reese and Garnett Newcombe, "Income Rights, Mothers' Rights, or Workers' Rights? Collective Action Frames, Organizational Ideologies, and the American Welfare Rights Movement," *Social Problems* 50 (2003): 294–318; Marshall Ganz, "Why David Sometimes Wins: Strategic Capacity in Social Movements," in *The Psychology of Leadership: New Perspectives and Research,* ed. David M. Messick and Roderick M. Kramer, 209–238 (Mahwah, N.J.: Lawrence Erlbaum, 2005).

25. Ash, *Social Movements in America,* 12.

26. Gamson, *Strategy of Social Protest,* 44–46. See also Homer R. Steedly and John

W. Foley, "The Success of Protest Groups: Multivariate Analyses." *Social Science Research* 8 (1979): 1–15.

27. Reese and Newcombe, "Income Rights, Mothers' Rights, or Workers' Rights?," 298, 313.

28. Bates, "Decline of a New Christian Right Movement," 30.

29. Ganz, "Why David Sometimes Wins," 221.

30. Marshall Ganz, "Resources and Resourcefulness: Strategic Capacity in the Unionization of California Agriculture, 1959–1966," *American Journal of Sociology* 105 (2000): 1012.

31. Wood, "Religious Culture and Political Action," 317, 326.

32. Elizabeth A. Armstrong, *Forging Gay Identities: Organizing Sexuality in San Francisco, 1950–1994* (Chicago: University of Chicago Press, 2002), 198.

33. Fligstein, "Social Skill and the Theory of Fields," 107, 116.

34. Wood, "Religious Culture and Political Action," 315.

35. Bates, "Decline of a New Christian Right Movement," 33.

36. Fred Kniss and Gene Burns, "Religious Movements," in *The Blackwell Companion to Social Movements,* ed. David A. Snow, Sarah A. Soule, and Hanspeter Kriesi (Malden, Mass.: Blackwell, 2004).

37. Charles Kurzman, "Structural Opportunity and Perceived Opportunity in Social Movement Theory: The Iranian Revolution of 1979," *American Sociological Review* 61 (1996): 153–170.

38. John L. Esposito, "Islam and Civil Society," in *Modernizing Islam: Religion in the Public Sphere in the Middle East and Europe,* ed. John L. Esposito and Francois Burgat, 71 (New Brunswick, N.J.: Rutgers University Press, 2003); Rebecca Kook, Michael Harris, and Gideon Doron, "In the Name of G-D and Our Rabbi: The Politics of the Ultra-Orthodox in Israel," *Israel Affairs* (August 1998): 16; Larry Derfner, "Social Concern," *Jerusalem Post Internet Edition,* May 24, 2000, http://www.jpost.com/Editions/2000/03/19/Features/Features.4223.html (accessed August 22, 2007); Ben Lynfield, "The Shas of Israel Rise to Prominence," *Christian Science Monitor,* April 4, 2000.

39. Gordon Urquhart, *The Pope's Armada: Unlocking the Secrets of Mysterious and Powerful New Sects in the Church* (Amherst, N.Y.: Prometheus Books, 1999), 330.

40. See, for example, Robert N. Bellah, Richard Madsen, William M. Sullivan, Ann Swidler, and Steven M. Tipton, *Habits of the Heart: Individualism and Commitment in American Life* (New York: Harper & Row, 1985); Robert D. Putnam, "The Strange Disappearance of Civic America," *American Prospect* (Winter, 1996): 34–48; Robert D. Putnam, *Bowling Alone: The Collapse and Revival of American Community* (New York: Simon & Schuster, 2000).

41. Sheri Berman, "Islam, Revolution, and Civil Society," *Perspectives on Politics* 1 (2003): 259.

42. Ghada Hashem Talhami, "Whither the Social Network of Islam," *Muslim World* 91 (2001): 311.

43. Omar Kamil, "The Synagogue as Civil Society, or How We Can Understand the Shas Party," *Mediterranean Quarterly* 12 (2001): 130.

44. Antonio Gramsci, *Prison Notebooks* (New York: International, 1971).

45. Christian Smith with Michael Emerson, Sally Gallagher, Paul Kennedy, and

David Sikkink, *American Evangelicalism: Embattled and Thriving* (Chicago: University of Chicago Press, 1998).

46. Davis and Robinson, "Are the Rumors of War Exaggerated?"; Davis and Robinson, "Their Brothers' Keepers"; Davis and Robinson, "Religious Cosmologies, Individualism, and Politics in Italy"; Davis and Robinson, "Theological Modernism, Cultural Libertarianism and Laissez-Faire Economics"; Davis and Robinson, "Egalitarian Face of Islamic Orthodoxy."

47. Doug McAdam, *Political Process and the Development of Black Insurgency, 1930–1970* (Chicago: University of Chicago Press, 1982); Doug McAdam, *Freedom Summer* (New York: Oxford University Press, 1988); Doug McAdam, John D. McCarthy, and Mayer N. Zald, "Opportunities, Mobilizing Structures, and Framing Processes— Toward a Synthetic, Comparative Perspective on Social Movements," in *Comparative Perspectives on Social Movements*, ed. Doug McAdam, John D. McCarthy, and Mayer N. Zald (New York: Cambridge University Press, 1996); Sidney Tarrow, *Power in Movement: Social Movements and Contentious Politics*, 2nd ed. (New York: Cambridge University Press, 1998).

48. Charles Kurzman, "Critics Within: Islamic Scholars' Protests against the Islamic State in Iran," *International Journal of Politics* 15 (2001): 341–359; Mansoor Moaddel, *Jordanian Exceptionalism: A Comparative Analysis of State-Religion Relationships in Egypt, Iran, Jordan and Syria* (New York: Palgrave Macmillan, 2002); Mohammed Hafez, *Why Muslims Rebel: Repression and Resistance in the Islamic World* (Boulder, Colo.: Lynne Rienner, 2003); Ronald A. Francisco, "The Dictator's Dilemma," in *Repression and Mobilization*, ed. Christian Davenport, Hank Johnston, and Carol Mueller (Minneapolis: University of Minnesota Press, 2005).

49. Karl-Dieter Opp and Wolfgang Roehl, "Repression, Micromobilization, and Political Protest," *Social Forces* 69 (1990): 521–547.

50. MaryJane Osa and Cristina Corduneanu-Huci, "Running Uphill: Political Opportunities in Non-Democracies," *Comparative Sociology* 2 (2003): 605–629.

51. Edward Crenshaw and Kristopher Robison, "Political Violence as an Object of Study: The Need for Taxonomic Clarity," in *Handbook of Politics: State and Society in Global Perspective*, ed. Kevin T. Leicht and J. Craig Jenkins (New York: Springer, 2010).

52. Nancy J. Davis and Robert V. Robinson, "The Roots of Political Activism in Six Muslim-Majority Nations." Paper given at the Workshop on Theoretical and Methodological Issues in the Study of Values in Islamic Countries, Cairo, Egypt, May 16–18, 2010.

53. Karen Rasler, "Concessions, Repression, and Political Protest in the Iranian Revolution," *American Sociological Review* 61 (1996): 132–152.

54. Charles D. Brockett, "A Protest-Cycle Resolution of the Repression/Popular-Protest Paradox," *Social Science History* 17 (1993): 457–484.

55. While multiparty elections seemingly existed in Egypt before the fall of Mubarak in early 2011, opposition parties were frequently shut down, their candidates arrested and imprisoned, and election results rigged. See "Another Flawed Election: Democracy in Egypt Has Stalled," *Economist*, June 14, 2007.

56. Edwin Amenta, Kathleen Dunleavy, and Mary Bernstein, "Stolen Thunder? Huey Long's 'Share Our Wealth,' Political Mediation, and the Second New Deal," *American Sociological Review* 59 (1994): 683.

57. John D. McCarthy, David W. Britt, and Mark Wolfson, "The Institutional Channeling of Social Movements by the State in the United States," *Research in Social Movements, Conflicts and Change* 13 (1991): 45–76.

58. McCarthy, Britt, and Wolfson, "Institutional Channeling," 54.

59. Elizabeth A. Armstrong and Mary Bernstein, "Culture, Power, and Institutions: A Multi-Institutional Politics Approach to Social Movements," *Sociological Theory* 26 (2008): 74–99.

2. THE MUSLIM BROTHERHOOD

Epigraph note: Quoted in Grace Halsell, "In Egypt the Real Struggle Is between Mubarak and the Muslim Brotherhood," *Washington Report on Middle Eastern Affairs,* January 1, 1996.

1. Brynjar Lia, *The Society of the Muslim Brothers in Egypt: The Rise of an Islamic Mass Movement, 1928–1942* (Beirut, Lebanon: Ithaca Press, 1998), 1.

2. Robert A. F. L. Woltering, "The Roots of Islamic Popularity," *Third World Quarterly* 23 (2002): 1135.

3. Barry Rubin, introduction, *The Muslim Brotherhood: The Organization and Policies of a Global Islamist Movement,* ed. Barry Rubin, (New York: Palgrave Macmillan, 2010), 3.

4. John Walsh, "Egypt's Muslim Brotherhood: Understanding Centrist Islam," *Harvard International Review* 24 (2003): 35; "America at Crossroads: Inside the Muslim Brotherhood," Public Broadcasting System, April 20, 2007; *Fresh Air with Terry Gross,* "Interview with Lawrence Wright," National Public Radio, February 8, 2011; Bari Weiss, "A Democrat's Triumphal Return to Cairo," *New York Times,* February 26, 2011.

5. Mary Anne Weaver, quoted in "Islam Rising: A Conversation with Mary Anne Weaver," *Atlantic Online,* February 17, 1999, http://www.theatlantic.com/unbound/bookauth/ba990217.htm (accessed March 27, 2011).

6. Ziad Munson, "Islamic Mobilization: Social Movement Theory and the Egyptian Muslim Brotherhood," *Sociological Quarterly* 42 (2001): 489.

7. Richard P. Mitchell, *The Society of the Muslim Brothers* (Oxford: Oxford University Press, 1969), 326, 234–235. Referring to the Brothers' strict interpretation of Islamic law (the shari'a), an International Crisis Group report noted that "They ignore the fact that Sharia allows room for interpretation . . . and vibrant debates across the Muslim world about how Sharia should be implemented." International Crisis Group, "Egypt's Muslim Brothers: Confrontation or Integration?," *Middle East/North Africa Report* (June 2008): 21.

8. Hasan al-Banna, *Ila al-Tullab* [*To Students*] (Alexandria, Egypt: Dar al-Da'wa, no date), 9–10.

9. Hasan al-Banna, *Memoirs of Hasan al-Banna,* trans. M. N. Shaikh (Karachi, Pakistan: International Islamic, 1981), 109.

10. Hasan al-Banna, *Five Tracts of Hasan al-Banna (1906–1949),* trans. Charles Wendell (Berkeley: University of California Press, 1978), 126–132.

11. Muslim Brotherhood, "The Role of Muslim Women in an Islamic Society," *Ikwanweb,* June 10, 2007, http://www.ikhwanweb.com/article.php?id=787 (accessed April 5, 2011).

12. Al-Banna, *Five Tracts,* 72; Lia, *Society of Muslim Brothers in Egypt,* 81.

13. Mitchell, *Society of Muslim Brothers*, 221, 250, 272–274; Munson, "Islamic Mobilization." For the Brotherhood's most recent position statement on economic issues, see Muslim Brotherhood, "The Electoral Programme of the Muslim Brotherhood for Shura Council in 2007," *Ikhwanweb*, June 14, 2007, http://www.ikhwanweb.com/Article.asp ?ID=822&SectionID=0 (accessed March 27, 2011).

14. United Nations Office for the Coordination of Humanitarian Affairs, "Egypt: Social Programs Bolster Appeal of Muslim Brotherhood," February 22, 2006, http://www .irinnews.org/report.aspx?reportid=26150 (accessed March 27, 2011).

15. Robert S. Leiken and Steven Brooke, "The Moderate Muslim Brotherhood," *Foreign Affairs* 86 (2007): 107–121.

16. Nancy J. Davis and Robert V. Robinson, "The Egalitarian Face of Islamic Orthodoxy: Support for Islamic Law and Economic Justice in Seven Muslim-Majority Nations," *American Sociological Review* 71 (2006): 167–190.

17. Al-Banna, *Five Tracts*, 46.

18. Sana Abed-Kotob, "The Accommodationists Speak: Goals and Strategies of the Muslim Brotherhood of Egypt," *International Journal of Middle East Studies* 27 (1995): 323.

19. Muslim Brotherhood, "Who We Are," http://www.ikhwanonline.com (accessed December 31, 2008, site discontinued).

20. Lia, *Society of Muslim Brothers in Egypt*, 85.

21. Munson, "Islamic Mobilization," 501–502

22. Mitchell, *Society of Muslim Brothers*, 234–235.

23. Karen Armstrong, *Islam: A Short History* (New York: Modern Library, 2000), 156; Mitchell, *Society of Muslim Brothers*, 30–31.

24. Mansoor Moaddel, *Jordanian Exceptionalism: A Comparative Analysis of State-Religion Relationships in Egypt, Iran, Jordan and Syria* (New York: Palgrave Macmillan, 2002).

25. Mitchell, *Society of Muslim Brothers*, 234.

26. Lia, *Society of Muslim Brothers in Egypt*, 21–43.

27. Lia, *Society of Muslim Brothers in Egypt*, 33–37.

28. Lia, *Society of Muslim Brothers in Egypt*, 33, 40–41, 54.

29. Lia, *Society of Muslim Brothers in Egypt*, 57.

30. Sheri Berman, "Islam, Revolution, and Civil Society," *Perspectives on Politics* 1 (2003): 261.

31. Munson, "Islamic Mobilization," 497–498.

32. Berman, "Islam, Revolution, and Civil Society," 260; Munson, "Islamic Mobilization," 502.

33. Lia, *Society of Muslim Brothers in Egypt*, 97–98, 109–110.

34. Mitchell, *Society of Muslim Brothers*, 274–277.

35. Munson, "Islamic Mobilization," 493.

36. Mitchell, *Society of Muslim Brothers*, 277.

37. Lia, *Society of Muslim Brothers in Egypt*, 111.

38. Mitchell, *Muslim Brothers*, 36–37.

39. John D. McCarthy, David W. Britt, and Mark Wolfson, "The Institutional Channeling of Social Movements by the State in the United States," *Research in Social Movements, Conflicts and Change* 13 (1991): 45–76.

40. Lia, *Society of Muslim Brothers in Egypt*, 111–112.

41. Armstrong, *Islam*, 19, 156; Lia, *Society of Muslim Brothers in Egypt*, 111; Barbara

H. E. Zollner, *The Muslim Brotherhood: Hasan al-Hudaybi and Ideology* (London: Routledge, 2009), 10.

42. For a more extensive treatment of this strategy as it was employed by the four movements considered here, see Nancy J. Davis and Robert V. Robinson, "Overcoming Movement Obstacles by the Religiously Orthodox: The Muslim Brotherhood in Egypt, Shas in Israel, Comunione e Liberazione in Italy, and the Salvation Army in the United States," *American Journal of Sociology* 114 (2009): 1302–1349.

43. Philip Selznick, *The Organizational Weapon: A Study of Bolshevik Strategy and Tactics* (Santa Monica, Calif.: Rand, 1952), 20.

44. Lia, *Society of Muslim Brothers in Egypt,* 108.

45. Mitchell, *Society of Muslim Brothers,* 183.

46. Lia, *Society of Muslim Brothers in Egypt,* 104.

47. Lia, *Society of Muslim Brothers in Egypt,* 244, 162, 177–180.

48. Mitchell, *Society of Muslim Brothers,* 62–65.

49. *Akhir Saʿa,* December 15, 1948, as cited in Mitchell, *Society of Muslim Brothers,* 66.

50. Munson, "Islamic Mobilization," 498.

51. John O. Voll, "Fundamentalism in the Sunni Arab World," in *Fundamentalisms Observed,* ed. Martin E. Marty and Scott Appleby, 489 (Chicago: University of Chicago Press 1991); Munson, "Islamic Mobilization," 489.

52. Alison Pargeter, *The Muslim Brotherhood: The Burden of Tradition* (London: SAQI, 2010), 31.

53. Zollner, *The Muslim Brotherhood,* 19, 50.

54. Mitchell, *Society of Muslim Brothers,* 293–294.

55. Mitchell, *Society of Muslim Brothers,* 101–109.

56. Mitchell, *Society of Muslim Brothers,* 112–113.

57. Voll, "Fundamentalism in the Arab World," 363.

58. Zollner, *The Muslim Brotherhood,* 37.

59. Ana Belén Soage and Jorge Fuentelsaz Franganillo, "The Muslim Brothers in Egypt," in *The Muslim Brotherhood: The Organization and Policies of a Global Islamist Movement,* ed. Barry Rubin, 41 (New York: Palgrave Macmillan, 2010).

60. Mitchell, *Society of Muslim Brothers,* 112–113, 151–162.

61. Munson, "Islamic Mobilization," 498, 501.

62. Martin E. Marty and R. Scott Appleby, *The Glory and the Power: The Fundamentalist Challenge to the Modern World* (Boston: Beacon Press, 1992), 154; Zollner, *The Muslim Brotherhood,* 58–59.

63. Sayyid Qutb, *Milestones* (Indianapolis, Ind.: American Trust, 1993), 50.

64. Rubin, introduction, 1.

65. Voll, "Fundamentalism in the Arab World," 373.

66. Hesham Al-Awadi, *In Pursuit of Legitimacy: The Muslim Brothers and Mubarak, 1982–2000* (London: Tauris Academic Studies, 2004), 178.

67. Rudolph Peters, "Divine Law or Man-Made Law? Egypt and the Application of the Shariʿa," *Arab Law Quarterly* 3 (1988): 231–253.

68. Lawrence Wright, *The Looming Tower: Al-Qaeda and the Road to 9/11* (New York: Vintage Books, 2006), 50–59.

69. Dan Murphy, "Egypt Reins in Democratic Voices," *Christian Science Monitor,* March 28, 2005.

70. Walsh, "Egypt's Muslim Brotherhood," 32–33; Carrie Rosefsky Wickham, *Mobilizing Islam: Religion, Activism and Political Change in Egypt* (New York: Columbia University Press, 2002), 114–115, 203.

71. Walsh, "Egypt's Muslim Brotherhood."

72. Wickham, *Mobilizing Islam,* 203.

73. Raymond William Baker, "Invidious Comparisons: Realism, Postmodern Globalism, and Centrist Islamic Movements in Egypt," in *Political Islam: Revolution, Radicalism, or Reform?,* ed. John L. Esposito, 124 (Boulder, Colo.: Lynne Rienner, 1997).

74. Wickham, *Mobilizing Islam,* 192; Walsh, "Egypt's Muslim Brotherhood," 34; Soage and Franganillo, "The Muslim Brotherhood in Egypt," 44.

75. Al-Awadi, *In Pursuit of Legitimacy,* 150.

76. Abdel-Halim Moussa, as quoted in Chris Hedges, "Cairo Journal: After the Earthquake, a Rumbling of Discontent," *New York Times,* October 21, 1992.

77. Al-Awadi, *In Pursuit of Legitimacy,* 92–94.

78. Berman, "Islam, Revolution, and Civil Society," 261.

79. Shahira Amin, "The Feminine Face of Egypt's Muslim Brotherhood," *CNN World,* August 3, 2011, http://articles.cnn.com/2011-08-03/world/egypt.muslim.sisterhood _1_egypt-s-muslim-brotherhood-charity-work-al-azhar-university?_s=PM:WORLD (accessed September 30, 2011).

80. Wickham, *Mobilizing Islam,* 27; Michael Slackman, "Stifled, Egypt's Young Turn to Islamic Fervor," *New York Times,* February 17, 2008.

81. Najib Ghadbian, "Political Islam and Violence," *New Political Science* 22 (2000): 77–88; Marc Sageman, *Understanding Terror Networks.* (Philadelphia: University of Pennsylvania Press, 2004), 95; Woltering, "The Roots of Islamic Popularity."

82. Janine A. Clark, *Islam, Charity, and Action: Middle-Class Networks and Social Welfare in Egypt, Jordan, and Yemen* (Bloomington: Indiana University Press, 2004), 62–64.

83. Mustafa Mashhur, as quoted in Al-Awadi, *In Pursuit of Legitimacy,* 181.

84. Soage and Franganillo, "The Muslim Brotherhood in Egypt," 47.

85. Asef Bayat, *Making Islam Democratic: Social Movements and the Post-Islamist Turn* (Stanford, Calif.: Stanford University Press, 2007), 143.

86. Denis J. Sullivan and Sana Abed-Kotob, *Islam in Contemporary Egypt: Civil Society vs. the State* (Boulder, Colo.: Lynne Rienner, 1999), 55.

87. Al-Awadi, *In Pursuit of Legitimacy,* 187.

88. Soage and Franganillo, "The Muslim Brotherhood in Egypt," 47.

89. Jeffrey Burton Russell, *The Prince of Darkness: Radical Evil and the Power of Good in History* (Ithaca, N.Y.: Cornell University Press, 1992), 13–15.

90. Al-Awadi, *In Pursuit of Legitimacy,* 156.

91. Bayat, *Making Islam Democratic,* 144.

92. Bayat, *Making Islam Democratic,* 145.

93. Leila J. Rupp and Verta Taylor, *Survival in the Doldrums: The American Women's Movement, 1945 to the 1960s* (New York: Oxford University Press, 1987).

94. Bayat, *Making Islam Democratic,* 145.

95. John L. Esposito, "Islam and Civil Society," in *Modernizing Islam: Religion in the Public Sphere in the Middle East and Europe,* ed. John L. Esposito and Francois Burgat, 71 (New Brunswick, N.J.: Rutgers University Press, 2003).

96. Sami Zubaida, "Trajectories of Political Islam: Egypt, Iran and Turkey," *Political*

Quarterly 71 (2000): 67; Munson, "Islamic Mobilization"; Esposito, "Islam and Civil Society," 75; Walsh, "Egypt's Muslim Brotherhood."

97. Esposito, "Islam and Civil Society," 75–77, 84.

98. Wickham, *Mobilizing Islam,* 170.

99. Egbert Harmsen, "Muslim NGOs: Between Empowerment and Paternalism," *ISIM Review* 20 (2007): 11.

100. Emad El-Din Shahin, "Political Islam: Ready for Engagement?" Paper presented at the Workshop on "Barcelona +10," Madrid, Spain, January 2005, 6.

101. Esposito, "Islam and Civil Society," 75.

102. Walsh, "Egypt's Muslim Brotherhood," 32.

103. Clark, *Islam, Charity, and Action.*

104. Wickham, *Mobilizing Islam,* 153.

105. Ghada Hashem Talhami, "Whither the Social Network of Islam," *Muslim World* 91 (2001): 311–324.

106. United Nations, "Egypt: Social Programs."

107. Wickham, *Mobilizing Islam,* 99.

108. Talhami, "Whither the Social Network of Islam."

109. Berman, "Islam, Revolution, and Civil Society," 261.

110. Wickham, *Mobilizing Islam,* 164.

111. International Crisis Group, "Egypt's Muslim Brothers," 4n14.

112. Mitchell, *Society of Muslim Brothers,* 27.

113. Al-Awadi, *In Pursuit of Legitimacy,* 114.

114. Samer Shehata and Joshua Stacher, "The Brotherhood Goes to Parliament," *Middle East Report* 240 (2006): 32–39.

115. Wickham, *Mobilizing Islam,* 217–222; Ursula Lindsey, "Egypt's Muslim Brotherhood: Widening Split between Young and Old," *Christian Science* Monitor, December 21, 2009; Evan Hill, "The Muslim Brotherhood in Flux," *Al Jazeera,* November 21, 2010, http://english.aljazeera.net/indepth/2010/11/2010111681527837704.html (accessed April 15, 2011); Mitch Potter, "Is the Muslim Brotherhood a Threat?," *Toronto Star,* February 3, 2011; David M. Farris and Stacey Philbrick Yadav, "Why Egypt's Muslim Brotherhood Isn't the Islamic Bogeyman," *Christian Science Monitor,* February 14, 2011; Deborah Amos, "In Egypt, Muslim Brotherhood's Youth Seek Voice," *Morning Edition,* National Public Radio, April 5, 2011.

116. Shehata and Stacher, "The Brotherhood Goes to Parliament"; James Traub, "Islamic Democrats?," *New York Times Magazine,* April 29, 2007.

117. International Crisis Group, "Egypt's Muslim Brothers," 1; Traub, "Islamic Democrats?"

118. Amin Saikal, *Islam and the West: Conflict or Cooperation?* (New York: Palgrave MacMillan, 2003), 20.

119. Wickham, *Mobilizing Islam,* 134–137.

120. Walsh, "Egypt's Muslim Brotherhood, 34.

121. United Nations, "Egypt: Social Programs."

122. Quoted in Walsh, "Egypt's Muslim Brothers," 34.

123. Nadine H. Abdalla, "Civil Society in Egypt: A Catalyst for Democratization?," *International Journal of Not-for-Profit Law* 10 (2008): 25–28; Berman, "Islam, Revolution, and Civil Society," 260.

124. "Islam Rising," *Atlantic Online*.

125. John L. Esposito, Robert E. Mazur, and Sibusiso Nkomo, *Political Islam: Revolution, Radicalism or Reform?* (Boulder, Colo.: Lynne Rienner, 1997), 9.

126. Al-Awadi, *In Pursuit of Legitimacy*, 196.

127. Gilles Kepel, *The Revenge of God: The Resurgence of Islam, Christianity and Judaism in the Modern World* (University Park: Pennsylvania State University Press, 1994), 43, 201; Lisa Anderson, "Fulfilling Prophecies: State Policy and Islamist Radicalism," in *Political Islam: Revolution, Radicalism or Reform?*, ed. John L. Esposito, 24 (Boulder, Colo.: Lynne Rienner, 1997), 24; Esposito, "Islam and Civil Society," 76.

128. International Crisis Group, "Egypt's Muslim Brothers," 11n.

129. Muslim Brotherhood, "Frequently Asked Questions" http://www.ummah.net/ikhwan/questions.html (accessed August 26, 2008, site discontinued).

130. Gamal Essam El-Din, "Brotherhood Steps into the Fray," *Al-Ahram Weekly Online*, March 11–17, 2004, http://weekly.ahram.org.eg/2004/681/eg3.htm (accessed March 27, 2011); Shehata and Stacher, "The Brotherhood Goes to Parliament"; Traub, "Islamic Democrats?"; Leiken and Brooke, "Moderate Muslim Brotherhood," 114.

131. Maamon Ahmad, "Summary of MB Performance in Egyptian Parliament since 2005," *Ikhwanweb*, August 14, 2006, http://www.ikhwanweb.com/article.php?id=3747 (accessed March 27, 2011).

132. Shehata and Stacher, "The Brotherhood Goes to Parliament," 11.

133. Walsh, "Egypt's Muslim Brothers," 34.

134. Nathan J. Brown, Michele Dunne, and Amr Hamzawy, "Egypt's Controversial Constitutional Amendments: A Textual Analysis," *Carnegie Endowment for International Peace*, March 23, 2007, http://www.carnegieendowment.org/files/egypt_constitution _webcommentary.pdf (accessed March 27, 2011); Traub, "Islamic Democrats?"

135. "Another Flawed Election: Democracy in Egypt Has Stalled," *Economist*, June 14, 2007.

136. Kanchan Gupta, "Egypt: Regime Targets Activists, NGOs," *The Pioneer, Demdigest.net-Egypt*, September 13, 2008, http://www.ikhwanweb.com/Article.asp?ID=17880 &SectionID=92 (accessed March 27, 2011).

137. United Nations, "Egypt: Social Programs."

138. United Nations, "Egypt: Social Programs"; Talhami, "Whither the Social Network of Islam."

139. Sullivan and Abed-Kotob, *Islam in Contemporary Egypt*, 123–124.

140. Kareem Fahim, "Slap to a Man's Pride Set Off Tumult in Tunisia," *New York Times*, January 21, 2011.

141. David D. Kirkpatrick and Michael Slackman, "Egyptian Youths Drive the Revolt against Mubarak," *New York Times*, January 26, 2011.

142. Ann Lesch, "Talking about a Revolution: Voices from the Margin?" Lecture given at DePauw University, Greencastle, Indiana, April 1, 2011.

143. Hadeel al-Shalchi, "Powerful Islamist Movement Sees Leadership Struggle," *Seattle Times*, October 30, 2009.

144. Jason Brownlee and Joshua Stacher, "Change of Leader, Continuity of System: Nascent Liberalism in Post-Mubarak Egypt," *Comparative Democratization*, May 2011.

145. "Revolution in Cairo," *Frontline*, PBS, February 22, 2011.

146. Weiss, "A Democrat's Triumphal Return."

147. Michael Slackman, "Islamist Group Is Rising Force in a New Egypt," *New York Times*, March 24, 2011; Yasmine El Rashidi, "The Battle for Egypt's Future," *New York Review of Books*, April 28, 2011.

148. Neil MacFarquhar, "Egyptian Voters Approve Constitutional Changes," *New York Times*, March 21, 2011.

149. Fredrick Kunkle, "In Egypt, Muslim Brotherhood's Charitable Works May Drive Political Support," *Washington Post*, April 9, 2011.

150. Slackman, "Islamist Group Is Rising Force in a New Egypt."

151. Stephen Glain, "Fault Lines in the Muslim Brotherhood," *Nation*, September 12, 2011.

152. Weiss, "A Democrat's Triumphal Return to Cairo."

153. Ben Wedeman, "Egypt's Muslim Brotherhood: Has Its Moment Arrived?," *CNN*, December 1, 2011, http://www.cnn.com/2011/12/01/world/meast/egypt-muslim -brotherhood/index.html?hpt=hp_t1 (accessed December 1, 2011); "Egypt's Islamist Parties Win Elections to Parliament," *BBC News*, January 21, 2012, http://www.bbc.co.uk/ news/world-middle-east-16665748 (accessed February 9, 2012).

154. Glain, "Fault Lines in the Muslim Brotherhood."

155. Omar Ashour, "Egypt Secularists and Liberals Afraid of Democracy?" *BBC News*, July 13, 2011, http://www.bbc.co.uk/news/world-middle-east-14112032 (accessed September 30, 2011).

156. Wickham, *Mobilizing Islam*, 174.

157. Neil Fligstein, "Social Skill and the Theory of Fields," *Sociological Theory* 19 (2001): 106.

3. THE SEPHARDI TORAH GUARDIANS

Epigraph note: Quoted in David Lehmann and Batia Siebzehner, *Remaking Israeli Judaism: The Challenge of Shas* (Oxford: Oxford University Press, 2006), 152.

1. Ezra Kopelowitz and Matthew Diamond, "Religion That Strengthens Democracy: An Analysis of Religious Political Strategies in Israel," *Theory and Society* 27 (1998): 673.

2. Lilly Weissbrod, "Shas: An Ethnic Religious Party," *Israel Affairs* 9 (2003): 81.

3. Rebecca Kook, Michael Harris, and Gideon Doron, "In the Name of G-D and Our Rabbi: The Politics of the Ultra-Orthodox in Israel," *Israel Affairs* (August 1998): 16; Graham Usher, "The Enigmas of Shas." *Middle East Report* 207 (1998): 34; Larry Derfner, "Social Concern," *Jerusalem Post Internet Edition*, May 24, 2000, http://www.jpost.com/ Editions/2000/03/19/Features/Features.4223.html (accessed August 22, 2007); Noah J. Efron, *Real Jews: Secular vs. Ultra-Orthodox and the Struggle for Jewish Identity in Israel* (New York: Basic, 2003), 51; Yaacov Yadgar, "Shas as a Struggle to Create a New Field: A Bourdieuan Perspective of an Israeli Phenomenon," *Sociology of Religion* 64 (2003): 223.

4. Etta Bick, "The Shas Phenomenon and Religious Parties in the 1999 Elections," *Israel Affairs* 7 (2001): 55–100.

5. Ethan Bronner and Isabel Kershner, "In Israeli Vote, with Two Parties Nearly Tied, the Winner Is Gridlock," *New York Times*, February 11, 2009.

6. We use Mizrahim (Jews of Middle Eastern or North African origin) in prefer-

ence to Sephardim (Jews of Spanish origin) because the former better reflects the broader target of Shas's appeal.

7. Lehmann and Siebzehner, *Remaking Israeli Judaism,* 238.

8. Yoav Peled, "Towards a Redefinition of Jewish Nationalism in Israel? The Enigma of Shas," *Ethnic and Racial Studies* 21 (1998): 701–726; Omar Kamil, "The Synagogue as Civil Society, or How We Can Understand the Shas Party," *Mediterranean Quarterly* 12 (2001): 128–143; Weissbrod, "Shas: An Ethnic Religious Party," 87–90.

9. Ella Shohat, "The Invention of the Mizrahim," *Journal of Palestinian Studies* 29 (1999): 5.

10. David Ben-Gurion, as quoted by Robert Moskin, "Prejudice in Israel," *Look,* October 5, 1965.

11. Usher, *The Enigma of Shas,* 34; Shohat, "The Invention of the Mizrahim," 14; Lehmann and Siebzehner, *Remaking Israeli Judaism,* 76.

12. "Factional and Government Make-Up of the Tenth Knesset," http://www.knesset .gov.il/history/eng/eng_hist10_s.htm (accessed March 16, 2011); "Factional and Government Make-Up of the Eleventh Knesset," http://www.knesset.gov.il/history/eng/eng_hist11 _s.htm (accessed March 16, 2011).

13. Quoted in Deborah Sontag, "A Rising Israeli Political Star Threatens Barak's Majority," *New York Times,* November 20, 1999.

14. Mizrahim constituted 47 percent of Jews in Israel in 2000. Peter Y. Medding, ed., *Sephardic Jewry and Mizrahi Jews,* Studies in Contemporary Jewry: An Annual, XXII (New York: Oxford University Press, 2007), ix.

15. Efron, *Real Jews,* 228.

16. Israel Kershner, "Some Israelis Question Benefits for Ultra-Religious," *New York Times,* December 28, 2010; Matti Friedman, "In Rise of Ultra-Orthodox, Challenges for Israel," *USA Today,* January 14, 2011.

17. Efron, *Real Jews,* 58–60.

18. Friedman, "In Rise of Ultra-Orthodox, Challenges for Israel."

19. Bick, "The Shas Phenomenon," 58–63.

20. Efron, *Real Jews,* 18–22; Weissbrod, "Shas: An Ethnic Religious Party," 91–92.

21. Quoted in Gershom Gorenberg, "Hot Shas," *New Republic,* January 25, 1999.

22. Gorenberg, "Hot Shas," 12.

23. Efron, *Real Jews,* 201.

24. Aaron P. Willis, "Shas—The Sephardic Torah Guardians: Religious 'Movement' and Political Power," in *The Elections in Israel—1992,* ed. Arian Asher and Michael Shamir, 11 (Albany, N.Y.: SUNY Press, 1995); Kook, Harris, and Doron, "In the Name of G-D," 7–8.

25. Weissbrod, "Shas: An Ethnic Religious Party," 98.

26. Gorenberg, "Hot Shas," 13.

27. Kopelowitz and Diamond, "Religion That Strengthens Democracy," 673; Efron, *Real Jews,* 187, 223; Weissbrod, "Shas: An Ethnic Religious Party," 80.

28. Kook, Harris, and Doron, "In the Name of G-D," 1.

29. Quoted in David Sharrock, "The Rise of the Torah's Guardians," *Guardian,* April 30, 1998.

30. Bick, "The Shas Phenomenon," 60.

31. Willis, "Shas—The Sephardic Torah Guardians," 10.

32. Lehmann and Siebzehner, *Remaking Israeli Judaism,* 121.

33. Kopelowitz and Diamond, "Religion That Strengthens Democracy," 690.

34. Efron, *Real Jews,* 201.

35. Yadgar, "Shas as a Struggle to Create a New Field," 232.

36. Gorenberg, "Hot Shas,"12; Kopelowitz and Diamond, "Religion That Strengthens Democracy," 690.

37. Suzanne Zima, "Religious Party Using Clout to Pressure Barak: Shas Seizes Chance to Build on Its Power Base in Israel," *SFGate.com,* July 13, 2000, http://articles .sfgate.com/2000-07-13/news/17654533_1_shas-spiritual-leader-shas-voters-israel-b-aliya -party (accessed April 8, 2011).

38. Lehmann and Siebzehner, *Remaking Israeli Judaism,* 71, 93.

39. Willis, "Shas—The Sephardic Torah Guardians," 6.

40. Yadgar, "Shas as a Struggle to Create a New Field," 225. Nissim Leon, "'Zikui Ha-rabim': Ovadia Yosef's Approach toward Religious Activism and His Place in the Haredi Movement within Mizrahi Jewry," in *Sephardic Jewry and Mizrahi Jews.* Studies in Contemporary Jewry, An Annual, XXII, ed. Peter Y. Medding, (Oxford: Oxford University Press, 2007).

41. Yossi Klein Halevi, "City of God," *New Republic,* September 29, 2003.

42. Leon, "'Zikui Harabim,'" 153.

43. http://www.shasnet.org.il/Front/Pages/pages.asp (accessed July 12, 2007, site discontinued). For a discussion of egalitarian discourse among Haredim, see Yohai Hakak, "Egalitarian Fundamentalism: Preventing Defection in the Israeli Haredi Community," *Journal of Contemporary Religion* 26 (2011): 291–310.

44. Yadgar, "Shas as a Struggle to Create a New Field," 235.

45. Lehmann and Siebzehner, *Remaking Israeli Judaism,* 79.

46. http://www.shasnet.org.il/Front/Pages/pages.asp (accessed July 12, 2007).

47. Bick, "The Shas Phenomenon"; Kamil, "The Synagogue as Civil Society"; Yadgar, "Shas as a Struggle to Create a New Field."

48. Lehmann and Siebzehner, *Remaking Israeli Judaism,* 117.

49. Lehmann and Siebzehner, *Remaking Israeli Judaism,* 117, 271.

50. Robby Berman, "Double Identity," *Jerusalem Post Internet Edition,* July 27, 1998, http://www.highbeam.com/doc/1P1-15582656.html (accessed March 16, 2011).

51. Ruth Sinai, "Abortion Issue Sparks Uproar in Knesset," *Israel Religious Action Center,* December 6, 2000, http://www.irac.org/article_e.asp?artid=377 (accessed January 15, 2007, site discontinued).

52. Yadgar, "Shas as a Struggle to Create a New Field," 236.

53. Kopelowitz and Diamond, "Religion That Strengthens Democracy," 673; Ethan Bronner, "Main Party in Israel Coalition Set to Choose Leader," *New York Times,* September 17, 2008; Nachman Ben-Yehuda, *Theocratic Democracy: The Social Construction of Religious and Secular Extremism* (Oxford: Oxford University Press, 2010), 207.

54. Willis, "Shas—The Sephardic Torah Guardians," 16; Kopelowitz and Diamond, "Religion That Strengthens Democracy," 690–693; Efron, *Real Jews,* 204.

55. Kopelowitz and Diamond, "Religion That Strengthens Democracy," 689–690.

56. Willis, "Shas—The Sephardic Torah Guardians"; Lehmann and Siebzehner, *Remaking Israeli Judaism,* 136.

57. http://www.knesset.gov.il/history/eng/eng_hist_all.htm (accessed March 16, 2011).

58. Lehmann and Siebzehner, *Remaking Israeli Judaism,* 96.

59. http://www.knesset.gov.il/history/eng/eng_hist_all.htm (accessed March 16, 2011).

60. Willis, "Shas—The Sephardic Torah Guardians," 13; Kamil, "The Synagogue as Civil Society," 129; Efron, *Real Jews,* 87–88; Weissbrod, "Shas: An Ethnic Religious Party," 83.

61. Lehmann and Siebzehner, *Remaking Israeli Judaism,* 4–5.

62. Lehmann and Siebzehner, *Remaking Israeli Judaism,* 5–8.

63. Kook, Harris, and Doron, "In the Name of G-D"; Bick, "The Shas Phenomenon"; Weissbrod, "Shas: An Ethnic Religious Party"; Efron, *Real Jews,* 203.

64. Bick, "The Shas Phenomenon," 55–58; Ben Lynfield, "Shas of Israel Rise to Prominence," *Christian Science Monitor,* April 4, 2000.

65. Lehmann and Siebzehner, *Remaking Israeli Judaism,* 79–80; Willis, "Shas—The Sephardic Torah Guardians."

66. Willis, "Shas—The Sephardic Torah Guardians," 122.

67. Lehmann and Siebzehner, *Remaking Israeli Judaism,* 88.

68. Ricky Tessler, "The Price of the Revolution," in *Shas: The Challenge of Israeliness* (Hebrew), ed. Yoav Peled, (Tel-Aviv: Yediot Aharonot, 2001).

69. Dov Elbaum and Anna Maria Tremonti, "Israel: A House Divided." *International Journal* 53 (Autumn 1998), 611–14; Kook, Harris, and Doron, "In the Name of G-D," 16; Yossi Klein Halevi, "Barak Must Confront Power Wielded by Ultra-Orthodox Party," *Los Angeles Times,* June 20, 1999; Lynfield, "The Shas of Israel Rise to Prominence," 6; Zima, "Religious Party Using Clout to Pressure Barak," 3; Friedman, "In Rise of Ultra-Orthodox, Challenges for Israel."

70. Lehmann and Siebzehner, *Remaking Israeli Judaism,* 5–8, 78.

71. Kamil, "The Synagogue as Civil Society," 130.

72. Efron, *Real Jews,* 51; see also Usher, "The Enigmas of Shas," 34.

73. Yadgar, "Shas as a Struggle to Create a New Field," 233.

74. Quoted in Lynfield, "Shas of Israel Rise to Prominence," 6.

75. Lehmann and Siebzehner, *Remaking Israeli Judaism,* 10.

76. Avi Machlis, "Shas Party's Growing Power Linked to Schools for Poor," *JWeekly* .com, June 4, 1999, http://www.jweekly.com/article/full/10952/shas-party-s-growing -power-linked-to-schools-for-poor/ (accessed April 8, 2011); Yadgar, "Shas as a Struggle to Create a New Field."

77. Kamil, "The Synagogue as Civil Society," 141; Yadgar, "Shas as a Struggle to Create a New Field"; Lehmann and Siebzehner, *Remaking Israeli Judaism,* 10, 173, 175.

78. Gorenberg, "Hot Shas," 13.

79. Quoted in Kamil, "The Synagogue as Civil Society," 128, 142.

80. Yair Ettinger, "Despite Opposition, English and Math Are Now Part of Haredi Curriculum," *Haaretz,* October 5, 2008; Amir Shoan, "The Haredi School Scam," *Ynetnews.com* July 12, 2010, http://www.ynetnews.com/articles/0,7340,L-3918220,00.html (accessed March 16, 2011).

81. Brenda Gazzar, "Ultra-Orthodox Israeli Women Reach for Better Jobs," *Women's eNews,* March 12, 2007, http://www.womensenews.org/story/070312/ultra-orthodox-israeli-women-reach-better-jobs (accessed April 6, 2011).

82. Tamar Rotem, "Some Revolutions Come in Modest Dress," *Haaretz.com,* March 4, 2009, http://www.haaretz.com/print-edition/features/some-revolutions-come-in-modest-dress-1.23124 (accessed April 8, 2011).

83. Lehmann and Siebzehner, *Remaking Israeli Judaism,* 195.

84. Weissbrod, "Shas: An Ethnic Religious Party," 83.

85. Lehmann and Siebzehner, *Remaking Israeli Judaism,* 196–197.

86. Kamil, "The Synagogue as Civil Society," 138.

87. Efron, *Real Jews,* 139–140.

88. Lehmann and Siebzehner, *Remaking Israeli Judaism,* 193.

89. Rifka Dzodin, "Aerial Terrorists or Cultural Bellwethers? Illegal Radio and the Fight for Israel's Airwaves," *NewVoices: National Jewish Student Magazine,* April 7, 2008.

90. Yaron Katz, "The 'Other Media'—Alternative Communications in Israel." *International Journal of Cultural Studies* 10 (2007): 384.

91. Zohar Blumenkrantz, "Police, Government Launch New Campaign to Fight Pirate Radio Broadcasters," *Haaretz,* June 21, 2007.

92. Katz, "The 'Other Media,'" 389.

93. Yechiel Spira, "Rav Ben-Atar to Begin Prison Sentence after Chanukah," *Yeshiva World News,* November 19, 2008, http://www.theyeshivaworld.com/article.php?p=26149 (accessed April 8, 2011).

94. Lehmann and Siebzehner, *Remaking Israeli Judaism,* 211.

95. Katz, "The 'Other Media,'" 388–389.

96. Barbara Sofer, "The World According to Shas," *Inside Magazine* (a supplement of the *Jewish Exponent*), Fall 2000.

97. Sarah Hershenson, "A Nurturing Spirit," *Jerusalem Post,* May 12, 2006.

98. Kook, Harris, and Doron, "In the Name of G-D," 16.

99. American Jewish Committee, "New American Jewish Committee Report Demystifies Israel's Shas Party for American Jews," *Charity Wire,* June 24, 1999, http://www.charitywire.com/charity11/00506.html (accessed April 17, 2011).

100. Sharrock, "The Rise of the Torah's Guardians."

101. Elbaum and Tremonti, "Israel: A House Divided," 616.

102. Kamil, "The Synagogue as Civil Society," 130.

103. Bick, "The Shas Phenomenon," 61, 67.

104. Usher, "The Enigmas of Shas," 35.

105. Lehmann and Siebzehner, *Remaking Israeli Judaism,* 166.

106. Bick, "The Shas Phenomenon," 58.

107. Quoted in Willis, "Shas—The Sephardic Torah Guardians," 6–7.

108. Lehmann and Siebzehner, *Remaking Israeli Judaism,* 248–249.

109. Lehmann and Siebzehner, *Remaking Israeli Judaism,* 190.

110. Lewis A. Coser, *Greedy Institutions: Patterns of Undivided Commitment* (New York: Free Press, 1974).

111. Karine Barzilai-Nahon and Gad Barzilai, "Cultured Technology: The Internet and Religious Fundamentalism," *Information Society* 21 (2005): 25–40.

112. Yadgar, "Shas as a Struggle to Create a New Field," 236.

113. Willis, "Shas—The Sephardic Torah Guardians"; Kook, Harris, and Doron, "In the Name of G-D"; Weissbrod, "Shas: An Ethnic Religious Party"; Yadgar, "Shas as a Struggle to Create a New Field."

114. Efron, *Real Jews*, 208.

115. Bick, "The Shas Phenomenon," 65.

116. Efron, *Real Jews*, 212.

117. Zima, "Religious Party Using Clout to Pressure Barak," 2.

118. Bick, "The Shas Phenomenon," 55–56.

119. Weissbrod, "Shas: An Ethnic Religious Party," 86.

120. Steve Bruce, *The Rise and Fall of the New Christian Right* (New York: Oxford University Press, 1988).

121. Gal Levy, "'And Thanks to the Ashkenazim . . .': The Politics of Mizrahi Ethnicity in Israel" (Hebrew), master's thesis, Tel Aviv University, 1995; Kamil, "The Synagogue as Civil Society," 139–140.

122. Quoted in Efron, *Real Jews*, 84.

123. Kamil, "The Synagogue as Civil Society," 139–140.

124. Efron, *Real Jews*, xiv.

125. Ruth Eglash, "Background: The Rights and Wrongs of Shas' Bid to Restore Child Allowances," *Jerusalem Post*, October 16, 2008.

126. Jonathan Spyer, "Special Issue: The 17th Knesset Elections," *Middle East Review of International Affairs*, April 10, 2006, http://meria.idc.ac.il/news/2006/06April10news.html (accessed March 16, 2011).

127. Quoted in Matthew Wagner, "Shas's Child Allowance Demands Face Tough Opposition," *Jerusalem Post*, August 7, 2008.

128. Marc de Chalvron and Annette Young, "The Spiritual—and Temporal—Heart of Shas" (videoclip), *France 24*, February 6, 2009, http://www.france24.com/en/20090206-spiritual-temporal-heart-shas-israel-elections-political-party (accessed April 17, 2011); Mazal Mualem, "Shas Won't Let Government Dry Out West Bank Settlements," *Haaretz.com*, March 6, 2009, http://www.haaretz.com/print-edition/news/shas-won-t-let-government-dry-out-west-bank-settlements-1.277170 (accessed October 4, 2011).

129. Ethan Bronner, "A Hard-Liner Gains Ground in Israel," *New York Times*, February 9, 2009.

130. Matthew Wagner, "Shas's Yosef: Voting for Israel Beiteinu an Unforgivable Sin," *Jerusalem Post*, February 9, 2009.

131. "Elections in Israel—2009," *Israel Ministry of Foreign Affairs*, http://www.mfa.gov.il/MFA/History/Modern+History/Historic+Events/Elections_in_Israel_February_2009.htm (accessed March 16, 2011); Ethan Bronner, "Netanyahu to Form New Israel Government," *New York Times* February 21, 2009.

132. Attila Somfalvi, "Shas: No Agreement with Likud Just Yet," *Ynetnews.com*, March 5, 2009, http://www.ynetnews.com/Ext/Comp/ArticleLayout/CdaArticlePrintPreview/1,2506,L-3682019,00.html (accessed March 16, 2011); Yair Ettinger and Shahar Ilan, "Shas-Likud Coalition Deal Includes Record Funding for Yeshivas, Boosts Child Allowances," *Haaretz.com*, March 23, 2009, http://www.haaretz.com/hasen/spages/1073472.html (accessed March 16, 2011).

133. Eli Berman, "Sect, Subsidy and Sacrifice: An Economist's View of Ultra-Orthodox Jews," *Quarterly Journal of Economics* 115 (2000): 905–953.

134. Quoted in Efron, *Real Jews*, 57; see also Kook, Harris, and Doron, "In the Name of G-D," 3.

135. Quoted in Ben-Yehuda, *Theocratic Democracy*, 23.

136. Weissbrod, "Shas: An Ethnic Religious Party," 87, 101.

137. Ilan Marciano, "Shas Election Jingles Reach Finals," *Ynetnews.com*, January 10, 2006, http://www.ynetnews.com/articles/0,7340,L-3197823,00.html (accessed March 16, 2011).

138. Aron Heller, "Israeli Change: Election Tone Is Obama-Like," *Chicago Tribune*, December 20, 2008.

139. http://www.shasnet.org.il/Front/Pages/pages.asp (accessed July 12, 2007, site discontinued).

140. Daniel B. Cornfield and Bill Fletcher, "Institutional Constraints on Social Movement 'Frame Extension': Shifts in the Legislative Agenda of the American Federation of Labor, 1881–1955," *Social Forces* 76 (1998): 1305–1321.

141. Herb Keinon and Rebecca Anna Stoil, "Cabinet Approves Stipend Limits to Most Yeshiva Students," *Jerusalem Post*, December 12, 2010; Kobi Nahshoni, "Yishai: Assurance of Income for University Students with Children," *Ynetnews.com*, November 4, 2010, http://www.ynetnews.com/Ext/Comp/ArticleLayout/CdaArticlePrintPreview/1,2506,L-3980045,00.html (accessed October 13, 2011).

142. Kershner, "Some Israelis Question Benefits for Ultra-Religious."

143. Friedman, "In Rise of Ultra-Orthodox, Challenges for Israel."

144. Kershner, "Some Israelis Question Benefits for Ultra-Religious."

145. Friedman, "In Rise of Ultra-Orthodox, Challenges for Israel."

146. Aryeh Dayan, "The Shas Enigma," *Jerusalem Post Online Edition*, July 19, 2010, http://www.jpost.com/JerusalemReport/Article.aspx?id=181927 (accessed October 19, 2011).

147. See the editorial by Shira Leibowitz Schmidt, "AAAs for Shas," *Jerusalem Post Online Edition*, February 7, 2009, http://www.jpost.com/Opinion/Op-EdContributors/Article.aspx?id=132037 (accessed March 16, 2011).

148. Lehmann and Siebzehner, *Remaking Israeli Judaism*, 201–202.

149. http://www.shasnet.org.il/Front/Pages/pages.asp (accessed July 12, 2007, site discontinued).

4. COMUNIONE E LIBERAZIONE

Epigraph note: Interviewed by Brandon Vaidyanathan, "A Rose by Any Other Name: Definitions of Religiosity among Volunteers in an Italian Cultural Festival." Paper presented at the eleventh annual Chicago Ethnography Conference, Chicago, February 28, 2009.

1. Salvatore Abbruzzese, "Religion et Modernité: Le Cas de 'Comunione e Liberazione,'" *Social Compass* 36 (1989): 13–32; Enzo Pace, "Fondamentalismo italiano: Il caso di Comunione e Liberazione," in *Il Regime della Verita: Il Fondamentalismo Religioso Contemporaneo*, ed. Enzo Pace, 87–103 (Bologna, Italy: Il Mulino, 1990); Gordon Urquhart, *The Pope's Armada: Unlocking the Secrets of Mysterious and Powerful New Sects in the Church* (Amherst, N.Y.: Prometheus Books, 1999), 9.

2. Mario B. Mignone, *Italy Today: Facing the Challenges of the New Millennium* (New York: Peter Lang, 2008), 289.

3. Compagnia delle Opere, *Executive Summary* (Milan, Italy: Compagnia delle Opere, 2009); Davide Rondoni, *Communion and Liberation: A Movement in the Church*, translated by Patrick Stevenson and Susan Scott (Montreal: McGill-Queen's University Press, 1998), 65, 87; Dario Zadra, "Comunione e Liberazione: A Fundamentalist Idea of Power," in *Accounting for Fundamentalisms: The Dynamic Character of Movements*, ed. Martin E. Marty and R. Scott Appleby, 140 (Chicago: University of Chicago Press, 1991); Urquhart, *Pope's Armada*, 256.

4. Rondoni, *Communion and Liberation*, 77.

5. Urquhart, *Pope's Armada*, 330.

6. http://www.clonline.org/storiatext/ita/adulti/cdo.htm (accessed March 14, 2011).

7. http://www.clonline.org/storiatext/ita/clrealta/carisma.htm (accessed March 14, 2011).

8. Zadra, "Comunione e Liberazione," 126.

9. Luigi Giussani, "What Kind of Life Gives Birth to Communion and Liberation?" *Traces*, May 1979.

10. Luigi Giussani, *The Christian Event* (Milan, Italy: Rizzoli, 1993), 49.

11. Julián Carrón, "Your Good Work Is a Good for All," *Traces*, December 1, 2009.

12. Giussani, *The Christian Event*, 49.

13. John L. Allen Jr., "Scouting Report: Three Soon-to-Be-Cardinals Range from Conservative to More Conservative to Unknown," *National Catholic Reporter*, January 11, 2002.

14. http://www.clonline.org/storiatext/eng/comlibe/tredimen.htm (accessed March 14, 2011).

15. http://www.clonline.org/storiatext/eng/comlibe/tredimen.htm (accessed March 14, 2011).

16. Zadra, "Comunione e Liberazione," 128.

17. Antonio Gaspari, "Communion and Liberation: Crusaders for Catholic Integrity," *Inside the Vatican*, February 1996, http://www.ewtn.com/library/ISSUES/COMLIB.TXT (accessed March 14, 2011).

18. Urquhart, *Pope's Armada*, 288.

19. http://www.clonline.org/storiatext/eng/comlibe/tredimen.htm (accessed March 14, 2011).

20. http://www.clonline.org/storiatext/eng/comlibe/tredimen.htm (accessed March 14, 2011).

21. Rondoni, *Communion and Liberation*, 55.

22. Urquhart, *Pope's Armada*, 174.

23. Quoted in Gaspari, "Communion and Liberation," 2.

24. Liugi Giussani, *Un avvenimento di vita, cioè una storia* (Rome, Italy: EDIT, 1993), 131.

25. Rondoni, *Communion and Liberation*, 43.

26. Urquhart, *Pope's Armada*, 119.

27. Luigi Giussani as quoted in Urquhart, *Pope's Armada*, 118.

28. Urquhart, *Pope's Armada*, 146.

29. "Testimonies," *Traces*, January 1, 2006.

30. Rondoni, *Communion and Liberation*, 45.

31. Rondoni, *Communion and Liberation*, 47.

32. http://www.clonline.org/storiatext/eng/comlibe/tredimen.htm (accessed March 14, 2011).

33. Urquhart, *Pope's Armada*, 200.

34. Rondoni, *Communion and Liberation*, 43.

35. Urquhart, *Pope's Armada*, 119.

36. Peter J. Rachleff, *Hard Pressed in the Heartland: The Hormel Strike and the Future of the Labor Movement* (Boston: South End Press, 1999).

37. John Hooper, "Father Liugi Giussani: Italian Priest and Founder of the Controversial Catholic Pressure Group, Communion and Liberation," *Guardian*, April 1, 2005.

38. Urquhart, *Pope's Armada*, 119.

39. Rondoni, *Communion and Liberation*, 52; Urquhart, *Pope's Armada*, 119–120.

40. Abbruzzese, "Religion et Modernité"; Roberto Cipriani, "'Diffused Religion' and New Values in Italy," in *The Changing Face of Religion*, ed. James A. Beckford and Thomas Luckmann, 24–49 (London: Sage, 1989); Zadra, "Comunione e Liberazione."

41. Urquhart, *Pope's Armada*, 120.

42. Zadra, "Comunione e Liberazione," 135.

43. http://www.clonline.org/storiatext/eng/storia.htm (accessed March 14, 2011).

44. Urquhart, *Pope's Armada*, 146.

45. Urquhart, *Pope's Armada*, 121, 289.

46. Urquhart, *Pope's Armada*, 191.

47. "The Pope's Youthful 'New Jesuits,'" *Time*, September 8, 1986, http://www.time.com/time/magazine/article/0,9171,962255,00.html (accessed March 14, 2011).

48. John L. Allen Jr., "Report from Rimini: Italy's Biggest Public Event," *National Catholic Reporter*, August 26, 2005; Luca Marcolivio, "Rimini '11 Closes with 800,000 Participants," *Zenit: the World Seen from Rome*, August 29, 2011, http://www.zenit.org/rssenglish-33312 (accessed October 15, 2011).

49. Gaspari, "Communion and Liberation," 8; Urquhart, *Pope's Armada*, 213.

50. Gaspari, "Communion and Liberation," 7.

51. Christian Smith with Michael Emerson, Sally Gallagher, Paul Kennedy, and David Sikkink, *American Evangelicalism: Embattled and Thriving* (Chicago: University of Chicago Press, 1998).

52. Urquhart, *Pope's Armada*, 327.

53. Rondoni, *Communion and Liberation*, 56.

54. "The Pope's Youthful 'New Jesuits,'" *Time*.

55. http://www.cusl.it/chisiamo/ (accessed April 5, 2011).

56. Uquhart, *Pope's Armada*, 333.

57. Zadra, "Comunione e Liberazione, 135.

58. Urquhart, *Pope's Armada*, 320.

59. Rondoni, *Communion and Liberation*, 55.

60. Zadra, "Comunione e Liberazione," 135.

61. http://www.clonline.org/storiatext/eng/storia.htm (accessed March 14, 2011).

62. Rondoni, *Communion and Liberation*, 56.

63. Zadra, "Comunione e Liberazione," 141.

64. Quoted in Urquhart, *Pope's Armada*, 270.

65. www.clonline.org/storiatext/ita/adulti/cdo.htm (accessed March 14, 2011).

66. Luigi Giussani, "Il 'potere' del laico, cioè del Cristiano: Intervista a Monsignor Luigi Giussani a cura di Angelo Scola," in *Come 2000 Anni Fa* (a supplement of *Il Sabato*), August 5, 1989.

67. http://www.clonline.org/storiatext/eng/storia.htm (accessed March 14, 2011).

68. Urquhart, *Pope's Armada*, 321.

69. Urquhart, *Pope's Armada*, 175.

70. Rondoni, *Communion and Liberation*, 65.

71. Joseph R. Gusfield, *Symbolic Crusade: Status Politics and the American Temperance Movement*, 2nd ed. (Urbana: University of Illinois Press, 1986).

72. Quoted in Gaspari, "Communion and Liberation," 10.

73. Urquhart, *Pope's Armada*, 139. See Melissa J. Wilde, *Vatican II: A Sociological Analysis of Religious Change* (Princeton, N.J.: Princeton University Press, 2007).

74. Allen, "Report from Rimini," 3; Gaspari, "Communion and Liberation," 8; Urquhart, *Pope's Armada*, 6.

75. Quoted in Gaspari, "Communion and Liberation," 9.

76. Zadra, "Comunione e Liberazione," 130.

77. Urquhart, *Pope's Armada*, 322.

78. Susan Cullinan, "Time Trail: Italy," *Time Europe*, September 8, 2000.

79. Gaspari, "Communion and Liberation," 11.

80. "Che bella vittoria!" (What a Great Victory!), *Tracce*, November 1999.

81. "Andreotti Cleared of Murder," *CNN.com/World*, October 30, 2003, http://edition.cnn.com/2003/WORLD/europe/10/30/italy.andreotti.reut/index.html (accessed April 17, 2011).

82. Gaspari, "Communion and Liberation," 9.

83. Antonio Gaspari, "A Change of Course?," *Catholic Information Network*, October 1996, http://www.catholic.net/RCC/Periodicals/Inside/10-96/Movement.html (accessed August 22, 2007); Rondoni, *Communion and Liberation*, 66.

84. Gaspari, "Change of Course."

85. http://www.clonline.org/storiatext/eng/comlibe/tredimen.htm (accessed March 14, 2011).

86. Rondoni, *Communion and Liberation*, 66.

87. Zadra, "Comunione e Liberazione," 140.

88. Urquhart, *Pope's Armada*, 9.

89. http://stats.oecd.org/wbos/Index.aspx?datasetcode=SOCX_REF (accessed March 14, 2011).

90. Rondoni, *Communion and Liberation*, 101.

91. Quoted in Urquhart, *Pope's Armada*, 269.

92. Urquhart, *Pope's Armada*, 271.

93. Urquhart, *Pope's Armada*, 330.

94. Zadra, "Comunione e Liberazione," 133.

95. Ferruccio Pinotti, Promotional video for *La Lobby di Dio: Fede, Affari, e Politica, La Prima Inchiesta su Comunione e Liberazione e Compagnia delle Opere*. Milan, Italy: Chiarelettere, 2010, http://www.youtube.com/watch?v=CW19B7R4xZ0 (accessed April 8, 2011).

96. Andrew Murray, "The Principle of Subsidiarity and the Church," *Australasian Catholic Record* 72 (1995): 163–172.

97. Tony Blair, "Speech at Rimini," August 27, 2009 http://www.laicidade.org/wp -content/uploads/2009/10/tony-blair-rimini.pdf (accessed October 6, 2011).

98. http://www.cdo.it/ (accessed March 14, 2011).

99. Urquhart, *Pope's Armada*, 277.

100. http://www.cdo.it/ (accessed March 14, 2011).

101. http://www.cdo.it/ (accessed March 14, 2011).

102. Zadra, "Comunione e Liberazione," 138.

103. Quoted in Urquhart, *Pope's Armada*, 317.

104. Luigi Giussani, "Il 'potere' del laico," 23.

105. Compagnia delle Opere, *Executive Summary*, 13.

106. http://www.avsi.org/ (accessed March 14, 2011).

107. Compagnia delle Opere, *Executive Summary*, 13; http://www.avsi.org/ (accessed March 14, 2011).

108. http://www.avsi.org/EN/ (accessed April 5, 2011).

109. http://www.avsi-usa.org/docs/pdf/Arvore%20da%20Vida%202008.pdf (accessed April 6, 2011).

110. http://www.famiglieperaccoglienza.it/index.asp (accessed March 14, 2011).

111. Compagnia delle Opere, *Executive Summary*, 13.

112. http://www.cdo.it/Home/BancoAlimentare/tabid/1496/Default.aspx (accessed March 14, 2011).

113. Compagnia delle Opere, *Executive Summary*, 13; http://www.foe.it/Objects/ Pagina.asp?ID=3&T=Chi%20Siamo (accessed March 14, 2011).

114. Urquhart, *Pope's Armada*, 256–257.

115. "Testimonies," *Traces*, January 1, 2006.

116. Compagnia delle Opere, *Executive Summary*, 13; http://www.foe.it/Objects/ Pagina.asp?ID=3&T=Chi%20Siamo (accessed March 14, 2011).

117. Compagnia delle Opere, *Executive Summary*, 13.

118. http://www.bancofarmaceutico.org/ (accessed March 14, 2011).

119. Compagnia delle Opere, *Executive Summary*, 5.

120. http://www.life-torino.it/eng/progetto/partner-nazionali/compagnia-opere.htm (accessed March 14, 2011).

121. http://www.cdo.it/ (accessed March 14, 2011).

122. "Marchionne parla al meeting di CL: 'L'Italia ha bisogno di guardare avanti,'" *Il Tempo*, August 26, 2010.

123. Bernard Scholz, "Work and the Person: Toward a New Education," speech delivered at Columbia University, October 29, 2009, http://www.crossroadsculturalcenter .org/storage/transcripts/2009-10-29-Human%20Capital-Scholz.pdf (accessed April 8, 2011).

124. Paola Bergamini, "Free Men behind Bars," *Traces*, January 1, 2006.

125. Bergamini, "Free Men behind Bars."

126. "Prisoners' Exhibit at Meeting 2008, Rimini," *Cahiers Péguy*, August 29, 2008.

127. Marcolivio, "Rimini '11 Closes with 800,000 Participants"; Susan Gately, "800,000 at Rimini Meeting," *CiNews*, September 10, 2011, http://www.cinews.ie/article .php?artid=8990 (accessed October 14, 2011).

128. Allen, "Italy's Biggest Public Event."

129. http://www.clonline.org/storiatext/eng/formevita/frater.htm (accessed March 14, 2011).

130. Zadra, "Comunione e Liberazione," 137.

131. http://www.clonline.org/memores/memoresEng.htm (accessed March 14, 2011).

132. Lewis A. Coser, *Greedy Institutions: Patterns of Undivided Commitment* (New York: Free Press, 1974).

133. Allen, "Report from Rimini."

134. Urquhart, *Pope's Armada,* 25.

135. http://www.clonline.org/it/testi/cl_mondo.asp (accessed March 14, 2011).

136. "You Have Brightened Egypt," *Traces,* November 1, 2010.

137. Allen, "Report from Rimini."

138. John L. Allen Jr., "Opposing Forces in Italian Church Try Détente," *National Catholic Reporter,* August 27, 2004.

139. John Zucchi, "Luigi Giussani, the Church, and Youth in the 1950s: A Judgment Born of an Experience," *Logos: A Journal of Catholic Thought and Culture* 10 (2007): 133.

140. Allen, "Report from Rimini," 2.

141. http://www.clonline.org/carron_eng.html (accessed March 14, 2011).

142. Amy Welborn, "In Communion," *Open Book,* March 24, 2007, http://amywelborn.typepad.com/openbook/2007/03/in_communion.html (accessed March 14, 2011).

143. John L. Allen Jr., "Report: Pope to Launch Pontifical Council for New Evangelization," *National Catholic Reporter,* April 25, 2010.

144. John D. McCarthy and Mayer N. Zald, "Resource Mobilization and Social Movements: A Partial Theory," *American Journal of Sociology* 82 (1977): 1212–1241; Daniel M. Cress and David A. Snow, "Mobilization at the Margins: Resources, Benefactors, and the Viability of Homeless Social Movement Organizations," *American Sociological Review* 61 (1996): 1089–1109.

145. Marcolivio, "Rimini '11 Closes with 800,000 Participants."

146. Giussani, "Il 'potere' del laico," 23.

5. THE SALVATION ARMY USA

Epigraph note: Evangeline Booth, *The American War Cry,* April 25, 1908, 13.

1. The Salvation Army was ranked first in net assets by *Forbes Magazine* in 2009; Shriners Hospital, with assets estimated at $7 billion, ranked second. Given our focus on institution-building, net assets is the best indicator of organization size. William P. Barrett, "America's 200 Largest Charities," *Forbes.com,* November 17, 2010, http://www.forbes.com/2010/11/16/forbes-charity-200-personal-finance-philanthropy-200-largest-charities-charity-10-intro.html (accessed March 13, 2011).

2. Salvation Army, *2010 Annual Report* (Alexandria, Va.: Salvation Army of the United States of America, 2010), 27.

3. Kate Pickert, "A Brief History of the Salvation Army," *Time,* December 2, 2008.

4. Salvation Army, *2010 Annual Report,* 21–23.

5. Salvation Army, *2010 Annual Report*, 22.

6. John W. Hazzard, "Marching on the Margins: An Analysis of the Salvation Army in the United States," *Review of Religious Research* 40 (1998): 121–141.

7. Robert A. Watson and Ben Brown, *"The Most Effective Organization in the U.S."*: *Leadership Secrets of the Salvation Army* (New York: Crown Business, 2001), 17.

8. Quoted in Susan Lee and Ashlea Ebeling, "Can You Top This for Cost-Efficient Management?," *Forbes*, April 20, 1998.

9. Lillian Taiz, *Hallelujah Lads & Lasses: Remaking the Salvation Army in America, 1880–1930* (Chapel Hill: University of North Carolina Press, 2001), 6, 9.

10. Roger J. Green, *The Life and Ministry of William Booth* (Nashville, Tenn.: Abingdon Press, 2005), 29.

11. Hazzard, "Marching on the Margins," 123.

12. Green, *Life and Ministry of William Booth*, 29.

13. Norman H. Murdoch, *Origins of the Salvation Army* (Knoxville: University of Tennessee Press, 1994), 19.

14. Green, *Life and Ministry of William Booth*, 117.

15. http://www.salvationarmyusa.org/usn/www_usn_2.nsf/vw-dynamic-index/ CE33D354A0544F368025732500314AF5?Opendocument (accessed March 14, 2011).

16. Rebecca Anne Allahyari, *Visions of Charity: Volunteer Workers and Moral Community* (Berkeley: University of California Press, 2000), 10.

17. Taiz, *Hallelujah Lads & Lasses*, 6.

18. Green, *Life and Ministry of William Booth*, 173.

19. http://www.salvationarmyusa.org/usn/www_usn_2.nsf/vw-dynamic-arrays/ B6F3F4DF3150F5B585257434004C177D?openDocument (accessed March 14, 2011).

20. Edward H. McKinley, *Marching to Glory: The History of The Salvation Army in the United States, 1880–1992*, 2nd ed. (Grand Rapids, Mich.: William B. Eerdmans, 1995), 40.

21. Watson and Brown, *"The Most Effective Organization in the U.S,"* 66.

22. Taiz, *Hallelujah Lads & Lasses*, 9.

23. Allahyari, *Visions of Charity*, 184.

24. Taiz, *Hallelujah Lads & Lasses*, 106–107.

25. Watson and Brown, *"The Most Effective Organization in the U.S,"* 38.

26. Quoted in J. Evan Smith, *Booth the Beloved* (Oxford: Oxford University Press, 1949), 123–124.

27. Green, *Life and Ministry of William Booth*, 204.

28. "End Times: Millennialism, Premillenialism, Dispensationalism," British Broadcasting Corporation, http://www.bbc.co.uk/religion/religions/christianity/beliefs/endtimes _1.shtml (accessed March 14, 2011).

29. "End Times," British Broadcasting Corporation.

30. Taiz, *Hallelujah Lads & Lasses*, 16.

31. Diane Winston, *Red Hot and Righteous: The Urban Religion of the Salvation Army* (Cambridge, Mass.: Harvard University Press, 1999), 2.

32. Evangeline Booth, *American War Cry*, April 25, 1908, 13.

33. http://www.salvationarmyusa.org/usn/www_usn_2.nsf/vw-dynamic-arrays/ B6F3F4DF3150F5B585257434004C177D?openDocument (accessed March 14, 2011).

34. http://www.salvationarmyusa.org/usn/www_usn_2.nsf/vw-dynamic-arrays/ B6F3F4DF3150F5B585257434004C177D?openDocument (accessed March 14, 2011).

35. Hazzard, "Marching on the Margins," 133.

36. http://www.salvationarmyusa.org/usn/www_usn_2.nsf/vw-dynamic-arrays/ B6F3F4DF3150F5B585257434004C177D?openDocument (accessed March 14, 2011).

37. Winston, *Red Hot and Righteous*, 46.

38. Beth M. Lewis, "Issues and Dilemmas in Faith-Based Social Service Delivery: The Case of the Salvation Army of Greater Philadelphia." *Administration in Social Work* 27 (2003): 94.

39. Murdoch, *Origins of the Salvation Army*; Hazzard, "Marching on the Margins," 124; Green, *Life and Ministry of William Booth*, 109.

40. Green, *Life and Ministry of William Booth*, 10.

41. William Booth, *In Darkest England and the Way Out* (Charleston, S.C.: Biblio-Bazaar, 2006 [1890]), 31.

42. Taiz, *Hallelujah Lads & Lasses*, 113–114.

43. Green, *Life and Ministry of William Booth*, 173; Winston, *Red Hot and Righteous*, 105–106.

44. http://www.salvationarmyusa.org/usn/www_usn_2.nsf/vw-dynamic-arrays/ B6F3F4DF3150F5B585257434004C177D?openDocument (accessed April 24, 2009).

45. Murdoch, *Origins of the Salvation Army*, 42, 47.

46. http://www.salvationarmyusa.org/usn/www_usn_2.nsf/vw-dynamic-arrays/ 816DE20E46B88B2685257435005070FA?openDocument (accessed March 14, 2011).

47. Green, *Life and Ministry of William Booth*, 106.

48. Green, *Life and Ministry of William Booth*, 113–114.

49. Green, *Life and Ministry of William Booth*, 131.

50. http://www.salvationarmyusa.org/usn/www_usn_2.nsf/vw-dynamic-arrays/ 7100A2893080C5238025732500315746?openDocument (accessed March 14, 2011).

51. Winston, *Red Hot and Righteous*, 10–11.

52. Henry Gariepy, *Christianity in Action: The International History of the Salvation Army* (Grand Rapids, Mich: William B. Eerdmans, 2009), 16.

53. Winston, *Red Hot and Righteous*, 15.

54. Taiz, *Hallelujah Lads & Lasses*, 74.

55. Winston, *Red Hot and Righteous*, 13, 33.

56. Quoted in Winston, *Red Hot and Righteous*, 13.

57. Taiz, *Hallelujah Lads & Lasses*, 67–68.

58. Winston, *Red Hot and Righteous*, 15.

59. Winston, *Red Hot and Righteous*, 15.

60. *War Cry*, September 1896, quoted in Winston, *Red Hot and Righteous*, 102.

61. Winston, *Red Hot and Righteous*; Lewis, "Issues and Dilemmas."

62. McKinley, *Marching to Glory*, 9.

63. McKinley, *Marching to Glory*, 81.

64. Green, *Life and Ministry of William Booth*, 134.

65. Taiz, *Hallelujah Lads & Lasses*, 29.

66. Taiz, *Hallelujah Lads & Lasses*, 29–32.

67. Taiz, *Hallelujah Lads & Lasses*, 3–34; Murdoch, *Origins of the Salvation Army*, 127.

68. Lewis A. Coser, *Greedy Institutions: Patterns of Undivided Commitment* (New York: Free Press, 1974).

69. McKinley, *Marching to Glory*, 36; Taiz, *Hallelujah Lads & Lasses*, 39–40.

70. Taiz, *Hallelujah Lads & Lasses*, 44–45.

71. Green, *Life and Ministry of William Booth*, 186.

72. McKinley, *Marching to Glory*, 102–103.

73. Green, *Life and Ministry of William Booth*, 189.

74. Doug McAdam, *Political Process and the Development of Black Insurgency, 1930–1970* (Chicago, University of Chicago Press, 1982); Doug McAdam, *Freedom Summer* (New York: Oxford University Press, 1988); Doug McAdam, John D. McCarthy, and Mayer N. Zald, "Opportunities, Mobilizing Structures, and Framing Processes—Toward a Synthetic, Comparative Perspective on Social Movements," in *Comparative Perspectives on Social Movements*, ed. by Doug McAdam, John D. McCarthy, and Mayer N. Zald, 1–20 (New York: Cambridge University Press, 1996); Sidney Tarrow, *Power in Movement: Social Movements and Contentious Politics*, 2nd ed. (New York: Cambridge University Press, 1998).

75. Joseph R. Gusfield, *Symbolic Crusade: Status Politics and the American Temperance Movement*, 2nd ed. (Urbana: University of Illinois Press, 1986), 164–165.

76. Leila Rupp and Verta Taylor, *Survival in the Doldrums: The American Women's Rights Movement, 1945 to the 1960s* (New York: Oxford University Press, 1987).

77. Sam Marullo, Ron Pagnucco, and Jackie Smith, "Frame Changes and Social Movement Contraction: U.S. Peace Movement Framing after the Cold War," *Sociological Inquiry* 36 (1996): 1–28.

78. Daniel Cornfield and Bill Fletcher, "Institutional Constraints on Social Movement 'Frame Extension': Shifts in the Legislative Agenda of the American Federation of Labor, 1881–1955," *Social Forces* 76 (1998): 1305–1321.

79. Watson and Brown, "*The Most Effective Organization in the U.S*," 14–15.

80. Murdoch, *Origins of the Salvation Army*; Hazzard, "Marching on the Margins," 124; Green, *Life and Ministry of William Booth*, 109.

81. William Booth, *In Darkest England*, 63.

82. Murdoch, *Origins of the Salvation Army*, 87.

83. Quoted in Murdoch, *Origins of the Salvation Army*, 97.

84. Murdoch, *Origins of the Salvation Army*, 126.

85. Murdoch, *Origins of the Salvation Army*, 113–114.

86. Marullo, Pagnucco, and Smith, "Frame Changes and Social Movement Contraction," 1–28.

87. Booth, *In Darkest England*; Taiz, *Hallelujah Lads & Lasses*, 106–107.

88. Green, *Life and Ministry of William Booth*, 166; Winston, *Red Hot and Righteous*, 60–61.

89. Murdoch, *Origins of the Salvation Army*, 160; Green, *Life and Ministry of William Booth*, 17.

90. Murdoch, *Origins of the Salvation Army*, 161–162.

91. Murdoch, *Origins of the Salvation Army*, 163.

92. Booth, *In Darkest England*, 30.

93. Quoted in Ann M. Woodall, *What Price the Poor? William Booth, Karl Marx and the London Residium* (Aldershot, England: Ashgate, 2005).

94. Quoted in Woodall, *What Price the Poor?*, 2.

95. Woodall, *What Price the Poor?*, 2.

96. Woodall, *What Price the Poor?*, 2; "Matches: A Story of Light and Dark," British Broadcasting Corporation, http://www.bbc.co.uk/dna/h2g2/classic/A798834 (accessed March 14, 2011); Salvation Army International Heritage Centre, "Lights in Darkest England," 2003, http://www.salvationarmy.org/heritage.nsf/36c107e27b0ba7a98025692e0032abaa/febeb0790e4da7508025690c0031fb01!OpenDocument (accessed October 24, 2011).

97. Fredrick Engels, 1892 English introduction to *Socialism: Utopian and Scientific*, translated by Edward Aveling, in *Marx/Engels Selected Works*, vol. 3 (Moscow: Progress, 1970).

98. Murdoch, *Origins of the Salvation Army*, 153.

99. Robert Sandall, *The History of the Salvation Army*, vol. 3: *Social Reform and Welfare Work* (New York: Salvation Army, 1979), 117–118.

100. Quoted in Taiz, *Hallelujah Lads & Lasses*, 113.

101. Green, *Life and Ministry of William Booth*, 173; McKinley, *Marching to Glory*, 76; Winston, *Red Hot and Righteous*, 105–106.

102. Taiz, *Hallelujah Lads & Lasses*, 111.

103. Winston, *Red Hot and Righteous*, 103.

104. Winston, *Red Hot and Righteous*, 117–118.

105. Taiz, *Hallelujah Lads & Lasses*, 137.

106. Edwin Gifford Lamb, "The Social Work of the Salvation Army," PhD diss., Columbia University, 1909), 10; Taiz, *Hallelujah Lads & Lasses*, 118; Winston, *Red Hot and Righteous*, 137–139.

107. Pickert, "A Brief History of the Salvation Army," 1.

108. Taiz, *Hallelujah Lads & Lasses*, 117.

109. Watson and Brown, "*The Most Effective Organization in the U.S.*," 17.

110. Murdoch, *Origins of the Salvation Army*, 154.

111. Taiz, *Hallelujah Lads & Lasses*, 144.

112. Taiz, *Hallelujah Lads & Lasses*, 145.

113. Taiz, *Hallelujah Lads & Lasses*, 162.

114. Quoted in McKinley, *Marching to Glory*, 142.

115. Max Weber, *Economy and Society: An Outline of Interpretive Sociology*, ed. Guenther Roth and Claus Wittich (Berkeley: University of California Press, 1978 [1922]).

116. McKinley, *Marching to Glory*, 210.

117. Hazzard, "Marching on the Margins," 131.

118. Salvation Army Indiana Division, "New Army Brand Unveiled Nationally," *County Line Newsletter*, Fall 2005.

119. http://www.salvationarmyusa.org (accessed April 17, 2011).

120. David E. Cedervall, "Writing Salvation Army Position Statements," *Good News!*, January 2005, http://www.sagoodnews.org/article.php?articleID=358 (accessed March 14, 2011).

121. Christopher Heredia, "Salvation Army Says No to Benefits for Partners: National Panel Overturns Regional Okay," *SFGate.com*, November 14, 2001, http://articles.sfgate.com/2001-11-14/news/17627593_1_partner-benefits-western-territory-domestic-partners (accessed April 17, 2011).

122. Oubai Shahbandar, "Salvation Army to Lose Funding over Domestic Partner Flap," *CNSNews.com: Cybercast News Service*, June 20, 2002, http://www.cnsnews.com/node/5096 (accessed March 14, 2011).

123. "Salvation Army in Chicago Reports 13 Percent Decline in Donations: Anti-Gay Stance at Root?," *HuffPost Chicago*, December 14, 2010, http://www.huffingtonpost.com/2010/12/14/salvation-army-in-chicago_n_796669.html (accessed April 2, 2011).

124. Salvation Army, "Fact Sheet: Salvation Army Organization and Structure," May 2010.

125. Salvation Army, *2010 Annual Report*.

126. Allahyari, *Visions of Charity*, 91.

127. Salvation Army, *2008 Annual Report* (Alexandria, Va.: Salvation Army of the United States of America, 2008), 3–4.

128. Clint Cooper, "Salvation Army Eyes New Kind of Homeless Outreach," *Chattanooga Times/Free Press*, March 6, 2011.

129. Kristin Hoppa, "Salvation Army Announces New Programs," *St. Joseph News-Press*, April 1, 2011.

130. Salvation Army, *2008 Annual Report*, 4.

131. http://kroccenter.org/ (accessed March 14, 2011).

132. Lewis, "Issues and Dilemmas in Faith-Based Social Service Delivery," 93.

133. Salvation Army, *2008 Annual Report*, 3. Heidi Rolland Unruh and Ronald J. Sider note that in their study of fifteen Philadelphia Protestant churches that were serving the community, the churches "consistently used the imagery of 'wholeness' to describe the integral relationship between spiritual and social ministry." Heidi Rolland Unruh and Ronald J. Sider, *Saving Souls, Serving Society: Understanding the Faith Factor in Church-Based Social Ministry*. (Oxford: Oxford University Press, 2005), 175.

134. David A. Snow and Leon Anderson, *Down on Their Luck: A Study of Homeless Street People* (Berkeley: University of California Press, 1993), 87.

135. Snow and Anderson, *Down on Their Luck*, 305–306.

136. Allahyari, *Visions of Charity*, 217–218.

137. Lewis, "Issues and Dilemmas in Faith-Based Social Service Delivery," 102.

138. Salvation Army, *2010 Annual Report*, 22.

139. Richard N. Ostling, "The Salvation Army: A Distinctive Corps Simultaneously Expands and Shrinks," *North County Times*, December 15, 2005.

140. "Oshkosh Salvation Army Capt. Johnny Harsh Terminated by Organization for Failure to Follow Rules, Insubordination," *Northwestern*, January 15, 2009.

141. William P. Barrett, "America's 200 Largest Charities," *Forbes.com*, November 17, 2010, http://www.forbes.com/2010/11/16/forbes-charity-200-personal-finance-philanthropy-200-largest-charities-charity-10-intro.html (accessed March 13, 2011).

142. Watson and Brown, "*The Most Effective Organization in the U.S,*" 99.

143. Quoted in Sandall, *History of the Salvation Army*, 263.

144. McKinley, *Marching to Glory*, 137.

145. Edwin Amenta, Kathleen Dunleavy, and Mary Bernstein, "Stolen Thunder? Huey Long's 'Share Our Wealth,' Political Mediation, and the Second New Deal," *American Sociological Review* 59 (1994), 683.

146. John D. McCarthy, David W. Britt, and Mark Wolfson, "The Institutional

Channeling of Social Movements by the State in the United States." *Research in Social Movements, Conflicts and Change* 13 (1991), 52–54.

147. McCarthy, Britt, and Wolfson, "Institutional Channeling," 52.

148. McCarthy, Britt, and Wolfson, "Institutional Channeling," 68.

149. McKinley, *Marching to Glory,* 284.

150. Michael P. Young, "Confessional Protest: The Religious Birth of U.S. National Social Movements," *American Sociological Review* 67 (2002): 663.

151. Elizabeth A. Armstrong and Mary Bernstein, "Culture, Power, and Institutions: A Multi-Institutional Politics Approach to Social Movements," *Sociological Theory* 26 (2008): 74–99.

152. Taiz, *Hallelujah Lads & Lasses,* 107; Allahyari, *Visions of Charity,* 80.

153. McKinley, *Marching to Glory,* 137, 179.

154. McKinley, *Marching to Glory,* 307.

155. Dana Milbank, "Charity Cites Bush Help in Fight against Hiring Gays," *Washington Post,* July 10, 2001, A01.

156. Quoted in McKinley, *Marching to Glory,* 78.

157. Winston, *Red Hot and Righteous,* 173.

158. *American War Cry,* July 17, 1897, 9.

159. McKinley, *Marching to Glory,* 66–67.

160. Todd Hawks, "What Would Jesus Do? Representing the Army on Capitol Hill," *Caring,* October 2008, 37.

161. Hawks, "What Would Jesus Do?," 38; Salvation Army, *2010 Annual Report,* 24.

162. Hawks, "What Would Jesus Do?," 37–38.

163. http://www.salvationarmyusa.org/usn/www_usn_2.nsf/vw-dynamic-arrays/ B6F3F4DF3150F5B585257434004C177D?openDocument (accessed March 14, 2011). See sociologist T. H. Marshall's classic essay on civil, political, and social rights, "Citizenship and Social Class," *Inequality and Society,* ed. Jeff Manza and Michael Sauder, 148–154 (New York: W. W. Norton, 2009).

164. Salvation Army, *2010 Annual Report,* 22.

165. Winston, *Red Hot and Righteous,* 13.

166. Adelle Banks, "Bush Touts His Faith-Based Initiative Despite Congressional Foot-Dragging," *Religion News Service,* June 2, 2004, http://pewforum.org/news/display .php?NewsID=3481 (accessed September 1, 2008).

167. "Office of Faith-Based and Neighborhood Partnerships," *Who Runs Government? From the Washington Post,* March 16, 2011, http://www.whorunsgov.com/Institutions/ White_House/Offices/OFB (accessed April 9, 2011).

168. Chad Terhune, "Along Battered Gulf, Katrina Aid Stirs Unintended Rivalry; Salvation Army Wins Hearts, Red Cross Faces Critics; Two Different Missions," *Wall Street Journal* (Eastern ed.), September 29, 2005.

169. Robert Wuthnow reports that 72 percent of respondents in his sample of Americans agreed that "Private charities are generally more effective than government programs." Robert Wuthnow, *Acts of Compassion: Caring for Others and Helping Ourselves* (Princeton, N.J.: Princeton University Press, 1991), 231.

170. Allahyari, *Visions of Charity,* 215; Jennifer R. Wolch, *The Shadow State: Government and Voluntary Sector in Transition* (New York: Foundation Center, 1990), xvi.

171. Steven Rathgeb Smith and Michael Lipsky, *Nonprofits for Hire: The Welfare State in the Age of Contracting* (Cambridge, Mass.: Harvard University Press, 1993).

172. Michael Lipsky, *Street-Level Bureaucracy: Dilemmas of the Individual in Public Service* (New York: Russell Sage Foundation, 1980).

173. Allahyari, *Visions of Charity*, 215–217.

174. Salvation Army, *2010 Annual Report*, 20.

175. Quoted in Lee and Ebeling, "Can You Top This for Cost-Efficient Management?"

176. Hazzard, "Marching on the Margins," 127; Lewis, "Issues and Dilemmas in Faith-Based Social Service Delivery," 102.

CONCLUSION

1. See, for example, Mona El-Ghobashy, "The Metamorphosis of the Egyptian Muslim Brothers," *International Journal of Middle East Studies* 37 (2005): 377; Robert S. Leiken and Steven Brooke, "The Moderate Muslim Brotherhood," *Foreign Affairs* 86 (2007): 112.

2. Elizabeth A. Armstrong and Mary Bernstein, "Culture, Power, and Institutions: A Multi-Institutional Politics Approach to Social Movements," *Sociological Theory* 26 (2008): 74–99.

3. Christian Smith with Michael Emerson, Sally Gallagher, Paul Kennedy, and David Sikkink, *American Evangelicalism: Embattled and Thriving* (Chicago: University of Chicago Press, 1998).

4. Operating at the grassroots level to allow members to work on local issues and concerns is a strategy used by many SMOs. For example, in a study of how the Service Employees International Union (SEIU) successfully organized low-wage nursing home employees and revitalized the union movement in western Pennsylvania, Steven Lopez finds that the union succeeded by combining "grassroots mobilization, face-to-face interaction, rank-and-file leadership, and a strong social justice orientation." These tactics addressed local concerns and built alliances with the broader community, in contrast to the less successful, nationally driven, legislative tactics of much of organized labor. Steven Henry Lopez, *Reorganizing the Rust Belt: An Inside Story of the American Labor Movement* (Berkeley: University of California Press, 2004), 9.

5. Lewis A. Coser, *Greedy Institutions: Patterns of Undivided Commitment* (New York: Free Press, 1974).

6. Debra C. Minkoff, "Bending with the Wind: Strategic Change and Adaptation by Women's and Racial Minority Organizations," *American Journal of Sociology* 104 (1999): 1666–1703.

7. See, e.g., Vernon L. Bates, "The Decline of a New Christian Right Social Movement Organization: Opportunities and Constraints," *Review of Religious Research* 42 (2000): 19–40.

8. *Fresh Air with Terry Gross*, "The Evangelicals Engaged in Spiritual Warfare," National Public Radio, August 24, 2011; *Fresh Air with Terry Gross*, "A Leading Figure in the New Apostolic Reformation," National Public Radio, October 3, 2011.

9. Armstrong and Bernstein, "Culture, Power, and Institutions."

10. Rosabeth Moss Kanter, *Commitment and Community: Communes and Utopias in Sociological Perspective* (Cambridge, Mass.: Harvard University Press, 1972).

11. James M. Jasper, *The Art of Moral Protest: Culture, Biography, and Creativity in Social Movements* (Chicago: University of Chicago Press, 1997).

12. JoNina M. Abron, "'Serving the People': The Survival Programs of the Black Panther Party," in *The Black Panther Party Reconsidered*, ed. Charles E. Jones, (Baltimore, Md.: Black Classic Press, 1998), 177–192.

13. Abron, "'Serving the People'"; Kit Kim Holder, "The History of the Black Panther Party 1966–1972: A Curriculum Tool for African-American Studies," PhD diss., University of Massachusetts, 1990.

14. Huey P. Newton, *To Die for the People* (New York: Writers and Publishers Edition, 1995).

15. Rebecca L. Bordt, *The Structure of Women's Non-Profit Organizations* (Bloomington: Indiana University Press, 1998); Debra C. Minkoff, "The Emergence of Hybrid Organizational Forms: Combining Identity-Based Service Provision and Political Action," *Non-Profit and Voluntary Sector Quarterly* 31 (2002): 377–401.

16. Benjamin Gidron, Stanley N. Katz, and Yeheskel Hasenfeld, eds., *Mobilizing for Peace: Conflict Resolution in Northern Ireland, Israel/Palestine, and South Africa* (New York: Oxford University Press, 2002).

BIBLIOGRAPHY

Abbruzzese, Salvatore. "Religion et Modernité: Le Cas de 'Comunione e Liberazione.'" *Social Compass* 36 (1989): 13–32.

Abdalla, Nadine H. "Civil Society in Egypt: A Catalyst for Democratization?" *International Journal of Not-for-Profit Law* 10 (2008): 25–29.

Abed-Kotob, Sana. "The Accommodationists Speak: Goals and Strategies of the Muslim Brotherhood of Egypt." *International Journal of Middle East Studies* 27 (1995): 321–339.

Abron, JoNina M. "'Serving the People': The Survival Programs of the Black Panther Party." In *The Black Panther Party Reconsidered*, edited by Charles E. Jones. Baltimore, Md.: Black Classic Press, 1998.

Ahmad, Maamon. "Summary of MB Performance in Egyptian Parliament since 2005." *Ikhwanweb*, August 14, 2006, http://www.ikhwanweb.com/article.php?id=3747 (accessed March 27, 2011).

Al-Awadi, Hersham. *In Pursuit of Legitimacy: The Muslim Brothers and Mubarak, 1982–2000*. London: Tauris Academic Studies, 2004.

Al-Banna, Hasan. *Five Tracts of Hasan al-Banna (1906–1949)*. Translated by Charles Wendell. Berkeley: University of California Press, 1978.

———. *Ila al-Tullab [To Students]*. Alexandria, Egypt: Dar al-Da'wa, no date.

———. *Memoirs of Hasan al-Banna*. Translated by M. N. Shaikh. Karachi, Pakistan: International Islamic, 1981.

Allahyari, Rebecca Anne. *Visions of Charity: Volunteer Workers and Moral Community*. Berkeley: University of California Press, 2000.

Allen, John L., Jr. "Opposing Forces in Italian Church Try Détente." *National Catholic Reporter*, August 27, 2004.

———. "Report from Rimini: Italy's Biggest Public Event." *National Catholic Reporter*, August 26, 2005.

———. "Report: Pope to Launch Pontifical Council for New Evangelization." *National Catholic Reporter*, April 25, 2010.

———. "Scouting Report: Three Soon-to-Be-Cardinals Range from Conservative to More Conservative to Unknown." *National Catholic Reporter*, January 11, 2002.

Almond, Gabriel A., R. Scott Appleby, and Emmanuel Sivan. *Strong Religion: The Rise of Fundamentalisms around the World*. Chicago: University of Chicago Press, 2003.

Al-Shalchi, Hadeel. "Powerful Islamist Movement Sees Leadership Struggle." *Seattle Times*, October 30, 2009.

Amenta, Edwin, Kathleen Dunleavy, and Mary Bernstein. "Stolen Thunder? Huey Long's

'Share Our Wealth,' Political Mediation, and the Second New Deal." *American Sociological Review* 59 (1994): 678–702.

"America at Crossroads: Inside the Muslim Brotherhood." Public Broadcasting System, April 20, 2007.

American Jewish Committee. "New American Jewish Committee Report Demystifies Israel's Shas Party for American Jews." *Charity Wire,* June 24, 1999, http://www.charitywire .com/charity11/00506.html (accessed April 17, 2011).

Amin, Shahira. "The Feminine Face of Egypt's Muslim Brotherhood." *CNN World,* August 3, 2011, http://articles.cnn.com/2011-08-03/world/egypt.muslim.sisterhood_1_egypt -s-muslim-brotherhood-charity-work-al-azhar-university?_s=PM:WORLD (accessed September 30, 2011).

Amos, Deborah. "In Egypt, Muslim Brotherhood's Youth Seek Voice." *Morning Edition,* National Public Radio, April 5, 2011.

Anderson, Lisa. "Fulfilling Prophecies: State Policy and Islamist Radicalism." In *Political Islam: Revolution, Radicalism or Reform?,* edited by John L. Esposito. Boulder, Colo.: Lynne Rienner, 1997.

"Andreotti Cleared of Murder." *CNN.com/World,* October 30, 2003, http://edition.cnn.com/ 2003/WORLD/europe/10/30/italy.andreotti.reut/index.html (accessed April 17, 2011).

"Another Flawed Election: Democracy in Egypt Has Stalled." *Economist,* June 14, 2007.

Armstrong, Elizabeth A. *Forging Gay Identities: Organizing Sexuality in San Francisco, 1950–1994.* Chicago: University of Chicago Press, 2002.

Armstrong, Elizabeth A., and Mary Bernstein. "Culture, Power, and Institutions: A Multi-Institutional Politics Approach to Social Movements." *Sociological Theory* 26 (2008): 74–99.

Armstrong, Karen. *Islam: A Short History.* New York: Modern Library, 2000.

Ash, Roberta. *Social Movements in America.* Chicago: Markham, 1972.

Ashour, Omar. "Egypt Secularists and Liberals Afraid of Democracy?" *BBC News,* July 13, 2011, http://www.bbc.co.uk/news/world-middle-east-14112032 (accessed September 30, 2011).

Baker, Raymond William. "Invidious Comparisons: Realism, Postmodern Globalism, and Centrist Islamic Movements in Egypt." In *Political Islam: Revolution, Radicalism, or Reform?,* edited by John L. Esposito. Boulder, Colo.: Lynne Rienner, 1997.

Banks, Adelle M. "Bush Touts His Faith-Based Initiative despite Congressional Foot-Dragging." *Religion News Service,* June 2, 2004, http://pewforum.org/news/display.php ?NewsID=3481 (accessed September 1, 2008, site discontinued).

Barrett, William P. "America's 200 Largest Charities." *Forbes.com,* November 17, 2010, http:// www.forbes.com/2010/11/16/forbes-charity-200-personal-finance-philanthropy-200 -largest-charities-charity-10-intro.html (accessed March 14, 2011).

Barzilai-Nahon, Karine, and Gad Barzilai. "Cultured Technology: The Internet and Religious Fundamentalism." *Information Society* 21 (2005): 25–40.

Bates, Vernon L. "The Decline of a New Christian Right Social Movement Organization: Opportunities and Constraints." *Review of Religious Research* 42 (2000): 19–40.

Bayat, Asef. *Making Islam Democratic: Social Movements and the Post-Islamist Turn.* Stanford, Calif.: Stanford University Press, 2007.

Bellah, Robert N., Richard Madsen, William M. Sullivan, Ann Swidler, and Steven M. Tipton, *Habits of the Heart: Individualism and Commitment in American Life.* New York: Harper & Row, 1985.

Ben-Yehuda, Nachman. *Theocratic Democracy: The Social Construction of Religious and Secular Extremism.* New York: Oxford University Press, 2010.

Bergamini, Paola. "Free Men behind Bars." *Traces,* January 1, 2006.

Berman, Eli. "Sect, Subsidy and Sacrifice: An Economist's View of Ultra-Orthodox Jews." *Quarterly Journal of Economics* 115 (2000): 905–953.

Berman, Robby. "Double Identity." *Jerusalem Post Internet Edition,* July 27, 1998, http://www.highbeam.com/doc/1P1-15582656.html (accessed March 17, 2011).

Berman, Sheri. "Islam, Revolution, and Civil Society." *Perspectives on Politics* 1 (2003): 257–272.

Bick, Etta. "The Shas Phenomenon and Religious Parties in the 1999 Elections." *Israel Affairs* 7 (2001): 55–100.

Blair, Tony. "Speech at Rimini." August 27, 2009, http://www.laicidade.org/wp-content/uploads/2009/10/tony-blair-rimini.pdf (accessed October 6, 2011).

Blouin, David, and Robert V. Robinson. "Are Religious People More Compassionate?" Paper presented at the joint annual meetings of the Midwest Sociological Society and the North Central Sociological Association, Chicago, April 2007.

Blumenkrantz, Zohar. "Police, Government Launch New Campaign to Fight Pirate Radio Broadcasters." *Haaretz,* June 21, 2007.

Bobbio, Norberto. *Left and Right: The Significance of a Political Distinction* (Destra e sinistra: Regioni e significati di una distinzione politica). Translated by Allan Cameron. Chicago: University of Chicago Press, 1996.

Booth, Evangeline. *The American War Cry,* April 25, 1908.

Booth, William. *In Darkest England and the Way Out.* Charleston, S.C.: BiblioBazaar, 2006 [1890].

Bordt, Rebecca L. *The Structure of Women's Non-Profit Organizations.* Bloomington: Indiana University Press, 1998.

Brockett, Charles D. "A Protest-Cycle Resolution of the Repression/Popular-Protest Paradox." *Social Science History* 17 (1993): 457–484.

Bronner, Ethan. "A Hard-Liner Gains Ground in Israel." *New York Times,* February 9, 2009.

———. "Main Party in Israel Coalition Set to Choose Leader." *New York Times,* September 17, 2008.

———. "Netanyahu to Form New Israel Government." *New York Times,* February 21, 2009.

Bronner, Ethan, and Isabel Kershner. "In Israeli Vote, with Two Parties Nearly Tied, the Winner Is Gridlock." *New York Times,* February 11, 2009.

Brown, Nathan J., Michele Dunne, and Amr Hamzawy. "Egypt's Controversial Constitutional Amendments: A Textual Analysis." *Carnegie Endowment for International Peace,* March 23, 2007, http://www.carnegieendowment.org/files/egypt_constitution _webcommentary.pdf (accessed March 27, 2011).

Bruce, Steve. *The Rise and Fall of the New Christian Right.* New York: Oxford University Press, 1988.

Carrón, Julián. "Your Good Work Is a Good for All." *Traces,* December 1, 2009.

Casanova, José. *Public Religions in the Modern World.* Chicago: University of Chicago Press, 1994.

Cavallaro, Renato. "Communion et Manipulation?" *Social Compass* 23 (1976): 259–261.

Cedervall, David E. "Writing Salvation Army Position Statements." *Good News!*, January 2005, http://www.sagoodnews.org/article.php?articleID=358 (accessed March 14, 2011).

"Che bella vittoria!" [What a great victory!]. *Tracce*, November 1999.

Cipriani, Roberto. "'Diffused Religion' and New Values in Italy." In *The Changing Face of Religion*, edited by James A. Beckford and Thomas Luckmann, 24–49. London: Sage, 1989.

Clark, Janine A. *Islam, Charity, and Action: Middle-Class Networks and Social Welfare in Egypt, Jordan, and Yemen*. Bloomington: Indiana University Press, 2004.

Compagnia delle Opere. *Executive Summary*. Milan, Italy: Compagnia delle Opere, 2009.

Cooper, Clint. "Salvation Army Eyes New Kind of Homeless Outreach." *Chattanooga Times/Free Press*, March 6, 2011.

Cornfield, Daniel B., and Bill Fletcher. "Institutional Constraints on Social Movement 'Frame Extension': Shifts in the Legislative Agenda of the American Federation of Labor, 1881–1955." *Social Forces* 76 (1998): 1305–1321.

Coser, Lewis A. *Greedy Institutions: Patterns of Undivided Commitment*. New York: Free Press, 1974.

Crenshaw, Edward, and Kristopher Robison. "Political Violence as an Object of Study: The Need for Taxonomic Clarity." In *Handbook of Politics: State and Society in Global Perspective*, edited by Kevin T. Leicht and J. Craig Jenkins. New York: Springer, 2010.

Cress, Daniel M., and David A. Snow. "Mobilization at the Margins: Resources, Benefactors, and the Viability of Homeless Social Movement Organizations." *American Sociological Review* 61 (1996): 1089–1109.

———. "The Outcomes of Homeless Mobilization: The Influence of Organization, Disruption, Political Mediation, and Framing." *American Journal of Sociology* 105 (2000): 1063–1104.

Cullinan, Susan. "Time Trail: Italy." *Time Europe*, September 8, 2000.

Davis, Nancy J., and Robert V. Robinson. "Are the Rumors of War Exaggerated? Religious Orthodoxy and Moral Progressivism in the United States." *American Journal of Sociology* 102 (1996): 756–787.

———. "The Egalitarian Face of Islamic Orthodoxy: Support for Islamic Law and Economic Justice in Seven Muslim-Majority Nations." *American Sociological Review* 71 (2006): 167–190.

———. "Overcoming Movement Obstacles by the Religiously Orthodox: The Muslim Brotherhood in Egypt, Shas in Israel, Comunione e Liberazione in Italy, and the Salvation Army in the United States." *American Journal of Sociology* 114 (2009): 1302–1349.

———. "Religious Cosmologies, Individualism, and Politics in Italy." *Journal for the Scientific Study of Religion* 38 (1999): 339–353.

———. "The Roots of Political Activism in Six Muslim-Majority Nations." Paper given at the Workshop on Theoretical and Methodological Issues in the Study of Values in Islamic Countries, Cairo, Egypt, May 16–18, 2010.

———. "Their Brothers' Keepers? Orthodox Religionists, Modernists and Economic Justice in Europe." *American Journal of Sociology* 104 (1999): 1631–1665.

———. "Theological Modernism, Cultural Libertarianism and Laissez-Faire Economics in Contemporary European Societies." *Sociology of Religion* 62 (2001): 23–50.

Dayan, Aryeh. "The Shas Enigma." *Jerusalem Post Online Edition*, July 19, 2010, http://www .jpost.com/JerusalemReport/Article.aspx?id=181927 (accessed October 19, 2011).

de Chalvron, Marc, and Annette Young. "The Spiritual—and Temporal—Heart of Shas." Videoclip. *France 24*, February 6, 2009, http://www.france24.com/en/20090206-spiritual -temporal-heart-shas-israel-elections-political-party (accessed April 17, 2011).

Derfner, Larry. "Social Concern." *Jerusalem Post Internet Edition*, May 24, 2000, http://www .jpost.com/Editions/2000/03/19/Features/Features.4223.html (accessed August 22, 2007).

Diamond, Sara. *Spiritual Warfare: The Politics of the Christian Right*. Montreal: Black Rose Books, 1990.

Dzodin, Rifka. "Aerial Terrorists or Cultural Bellwethers? Illegal Radio and the Fight for Israel's Airwaves." *New Voices: National Jewish Student Magazine*, April 7, 2008.

Efron, Noah J. *Real Jews: Secular vs. Ultra-Orthodox and the Struggle for Jewish Identity in Israel*. New York: Basic, 2003.

Eglash, Ruth. "Background: The Rights and Wrongs of Shas' Bid to Restore Child Allowances." *Jerusalem Post*, October 16, 2008.

"Egypt's Islamist Parties Win Elections to Parliament." *BBC News*, January 21, 2012, http:// www.bbc.co.uk/news/world-middle-east-16665748 (accessed February 9, 2012).

Elbaum, Dov, and Anna Maria Tremonti. "Israel: A House Divided." *International Journal* 53 (Autumn 1998): 609–621.

El-Din, Gamal Essam. "Brotherhood Steps into the Fray." *Al-Ahram Weekly Online*, March 11–17, 2004, http://weekly.ahram.org.eg/2004/681/eg3.htm (accessed March 27, 2011).

"Elections in Israel—2009." *Israel Ministry of Foreign Affairs*. http://www.mfa.gov.il/MFA/ History/Modern+History/Historic+Events/Elections_in_Israel_February_2009.htm (accessed March 17, 2011).

El-Ghobashy, Mona. "The Metamorphosis of the Egyptian Muslim Brothers." *International Journal of Middle East Studies* 37 (2005): 373–395.

El Rashidi, Yasmine. "The Battle for Egypt's Future." *New York Review of Books*, April 28, 2011.

Engels, Fredrick. 1892 English introduction to *Socialism: Utopian and Scientific*, translated by Edward Aveling. In *Marx/Engels Selected Works*, Vol. 3. Moscow: Progress, 1970.

Entous, Adam. "U.S.-Backed Campaign against Hamas Expands to Charities." Reuters, August 20, 2007, http://www.reuters.com/article/worldNews/idUSL2027514420070820 (accessed April 15, 2011).

Esposito, John L. "Islam and Civil Society." In *Modernizing Islam: Religion in the Public Sphere in the Middle East and Europe*, edited by John L. Esposito and Francois Burgat. New Brunswick, N.J.: Rutgers University Press, 2003.

———. *The Oxford Dictionary of Islam*. New York: Oxford University Press, 2003.

Esposito, John L., Robert E. Mazur, and Sibusiso Nkomo. *Political Islam: Revolution, Radicalism or Reform?* Boulder, Colo.: Lynne Rienner, 1997.

Ettinger, Yair. "Despite Opposition, English and Math Are Now Part of Haredi Curriculum." *Haaretz*, October 5, 2008.

Ettinger, Yair, and Shahar Ilan. "Shas-Likud Coalition Deal Includes Record Funding for Yeshivas, Boosts Child Allowances." *Haaretz.com*, March 23, 2009, http://www.haaretz .com/hasen/spages/1073472.html (accessed March 17, 2011).

"Factional and Government Make-Up of the Tenth Knesset." *Knesset*. http://www.knesset .gov.il/history/eng/eng_hist10_s.htm (accessed March 16, 2011).

"Factional and Government Make-Up of the Eleventh Knesset." *Knesset*. http://www.knesset .gov.il/history/eng/eng_hist11_s.htm (accessed March 16, 2011).

Fahim, Kareem. "Slap to a Man's Pride Set Off Tumult in Tunisia." *New York Times*, January 21, 2011.

Farris, David M., and Stacey Philbrick Yadav. "Why Egypt's Muslim Brotherhood Isn't the Islamic Bogeyman." *Christian Science Monitor*, February 14, 2011.

Fligstein, Neil. "Social Skill and the Theory of Fields." *Sociological Theory* 19 (2001): 105–125.

Francisco, Ronald A. "The Dictator's Dilemma." In *Repression and Mobilization*, edited by Christian Davenport, Hank Johnston, and Carol Mueller. Minneapolis: University of Minnesota Press, 2005.

Fresh Air with Terry Gross. "The Evangelicals Engaged in Spiritual Warfare." National Public Radio, August 24, 2011.

Fresh Air with Terry Gross. "Interview with Lawrence Wright." National Public Radio, February 8, 2011.

Fresh Air with Terry Gross. "A Leading Figure in the New Apostolic Reformation." National Public Radio, October 3, 2011.

Friedman, Matti. "In Rise of Ultra-Orthodox, Challenges for Israel." *USA Today*, January 14, 2011.

Gamson, William. *The Strategy of Social Protest*. 2nd ed. Belmont, Calif.: Wadsworth, 1990.

Ganz, Marshall. "Resources and Resourcefulness: Strategic Capacity in the Unionization of California Agriculture, 1959–1966." *American Journal of Sociology* 105 (2000): 1003–1062.

———. "Why David Sometimes Wins: Strategic Capacity in Social Movements." In *The Psychology of Leadership: New Perspectives and Research*, edited by David M. Messick and Roderick M. Kramer, 209–238. Mahwah, N.J.: Lawrence Erlbaum, 2005.

Gariepy, Henry. *Christianity in Action: The International History of the Salvation Army*. Grand Rapids, Mich.: William B. Eerdmans, 2009.

Gaspari, Antonio. "A Change of Course?" *Catholic Information Network*, October 1996, http://www.catholic.net/RCC/Periodicals/Inside/10-96/Movement.html (accessed August 22, 2007; site discontinued).

———. "Communion and Liberation: Crusaders for Catholic Integrity." *Inside the Vatican*, February 1996, http://www.ewtn.com/library/ISSUES/COMLIB.TXT (accessed March 14, 2011).

Gately, Susan. "800,000 at Rimini Meeting." *CiNews*, September 10, 2011, http://www.cinews .ie/article.php?artid=8990 (accessed October 14, 2011).

Gazzar, Brenda. "Ultra-Orthodox Israeli Women Reach for Better Jobs." *Women's eNews*, March 12, 2007, http://www.womensenews.org/story/070312/ultra-orthodox-israeli -women-reach-better-jobs (accessed April 6, 2011).

Ghadbian, Najib. "Political Islam and Violence." *New Political Science* 22 (2000): 77–88.

Giddens, Anthony. *Beyond Left and Right: The Future of Radical Politics*. Cambridge: Polity Press, 1994.

Gidron, Benjamin, Stanley N. Katz, and Yeheskel Hasenfeld, eds. *Mobilizing for Peace: Con-*

flict Resolution in Northern Ireland, Israel/Palestine, and South Africa. New York: Oxford University Press, 2002.

Giugni, Marco G. "Was It Worth the Effort? The Outcomes and Consequences of Social Movements." *Annual Review of Sociology* 98 (1998): 371–393.

Giussani, Luigi. *The Christian Event*. Milan, Italy: Rizzoli, 1993.

———. "Il 'potere' del laico, cioè del Cristiano: Intervista a Monsignor Luigi Giussani a cura di Angelo Scola." *Come 2000 Anni Fa*, a supplement of *Il Sabato*, August 5, 1989.

———. *Un avvenimento di vita, cioè una storia*. Rome, Italy: EDIT, 1993.

———. "What Kind of Life Gives Birth to Communion and Liberation?" *Traces*, May 1979.

Glain, Stephen. "Fault Lines in the Muslim Brotherhood." *Nation*, September 12, 2011.

"God's Warriors: Jewish Warriors, Muslim Warriors, Christian Warriors." *CNN*, reported by Christiane Amanpour. August 21–23, 2007.

Gorenberg, Gershom. "Hot Shas." *New Republic*, January 25, 1999.

Gramsci, Antonio. *Prison Notebooks*. New York: International, 1971.

Green, Roger J. *The Life and Ministry of William Booth*. Nashville, Tenn.: Abingdon Press, 2005.

Gupta, Kanchan. "Egypt: Regime Targets Activists, NGOs." *The Pioneer, Demdigest.net-Egypt*, September 13, 2008, http://www.ikhwanweb.com/Article.asp?ID=17880&SectionID= 92 (accessed March 27, 2011).

Gusfield, Joseph R. *Symbolic Crusade: Status Politics and the American Temperance Movement*. 2nd ed. Urbana: University of Illinois Press, 1986.

Hafez, Mohammed. *Why Muslims Rebel: Repression and Resistance in the Islamic World*. Boulder, Colo.: Lynne Rienner, 2003.

Hakak, Yohai, "Egalitarian Fundamentalism: Preventing Defection in the Israeli Haredi Community." *Journal of Contemporary Religion* 26 (2011): 291–310.

Halevi, Yossi Klein. "Barak Must Confront Power Wielded by Ultra-Orthodox Party." *Los Angeles Times*, June 20, 1999.

———. "City of God." *New Republic*, September 29, 2003.

Halsell, Grace. "In Egypt the Real Struggle Is between Mubarak and the Muslim Brotherhood." *Washington Report on Middle Eastern Affairs*, January 1, 1996.

Harmsen, Egbert. "Muslim NGOs: Between Empowerment and Paternalism." *ISIM Review* 20 (2007): 10–11.

Hart, Stephen. *What Does the Lord Require? How American Christians Think about Economic Justice*. New York: Oxford University Press, 1992.

Hawks, Todd. "What Would Jesus Do? Representing the Army on Capitol Hill." *Caring*, October 2008.

Hazzard, John W. "Marching on the Margins: An Analysis of the Salvation Army in the United States." *Review of Religious Research* 40 (1998): 121–141.

Hedges, Chris. "Cairo Journal: After the Earthquake, a Rumbling of Discontent." *New York Times*, October 21, 1992.

Heller, Aron. "Israeli Change: Election Tone Is Obama-Like." *Chicago Tribune*, December 20, 2008.

Heredia, Christopher. "Salvation Army Says No to Benefits for Partners: National Panel Overturns Regional Okay." *SFGate.com*, November 14, 2001, http://articles.sfgate.com/

2001-11-14/news/17627593_1_partner-benefits-western-territory-domestic-partners (accessed April 17, 2011).

Hershenson, Sarah. "A Nurturing Spirit." *Jerusalem Post,* May 12, 2006.

Hill, Evan. "The Muslim Brotherhood in Flux." *Al Jazeera,* November 21, 2010, http://english.aljazeera.net/indepth/2010/11/2010111681527837704.html (accessed April 15, 2011).

Hoffman, Bruce. *Inside Terrorism.* New York: Columbia University Press, 2006.

Holder, Kit Kim. "The History of the Black Panther Party 1966–1972: A Curriculum Tool for African-American Studies." PhD diss., University of Massachusetts, 1990.

Hooper, John. "Father Liugi Giussani: Italian Priest and Founder of the Controversial Catholic Pressure Group, Communion and Liberation." *Guardian,* April 1, 2005.

Hoppa, Kristin. "Salvation Army Announces New Programs." *St. Joseph News-Press,* April 1, 2011.

Hunter, James Davison. *Culture Wars: The Struggle to Define America.* New York: Basic Books, 1991.

International Crisis Group. "Egypt's Muslim Brothers: Confrontation or Integration?" *Middle East/North Africa Report* 76 (2008): 1–32.

"Islam Rising: A Conversation with Mary Anne Weaver." *Atlantic Online,* February 17, 1999, http://www.theatlantic.com/unbound/bookauth/ba990217.htm (accessed March 27, 2011).

"Israel's Netanyahu Signs Up Shas." *BBC News,* March 23, 2009, http://news.bbc.co.uk/2/hi/middle_east/7958747.stm (accessed March 17, 2011).

Jasper, James M. *The Art of Moral Protest: Culture, Biography, and Creativity in Social Movements.* Chicago: University of Chicago Press, 1997.

Jelen, Ted. "Religious Belief and Attitude Constraint." *Journal for the Scientific Study of Religion* 29 (1990): 118–125

Juergensmeyer, Mark. *Terror in the Mind of God: The Global Rise of Religious Violence.* 3rd ed. Berkeley: University of California Press, 2003.

Junisbai, Azamat. "Understanding Economic Justice Attitudes in Two Countries: Kazakhstan and Kyrgyzstan." *Social Forces* 88 (2010): 1677–1702.

Kamil, Omar. "The Synagogue as Civil Society, or How We Can Understand the Shas Party." *Mediterranean Quarterly* 12 (2001): 128–143.

Kanter, Rosabeth Moss. *Commitment and Community: Communes and Utopias in Sociological Perspective.* Cambridge, Mass.: Harvard University Press, 1972.

Katz, Yaron. "The 'Other Media'—Alternative Communications in Israel." *International Journal of Cultural Studies* 10 (2007): 383–400.

Keinon, Herb, and Rebecca Anna Stoil. "Cabinet Approves Stipend Limits to Most Yeshiva Students." *Jerusalem Post,* December 12, 2010.

Kepel, Gilles. *The Revenge of God: The Resurgence of Islam, Christianity and Judaism in the Modern World.* University Park: Pennsylvania State University Press, 1994.

Kershner, Israel. "Some Israelis Question Benefits for Ultra-Religious." *New York Times,* December 28, 2010.

King, Winston L. "Eastern Religions: A New Interest and Influence." *Annals of the American Academy of Political and Social Science* 381 (1970): 66–76.

Kirkpatrick, David D., and Michael Slackman. "Egyptian Youths Drive the Revolt against Mubarak." *New York Times,* January 26, 2011.

Klatch, Rebecca. "Complexities of Conservatism: How Conservatives Understand the World." In *America at Century's End,* edited by Alan Wolfe. Berkeley: University of California Press, 1992.

Kniss, Fred. "Culture Wars: Remapping the Battleground." In *Cultural Wars in American Politics: Critical Reviews of a Popular Myth,* edited by Rhys H. Williams, 331–347. New York: Aldine de Gruyter, 1997.

Kniss, Fred, and Gene Burns. "Religious Movements." In *The Blackwell Companion to Social Movements,* edited by David A. Snow, Sarah A. Soule, and Hanspeter Kriesi, 694–715. Malden, Mass.: Blackwell, 2004.

Kook, Rebecca, Michael Harris, and Gideon Doron. "In the Name of G-D and Our Rabbi: The Politics of the Ultra-Orthodox in Israel." *Israel Affairs* (August 1998): 1–18.

Kopelowitz, Ezra, and Matthew Diamond. "Religion That Strengthens Democracy: An Analysis of Religious Political Strategies in Israel." *Theory and Society* 27 (1998): 671–708.

Kunkle, Fredrick. "In Egypt, Muslim Brotherhood's Charitable Works May Drive Political Support." *Washington Post,* April 9, 2011

Kurzman, Charles. "Critics Within: Islamic Scholars' Protests against the Islamic State in Iran." *International Journal of Politics* 15 (2001): 341–359.

———. "Structural Opportunity and Perceived Opportunity in Social Movement Theory: The Iranian Revolution of 1979." *American Sociological Review* 61 (1996): 153–170.

Lamb, Edwin Gifford. "The Social Work of the Salvation Army." PhD diss., Columbia University, 1909.

Lee, Susan, and Ashlea Ebeling. "Can You Top This for Cost-Efficient Management?" *Forbes,* April 20, 1998.

Lehmann, David, and Batia Siebzehner. *Remaking Israeli Judaism: The Challenge of Shas.* Oxford: Oxford University Press, 2006.

Leiken, Robert S., and Steven Brooke. "The Moderate Muslim Brotherhood." *Foreign Affairs* 86 (2007): 107–121.

Leon, Nissim. "'Zikui Harabim': Ovadia Yosef's Approach toward Religious Activism and His Place in the Haredi Movement within Mizrahi Jewry." In *Sephardic Jewry and Mizrahi Jews. Studies in Contemporary Jewry, an Annual, XXII,* edited by Peter Y. Medding. Oxford: Oxford University Press, 2007.

Lesch, Ann. "Talking about a Revolution: Voices from the Margin?" Lecture given at DePauw University, Greencastle, Indiana, April 1, 2011.

Levy, Gal. "'And Thanks to the Ashkenazim . . .': The Politics of Mizrahi Ethnicity in Israel" (Hebrew). Master's thesis, Tel Aviv University, 1995.

Lewis, Beth M. "Issues and Dilemmas in Faith-Based Social Service Delivery: The Case of the Salvation Army of Greater Philadelphia." *Administration in Social Work* 27 (2003): 87–106.

Lia, Brynjar. *The Society of the Muslim Brothers in Egypt: The Rise of an Islamic Mass Movement, 1928–1942.* Beirut, Lebanon: Ithaca Press, 1998.

Lindsey, Ursula. "Egypt's Muslim Brotherhood: Widening Split between Young and Old." *Christian Science* Monitor, December 21, 2009.

Lipset, Seymour Martin. *Political Man*. New York: Free Press, 1981.

Lipsky, Michael. *Street-Level Bureaucracy: Dilemmas of the Individual in Public Service*. New York: Russell Sage Foundation, 1980.

Lopez, Steven Henry. *Reorganizing the Rust Belt: An Inside Story of the American Labor Movement*. Berkeley: University of California Press, 2004.

Lynfield, Ben. "The Shas of Israel Rise to Prominence." *Christian Science Monitor*, April 4, 2000.

MacFarquhar, Neil. "Egyptian Voters Approve Constitutional Changes." *New York Times*, March 21, 2011.

Machlis, Avi. "Shas Party's Growing Power Linked to Schools for Poor." *JWeekly.com*, June 4, 1999, http://www.jweekly.com/article/full/10952/shas-party-s-growing-power-linked -to-schools-for-poor/ (accessed April 8, 2011).

"Marchionne parla al meeting di CL: 'L'Italia ha bisogno di guardare avanti.'" *Il Tempo*, August 26, 2010.

Marciano, Ilan. "Shas Election Jingles Reach Finals." *Ynetnews.com*, January 10, 2006, http:// www.ynetnews.com/articles/0,7340,L-3197823,00.html (accessed March 16, 2011).

Marcolivio, Luca. "Rimini '11 Closes with 800,000 Participants." *Zenit: The World Seen from Rome*, August 29, 2011, http://www.zenit.org/rssenglish-33312 (accessed October 15, 2011).

Marshall, T. H. "Citizenship and Social Class." In *Inequality and Society*, edited by Jeff Manza and Michael Sauder, 148–154. New York: W. W. Norton, 2009.

Marty, Martin E., and R. Scott Appleby. *The Glory and the Power: The Fundamentalist Challenge to the Modern World*. Boston: Beacon Press, 1992.

Marullo, Sam, Ron Pagnucco, and Jackie Smith. "Frame Changes and Social Movement Contraction: U.S. Peace Movement Framing after the Cold War." *Sociological Inquiry* 36 (1996): 1–28.

"Matches: A Story of Light and Dark." *British Broadcasting Corporation*. http://www.bbc .co.uk/dna/h2g2/classic/A798834 (accessed March 14, 2011).

McAdam, Doug. *Freedom Summer*. New York: Oxford University Press, 1988.

———. *Political Process and the Development of Black Insurgency, 1930–1970*. Chicago: University of Chicago Press, 1982.

McAdam, Doug, John D. McCarthy, and Mayer N. Zald. "Opportunities, Mobilizing Structures, and Framing Processes—Toward a Synthetic, Comparative Perspective on Social Movements." In *Comparative Perspectives on Social Movements*, edited by Doug McAdam, John D. McCarthy, and Mayer N. Zald, 1–20. New York: Cambridge University Press, 1996.

McCarthy, John D., David W. Britt, and Mark Wolfson. "The Institutional Channeling of Social Movements by the State in the United States." *Research in Social Movements, Conflicts and Change* 13 (1991): 45–76.

McCarthy, John D. and Mayer N. Zald. "Resource Mobilization and Social Movements: A Partial Theory." *American Journal of Sociology* 82 (1977): 1212–1241.

McKinley, Edward H. *Marching to Glory: The History of The Salvation Army in the United States, 1880–1992*. 2nd ed. Grand Rapids, Mich.: William B. Erdmans, 1995.

Medding, Peter Y., ed. *Sephardic Jewry and Mizrahi Jews*. Studies in Contemporary Jewry: An Annual, XXII. New York: Oxford University Press, 2007.

Mignone, Mario B. *Italy Today: Facing the Challenges of the New Millennium.* New York: Peter Lang, 2008.

Milbank, Dana. "Charity Cites Bush Help in Fight against Hiring Gays." *Washington Post,* July 10, 2001.

Minkoff, Debra C. "Bending with the Wind: Strategic Change and Adaptation by Women's and Racial Minority Organizations." *American Journal of Sociology* 104 (1999): 1666–1703.

———. "The Emergence of Hybrid Organizational Forms: Combining Identity-Based Service Provision and Political Action." *Non-profit and Voluntary Sector Quarterly* 31 (2002): 377–401.

Mitchell, Richard P. *The Society of the Muslim Brothers.* Oxford: Oxford University Press, 1969.

Moaddel, Mansoor. *Jordanian Exceptionalism: A Comparative Analysis of State-Religion Relationships in Egypt, Iran, Jordan, and Syria.* New York: Palgrave Macmillan, 2002.

Moskin, Robert. "Prejudice in Israel." *Look,* October 5, 1965.

Mualem, Mazal. "Shas Won't Let Government Dry Out West Bank Settlements." *Haaretz.com,* March 6, 2009, http://www.haaretz.com/print-edition/news/shas-won-t-let-government-dry-out-west-bank-settlements-1.277170 (accessed October 4, 2011).

Munson, Ziad. "Islamic Mobilization: Social Movement Theory and the Egyptian Muslim Brotherhood." *Sociological Quarterly* 42 (2001): 487–510.

Murdoch, Norman H. *Origins of the Salvation Army.* Knoxville: University of Tennessee Press, 1994.

Murphy, Dan. "Egypt Reins in Democratic Voices." *Christian Science Monitor,* March 28, 2005.

Murray, Andrew. "The Principle of Subsidiarity and the Church." *Australasian Catholic Record* 72 (1995): 163–172.

Muslim Brotherhood. "The Electoral Programme of the Muslim Brotherhood for Shura Council in 2007." *Ikhwanweb,* June 14, 2007, http://www.ikhwanweb.com/Article.asp?ID=822&SectionID=0 (accessed March 27, 2011).

———. "Frequently Asked Questions." *Ikhwanweb.* http://www.ummah.net/ikhwan/questions.html (accessed August 26, 2008; site discontinued).

———. "The Role of Muslim Women in an Islamic Society." *Ikhwanweb,* June 10, 2007, http://www.ikhwanweb.com/article.php?id=787 (accessed April 5, 2011).

———. "Who We Are." *Ikhwanweb.* http://www.ikhwanonline.com (accessed December 31, 2008).

Nahshoni, Kobi. "Yishai: Assurance of Income for University Students with Children." *Ynetnews.com,* November 4, 2010, http://www.ynetnews.com/Ext/Comp/ArticleLayout/CdaArticlePrintPreview/1,2506,L-3980045,00.html (accessed October 13, 2011).

Newton, Huey P. *To Die for the People.* New York: Writers and Publishers Edition, 1995.

"Office of Faith-Based and Neighborhood Partnerships." *Who Runs Government? From the Washington Post,* March 16, 2011, http://www.whorunsgov.com/Institutions/White_House/Offices/OFB (accessed April 9, 2011).

Opp, Karl-Dieter, and Wolfgang Roehl. "Repression, Micromobilization, and Political Protest." *Social Forces* 69 (1990): 521–547.

Osa, MaryJane, and Cristina Corduneanu-Huci. "Running Uphill: Political Opportunities in Non-Democracies." *Comparative Sociology* 2 (2003): 605–629.

"Oshkosh Salvation Army Capt. Johnny Harsh Terminated by Organization for Failure to Follow Rules, Insubordination." *Northwestern,* January 15, 2009.

Ostling, Richard N. "The Salvation Army: A Distinctive Corps Simultaneously Expands and Shrinks." *North County Times,* December 15, 2005.

Pace, Enzo. "Fondamentalismo italiano: Il caso di Comunione e Liberazione." In *Il Regime della Verita: Il Fondamentalismo Religioso Contemporaneo,* edited by Enzo Pace. Bologna, Italy: Il Mulino, 1990.

Pargeter, Alison. *The Muslim Brotherhood: The Burden of Tradition.* London: SAQI, 2010.

Peled, Yoav. "Towards a Redefinition of Jewish Nationalism in Israel? The Enigma of Shas." *Ethnic and Racial Studies* 21 (1998): 701–726.

Peters, Rudoph. "Divine Law or Man-Made Law? Egypt and the Application of the Shari'a." *Arab Law Quarterly* 3 (1988): 231–253.

Pickert, Kate. "A Brief History of the Salvation Army." *Time,* December 2, 2008.

Pinotti, Ferruccio. Promotional video for *La Lobby di Dio: Fede, Affari, e Politica, La Prima Inchiesta su Comunione e Liberazione e Compagnia delle Opere.* Milan, Italy: Chiarelettere, 2010. http://www.youtube.com/watch?v=CW19B7R4xZ0 (accessed April 8, 2011).

Platt, Gerald M., and Rhys H. Williams. "Ideological Language and Social Movement Mobilization: A Sociolinguistic Analysis of Segregationists' Ideologies." *Sociological Theory* 20 (2002): 328–359.

"The Pope's Youthful 'New Jesuits,'" *Time,* September 8, 1986.

Potter, Mitch. "Is the Muslim Brotherhood a Threat?" *Toronto Star,* February 3, 2011.

"Prisoners' Exhibit at Meeting 2008, Rimini." *Cahiers Péguy,* August 29, 2008.

Prusher, Ileen R. "Israel's 'Religious Right' Gains Clout, Complicating Peace with Palestinians." *Christian Science Monitor,* March 19, 2008.

Putnam, Robert D. *Bowling Alone: The Collapse and Revival of American Community.* New York: Simon & Schuster, 2000.

———. "The Strange Disappearance of Civic America." *American Prospect* (Winter, 1996): 34–48.

Qutb, Sayyid. *Milestones.* Indianapolis, Ind.: American Trust, 1993.

Rachleff, Peter J. *Hard Pressed in the Heartland: The Hormel Strike and the Future of the Labor Movement.* Boston: South End Press, 1999.

Rasler, Karen. "Concessions, Repression, and Political Protest in the Iranian Revolution." *American Sociological Review* 61 (1996): 132–152.

Reese, Ellen, and Garnett Newcombe. "Income Rights, Mothers' Rights, or Workers' Rights? Collective Action Frames, Organizational Ideologies, and the American Welfare Rights Movement." *Social Problems* 50 (2003): 294–318.

Regnerus, Mark, Christian Smith, and David Sikkink. "Who Gives to the Poor? The Influence of Religious Tradition and Political Location on the Personal Generosity of Americans toward the Poor." *Journal for the Scientific Study of Religion* 37 (1998): 481–493.

"Revolution in Cairo." *Frontline,* PBS, February 22, 2011.

Rondoni, Davide. *Communion and Liberation: A Movement in the Church.* Translated by Patrick Stevenson and Susan Scott. Montreal: McGill-Queen's University Press, 1998.

Rotem, Tamar. "Some Revolutions Come in Modest Dress." *Haaretz.com,* March 4, 2009, http://www.haaretz.com/print-edition/features/some-revolutions-come-in-modest -dress-1.23124 (accessed April 8, 2011).

Rubin, Barry. Introduction. In *The Muslim Brotherhood: The Organization and Policies of a Global Islamist Movement*, edited by Barry Rubin. New York: Palgrave Macmillan, 2010.

Rupp, Leila, and Verta Taylor. *Survival in the Doldrums: The American Women's Rights Movement, 1945 to the 1960s*. New York: Oxford University Press, 1987.

Russell, Jeffrey Burton. *The Prince of Darkness: Radical Evil and the Power of Good in History*. Ithaca, N.Y.: Cornell University Press, 1992.

Ryle, Robyn R., and Robert V. Robinson. "Ideology, Moral Cosmology, and Community in the United States." *City & Community* 5 (2006): 53–69.

Sageman, Marc. *Understanding Terror Networks*. Philadelphia: University of Pennsylvania Press, 2004.

Saikal, Amin. *Islam and the West: Conflict or Cooperation?* New York: Palgrave MacMillan, 2003.

Salvation Army. *2008 Annual Report*. Alexandria, Va.: Salvation Army of the United States of America, 2008.

Salvation Army. *2010 Annual Report*. Alexandria, Va.: Salvation Army of the United States of America, 2010.

Salvation Army. "Fact Sheet: Salvation Army Organization and Structure." May 2010.

"Salvation Army in Chicago Reports 13 Percent Decline in Donations: Anti-Gay Stance at Root?" *HuffPost Chicago,* December 14, 2010, http://www.huffingtonpost.com/2010/ 12/14/salvation-army-in-chicago_n_796669.html (accessed April 2, 2011).

Salvation Army Indiana Division. "New Army Brand Unveiled Nationally." *County Line Newsletter,* Fall 2005.

Salvation Army International Heritage Centre, "Lights in Darkest England." 2003, http://www.salvationarmy.org/heritage.nsf/36c107e27b0ba7a98025692e0032abaa/ febeb0790e4da7508025690c0031fb01!OpenDocument (accessed October 24, 2011).

Sandall, Robert. *The History of the Salvation Army*. Vol. 3: *Social Reform and Welfare Work*. New York: Salvation Army, 1979.

Schmidt, Shira Leibowitz. "AAAs for Shas." *Jerusalem Post Online Edition,* February 7, 2009, http://www.jpost.com/Opinion/Op-EdContributors/Article.aspx?id=132037 (accessed March 16, 2011).

Scholz, Bernard. "Work and the Person: Toward a New Education." Speech delivered at Columbia University, October 29, 2009, http://www.crossroadsculturalcenter.org/ storage/transcripts/2009-10-29-Human%20Capital-Scholz.pdf (accessed April 8, 2011).

Selznick, Philip. *The Organizational Weapon: A Study of Bolshevik Strategy and Tactics*. Santa Monica, Calif.: Rand, 1952.

Shaeffer, Frank. *Crazy for God: How I Grew Up as One of the Elect, Helped Found the Religious Right, and Lived to Take All (or Almost All) of It Back*. New York: Carroll and Graf, 2007.

Shahbandar, Oubai. "Salvation Army to Lose Funding over Domestic Partner Flap." *CNSNews .com: Cybercast News Service,* June 20, 2002, http://www.cnsnews.com/node/5096 (accessed March 14, 2011).

Shahin, Emad El-Din. "Political Islam: Ready for Engagement?" Paper presented at the Workshop on "Barcelona +10." Madrid, Spain, January 2005.

Sharrock, David. "The Rise of the Torah's Guardians." *Guardian,* April 30, 1998.

Shehata, Samer, and Joshua Stacher. "The Brotherhood Goes to Parliament." *Middle East Report* 240 (2006): 32–39.

Shoan, Amir, "The Haredi School Scam." *Ynetnews.com,* July 12, 2010, http://www.ynetnews.com/articles/0,7340,L-3918220,00.html (accessed March 16, 2011).

Shohat, Ella. "The Invention of the Mizrahim." *Journal of Palestinian Studies* 29 (1999): 5–20.

Sinai, Ruth. "Abortion Issue Sparks Uproar in Knesset." *Israel Religious Action Center,* December 6, 2000, http://www.irac.org/article_e.asp?artid=377 (accessed January 15, 2007; site discontinued.).

Slackman, Michael. "Islamist Group Is Rising Force in a New Egypt." *New York Times,* March 24, 2011.

———. "Mohamed Sayed Tantawi, Top Cleric, Dies at 81." *New York Times,* March 10, 2010.

———. "Stifled, Egypt's Young Turn to Islamic Fervor." *New York Times,* February 17, 2008.

Smith, Christian, with Michael Emerson, Sally Gallagher, Paul Kennedy, and David Sikkink. *American Evangelicalism: Embattled and Thriving.* Chicago: University of Chicago Press, 1998.

Smith, J. Evan. *Booth the Beloved.* Oxford: Oxford University Press, 1949.

Smith, Steven Rathgeb, and Michael Lipsky. *Nonprofits for Hire: The Welfare State in the Age of Contracting.* Cambridge, Mass.: Harvard University Press, 1993.

Snow, David A., and Leon Anderson. *Down on Their Luck: A Study of Homeless Street People.* Berkeley: University of California Press, 1993.

Snow, David A., and Scott C. Byrd. "Ideology, Framing Processes, and Islamic Terrorist Movements." *Mobilization* 12 (2007): 119–136.

Soage, Ana Belén, and Jorge Fuentelsaz Franganillo. "The Muslim Brothers in Egypt." In *The Muslim Brotherhood: The Organization and Policies of a Global Islamist Movement,* edited by Barry Rubin. New York: Palgrave Macmillan, 2010.

Sofer, Barbara. "The World According to Shas." *Inside Magazine,* a supplement of *Jewish Exponent,* Fall 2000.

Somfalvi, Attila. "Shas: No Agreement with Likud Just Yet." *Ynetnews.com,* March 5, 2009, http://www.ynetnews.com/Ext/Comp/ArticleLayout/CdaArticlePrintPreview/1,2506,L-3682019,00.html (accessed March 16, 2011).

Sontag, Deborah. "A Rising Israeli Political Star Threatens Barak's Majority." *New York Times,* November 20, 1999.

Spira, Yechiel. "Rav Ben-Atar to Begin Prison Sentence after Chanukah." *Yeshiva World News,* November 19, 2008, http://www.theyeshivaworld.com/article.php?p=26149 (accessed April 8, 2011).

Spyer, Jonathan. "Special Issue: The 17th Knesset Elections." *Middle East Review of International Affairs,* April 10, 2006, http://meria.idc.ac.il/news/2006/06April10news.html (accessed March 16, 2011; site discontinued).

Starks, Brian, and Robert V. Robinson. "Moral Cosmology, Religion, and Adult Values for Children." *Journal for the Scientific Study of Religion* 46 (2007): 17–35.

———. "Two Approaches to Religion and Politics: Moral Cosmology and Subcultural Identity." *Journal for the Scientific Study of Religion* 48 (2009): 650–669.

Steedly, Homer R., and John W. Foley. "The Success of Protest Groups: Multivariate Analyses." *Social Science Research* 8 (1979): 1–15.

Stern, Jessica. *Terror in the Name of God: Why Religious Militants Kill.* New York: Harper Perennial, 2004.

Sullivan, Denis J., and Sana Abed-Kotob. *Islam in Contemporary Egypt: Civil Society vs. the State.* Boulder, Colo.: Lynne Rienner, 1999.

Taiz, Lillian. *Hallelujah Lads & Lasses: Remaking the Salvation Army in America, 1880–1930.* Chapel Hill: University of North Carolina Press, 2001.

Talhami, Ghada Hashem. "Whither the Social Network of Islam." *Muslim World* 91 (2001): 311–324.

Tamney, Joseph B., Ronald Burton, and Stephen D. Johnson. "Fundamentalism and Economic Restructuring." In *Religion and Political Behavior in the United States,* edited by Ted G. Jelen. New York: Praeger, 1989.

Tarrow, Sidney. *Power in Movement: Social Movements and Contentious Politics.* 2nd ed. New York: Cambridge University Press, 1998.

Terhune, Chad. "Along Battered Gulf, Katrina Aid Stirs Unintended Rivalry; Salvation Army Wins Hearts, Red Cross Faces Critics; Two Different Missions." *Wall Street Journal* (Eastern ed.), September 29, 2005.

Tessler, Ricky. "The Price of the Revolution." In *Shas: The Challenge of Israeliness* (Hebrew), edited by Yoav Peled. Tel-Aviv: Yediot Aharonot, 2001.

"Testimonies." *Traces,* January 1, 2006.

Traub, James. "Islamic Democrats?" *New York Times Magazine,* April 29, 2007.

United Nations Office for the Coordination of Humanitarian Affairs. "Egypt: Social Programs Bolster Appeal of Muslim Brotherhood." February 22, 2006, http://www.irinnews.org/report.aspx?reportid=26150 (accessed March 27, 2011).

Unruh, Heidi Rolland, and Ronald J. Sider. *Saving Souls, Serving Society: Understanding the Faith Factor in Church-Based Social Ministry.* Oxford: Oxford University Press, 2005.

Urquhart, Gordon. *The Pope's Armada: Unlocking the Secrets of Mysterious and Powerful New Sects in the Church.* Amherst, N.Y.: Prometheus Books, 1999.

Usher, Graham. "The Enigmas of Shas." *Middle East Report* 207 (1998): 34–36.

Vaidyanathan, Brandon. "A Rose by Any Other Name: Definitions of Religiosity among Volunteers in an Italian Cultural Festival." Paper presented at the eleventh annual Chicago Ethnography Conference. Chicago, February 28, 2009.

Voll, John O. "Fundamentalism in the Sunni Arab World." In *Fundamentalisms Observed,* edited by Martin E. Marty and Scott Appleby. Chicago: University of Chicago Press, 1991.

Wagner, Matthew. "Shas's Child Allowance Demands Face Tough Opposition." *Jerusalem Post,* August 7, 2008.

———. "Shas's Yosef: Voting for Israel Beiteinu an Unforgivable Sin." *Jerusalem Post,* February 9, 2009.

Walsh, John. "Egypt's Muslim Brotherhood: Understanding Centrist Islam." *Harvard International Review* 24 (2003): 32–36.

Watson, Robert A., and Ben Brown. *"The Most Effective Organization in the U.S.": Leadership Secrets of the Salvation Army.* New York: Crown Business, 2001.

Weber, Max. *Economy and Society: An Outline of Interpretive Sociology,* edited by Guenther Roth and Claus Wittich. Berkeley: University of California Press, 1978 (1922).

Wedeman, Ben. "Egypt's Muslim Brotherhood: Has Its Moment Arrived?" *CNN,* December 1,

2011, http://www.cnn.com/2011/12/01/world/meast/egypt-muslim-brotherhood/index
.html?hpt=hp_t1 (accessed December 1, 2011).

Weiss, Bari. "A Democrat's Triumphal Return to Cairo." *New York Times,* February 26, 2011.

Weissbrod, Lilly. "Shas: An Ethnic Religious Party." *Israel Affairs* 9 (2003): 79–104.

Welborn, Amy. "In Communion." *Open Book,* March 24, 2007, http://amywelborn.typepad
.com/openbook/2007/03/in_communion.html (accessed March 14, 2011).

Wickham, Carrie Rosefsky. *Mobilizing Islam: Religion, Activism and Political Change in
Egypt.* New York: Columbia University Press, 2002.

Wilde, Melissa J. *Vatican II: A Sociological Analysis of Religious Change.* Princton, N.J.:
Princeton University Press, 2007.

Williams, Rhys H. "Movement Dynamics and Social Change: Transforming Fundamen-
talist Ideology and Organization." In *Accounting for Fundamentalisms: The Dynamic
Character of Movements,* edited by Martin E. Marty and R. Scott Appleby, 785–833.
Chicago: University of Chicago Press, 1994.

———. "Public Religion and Hegemony: Contesting the Language of the Common Good."
In *The Power of Religious Publics: Staking Claims in American Society,* edited by William
H. Swatos Jr. and James K. Wellman Jr. Westport, Conn.: Praeger, 1999.

Willis, Aaron P. "Shas—The Sephardic Torah Guardians: Religious 'Movement' and Political
Power." In *The Elections in Israel—1999,* edited by Arian Asher and Michael Shamir.
Albany, N.Y.: SUNY Press, 1995.

Wilson, Scott. "Hamas Sweeps Palestinian Elections." *Washington Post,* January 27, 2006.

Winston, Diane. *Red Hot and Righteous: The Urban Religion of the Salvation Army.* Cambridge, Mass.: Harvard University Press, 1999.

Wolch, Jennifer R. *The Shadow State: Government and Voluntary Sector in Transition.* New
York: Foundation Center, 1990.

Woltering, Robert A. F. L. "The Roots of Islamic Popularity." *Third World Quarterly* 23
(2002): 1133–1143.

Wood, Richard L. "Religious Culture and Political Action." *Sociological Theory* 17 (1999):
307–332.

Woodall, Ann M. *What Price the Poor? William Booth, Karl Marx and the London Residium.*
Aldershot, U.K.: Ashgate, 2005.

Wright, Lawrence. *The Looming Tower: Al-Qaeda and the Road to 9/11.* New York: Vintage Books, 2006.

Wuthnow, Robert. *Acts of Compassion: Caring for Others and Helping Ourselves.* Princeton,
N.J.: Princeton University Press, 1991.

Yadgar, Yaacov. "Shas as a Struggle to Create a New Field: A Bourdieuan Perspective of an
Israeli Phenomenon." *Sociology of Religion* 64 (2003): 223–246.

"You Have Brightened Egypt." *Traces,* November 1, 2010.

Young, Michael P. "Confessional Protest: The Religious Birth of U.S. National Social Movements." *American Sociological Review* 67 (2002): 660–686.

Zadra, Dario. "Comunione e Liberazione: A Fundamentalist Idea of Power." In *Accounting
for Fundamentalisms: The Dynamic Character of Movements,* edited by Martin E. Marty
and R. Scott Appleby. Chicago: University of Chicago Press, 1991.

Zima, Suzanne. "Religious Party Using Clout to Pressure Barak: Shas Seizes Chance to
Build on Its Power Base in Israel." *SFGate.com,* July 13, 2000, http://articles.sfgate.com/

2000-07-13/news/17654533_1_shas-spiritual-leader-shas-voters-israel-b-aliya-party (accessed April 8, 2011; site discontinued).

Zollner, Barbara H. E. *The Muslim Brotherhood: Hasan al-Hudaybi and Ideology.* London: Routledge, 2009.

Zubaida, Sami. "Trajectories of Political Islam: Egypt, Iran, and Turkey." *Political Quarterly* 71 (2000): 60–78.

Zucchi, John. "Luigi Giussani, the Church, and Youth in the 1950s: A Judgment Born of an Experience." *Logos: A Journal of Catholic Thought and Culture* 10 (2007): 131–150.

INDEX

NANCY J. DAVIS
is Lester Martin Jones Professor of Sociology at DePauw University.

ROBERT V. ROBINSON
is the Class of 1964 Chancellor's Professor of Sociology at Indiana University, Bloomington.

Together, they have published on religion and politics in the *American Sociological Review,* the *American Journal of Sociology,* and *Contexts,* winning recognition from the Society for the Scientific Study of Religion's and the American Sociological Association's sections on the sociology of religion and collective behavior and social movements.

Printed and bound by CPI Group (UK) Ltd, Croydon, CR0 4YY

13/04/2025

14656544-0002